Stretchers Not Available

The Wartime Story of Dr Jim Rickett

John Rickett

Jim Rickett 1942

authorHOUSE

AuthorHouse™ UK Ltd.
1663 Liberty Drive
Bloomington, IN 47403
www.authorhouse.co.uk
Phone: 1-800-839-8640

© 2012, 2014 by John Rickett. All rights reserved.

No part of this book may be reproduced, stored in a retrieval system, or transmitted by any means without the written permission of the author.

Published by AuthorHouse   01/16/2012

ISBN: 978-1-4670-0898-3 (softcover)
ISBN: 978-1-4772-5042-6 (audio)
ISBN: 978-1-4670-0899-0 (e-book)

Printed in the United States of America

Any people depicted in stock imagery provided by Thinkstock are models, and such images are being used for illustrative purposes only.
Certain stock imagery © Thinkstock.

This book is printed on acid-free paper.

Because of the dynamic nature of the Internet, any web addresses or links contained in this book may have changed since publication and may no longer be valid. The views expressed in this work are solely those of the author and do not necessarily reflect the views of the publisher, and the publisher hereby disclaims any responsibility for them.

Stretchers Not Available

DEDICATION

To my sister Pip, sadly no longer with us

Author's acknowledgements

In Part Two the account of 1944 was written by Jim Rickett when he was back in Italy in 1945 with the detail still fresh in his mind. In addition some material was taken from 'The Island of Terrible Friends' written by Bill Strutton, published in 1961. Some stories were told to me Jim Rickett himself. Some information about the Commando fighting on Vis was taken from 'Commando Crusade' by Brigadier Tom Churchill and about the Brac raid from 'Royal Marine Commandos' by John Parker and from Commando Subaltern at War by WG Jenkins. Details of the work of the Coastal Forces RN was from 'Dog Boats at War' by Leonard C Reynolds. Information about Tito and the Partisans came from 'Tito's Partisans' by Velimir Vuksik and from 'Eastern Approaches' by Fitzroy Maclean. I am also grateful to Charles Messenger whose book 'World War Two-Chronological Atlas' provided much useful information. I am grateful to all those who gave advice including my brother Barney, Gill Brown, John Sladden, Annette Vaitkus, Eileen Atkinson, Sue Lloyd Roberts, Peter Trott, Peter Bickmore of Coastal Forces Veterans, and countless others over a considerable period of time.

Introduction

Realising the seriousness of the war after the damage to morale caused by Dunkirk in June 1940 and thinking that there would be another and more serious German offensive, Jim Rickett started to keep a diary of his work as a GP near Portsmouth. Bombing during the blitz was intense as the diary relates.

At the end of the day, often with the sound of a bombing raid in the background, he reflected on his day's work. Much of what is written is verbatim, but there were times when, for the sake of clarity and better English, the text has been altered to make it more readable. The aim was to keep just what Jim Rickett wanted to say. The diaries of that time are supplemented by letters written to Dorothy, his wife, who had evacuated with the three children, to the safety of Scotland.

In January 1941 the raids were particularly heavy, and as a consequence the work increased to the extent that the diary suffered. However, he continued to write frequent letters to Dorothy, describing the scene locally. The record of that time is solely from these letters.

In writing the account, some comments have been added concerning the historical detail and sometimes also of certain medical aspects. These comments are in a different typescript.

Part Two is an account written by Jim Rickett in 1945 of the time he was posted to join the SOE commandos on the Adriatic island of Vis. This part of the book is supplemented with stories both told by commandos with whom he was working and related to me, his son, after the war.

PART ONE
CHAPTER 1

After returning to England in 1945, Jim Rickett wrote of the events of 1944. He had been working in a hospital in Italy when he received his posting to join the commandos on the island of Vis in February of that year. This was at the start of the Vis campaign, during which the island became the strategic base for the Balkan campaign. Churchill was planning the Normandy landings. Hitler's supplies from the Mediterranean were very much dependent on the Adriatic Sea route, for which the Naval forces in the harbours and the commandos on the island held the key.

It was a dull, cold February day, and I was just finishing a routine operating list, when Major Jones, the registrar, stuck his head round the door of the theatre and expressed a wish to see me at the earliest moment possible. This was unusual in itself, and in addition he seemed rather intense, which led me to wonder what might be coming. In the army one becomes ready for immediate postings which can sometimes appear completely out of the blue. Then there are orders, delivered with apparent extreme urgency, which later may be cancelled, altered, or postponed times without number. I was not unduly curious therefore about this summons to the hospital office, though I did wonder what exactly might be thrust upon me.

The fighting was proving tough going in Italy. The commandos had a hard time establishing a beachhead at Anzio and were still struggling on their way towards Rome. We had little direct information about the progress they were making, but we would have got the news of the fall of Rome when it happened, as it was a mere thirty miles from Anzio. I have to admit I was not enamoured of the idea of joining the front line, which would be under canvas, and with a completely new team I had never met. It would be very hard work in a most stressful situation.

The hospital where I had been working was at Trani, a town some thirty miles north of Bari on the Adriatic coast of Italy. Despite being in the "sunny Med", as we would think of it, the weather was no warmer than one would find in England at that time of the year. It rained a great deal, though when the sun did shine, it was beautifully warm and showed this part of Italy at its best.

It was raining steadily as I crossed from the surgical block to the Scuole Elementari, in the ruins of which the administrative offices of the hospital were situated. The two other blocks of the Nazi schools had been left untouched by the Germans in their hurried retreat.

Major Jones was waiting for me with an Allied Force Headquarters posting for me to be attached to the Special Operations Executive (SOE) Force 133 and to report to HQ No. 2 District at once, together with 40 lbs. of kit. At this time I had not heard of Force 133 and knew nothing of the SOE, except that everything about it was Churchill's baby and was top secret. Though I was glad of the challenge of a fresh posting, I feared that it might mean Anzio, which was not going along too happily at the time. I welcomed a change, but Anzio was not an exciting prospect. Performing forward surgery in tents in the cold in both rain and mud, whilst subjected all the while to fairly heavy shell fire, did not offer enormous appeal.

I went back to the theatre to tell the news, which was received without enthusiasm. We were a happy unit with a well-run operating theatre team. My posting meant that another surgeon would have to take my place. He would be an unknown quantity, and until he arrived to take charge of the surgical division, Jimmy Mason-Brown was going to be left as the only surgeon for as many as four hundred beds. This daunting thought came to me, but one thing that the Army does teach you is that nobody is indispensable. Keeping staff on the move has the advantage of bringing in new blood and new ideas. As a result, I have to admit I had little compunction in leaving him with a job that I knew he could not manage on his own. With backing from the War Office, they would sort something out.

After getting a few belongings together, I went again to the office to get the latest instructions and orders. There I found Colonel "Black Jack" Donnelly, our CO. He at once broke into wild plans, as he recognised that Force 133 meant a posting to the German-occupied east side of the Adriatic. All information about Force 133 was classified, and he had no other details. He explained that now we had landed in southern Italy, Hitler had lost his trade route from the south. So he had decided to occupy the Adriatic islands in order to preserve the sea trade. This was therefore an important assignment.

Black Jack was a roughneck and had been born out of his time. Had he been born in the days of Robin Hood, he would have become famous. As a colonel in the RAMC he was a misfit. His quick brain leapt at once to the possibilities. Quite obviously we would be in a front-line situation with doubtful supplies. He added some valuable things to my kit. In addition, he took the opportunity of selling me a bag of Italian flour which he thought I might need and, more usefully, gave me a paraffin vapour Tilley lamp. I found these were almost unobtainable and were vital as a source of heat and light when under canvas. I was extremely grateful.

I managed to get hold of an ambulance and set off in it with mixed and somewhat confused feelings. Eventually I trundled into Bari along that long, straight, and boring flat coast road. I had spent just over a year overseas and not much more than that in the Army, so I was, in terms of army experience, fairly green when I got to the HQ. I did not have much of a clue what to expect or how to obtain things on my own. I was to learn quickly about the way things were run, and the lesson was decidedly painful.

I underwent a medical at No. 2 District, and afterwards I was shown in to meet the Deputy Director of Medical Supplies, Brigadier Cameron. He was a most dynamic little brigadier. He was very brief and to the point in what he had to tell me, partly as a matter of habit and partly, I suspect, because he only had a sketchy idea of what I had been posted to do. He told me that there was an island—and here he referred to a paper-called Vis. He thought that I was to do surgery on casualties occurring amongst British troops. He told me the island was technically behind enemy lines and in the hands of Tito's partisans and that we had sent across a bunch of commandos to hold it against a German attack that was reported to be imminent. The commandos would carry out harassing raids on neighbouring islands, and I was to get what I thought was necessary and go across and set up a field hospital to look after the British troops who would be wounded in the raids. Speed was of the essence. I must take out with me everything I would need, as providing supplies to the island would be very difficult, if not impossible. The island was relatively close to the Yugoslav mainland and amongst other islands which were under German occupation. We would have to get there by night in order to avoid the Luftwaffe, which at the time dominated the air during the day.

I was needed out there right away. I must get things organised and embark without delay. He said there was already a young medical officer over there. He was treating the partisans in the one small permanent hospital on the island. I could help him with the partisan wounded if I liked. Being young and lacking experience, he was not recognised by the Army as a surgeon, and that was the reason I was to go to support him, but my main concern was to sort out the British personnel. He told me to go to the HQ of Force 133, where I would hear more details.

Brigadier Cameron was very good to me. I told him I was happy about taking on the surgical side, but having been simply a GP before the war, I was very inexperienced in administration. I had never set up a surgical unit and would need a lot of help in doing so; otherwise I would probably slip up badly. As a result of my request and to speed me on my way, he lent me his own car and driver and sent me off.

When I found the HQ in Torre a Mare, a small fishing village south of Bari, I went inside to report and get a briefing. However, I was in for a shock. Force 133 was known as "The Firm". It was only at that point that I learned that, as part of the SOE, everything was "top secret". It was under the direct control of the Foreign Office and was therefore outside the immediate remit of the War Office. As a result of this, the normal army methods of administration did not apply; most things were accomplished very differently, and often by what seemed to me to be the "old boy" method. It brought about a curious atmosphere. More arresting was the presence of a number of lovely ladies, all in mufti and all very much a part of the scene. Initially I thought they were friends *and relatives of the staff, but I came later to realise they were FANYs and were working for the SOE[1].*

All the staff were addressed by their Christian names. Amongst them was a collection of very keen young men. They were tough and parachute-trained, and they were used to working under the worst conditions in the field. Others seemed to be from a different stable, though not lacking in social skills judging by the attention given to the female members.

I sought out and found the colonel at HQ. I learnt from him that No. 2 Commando under Colonel Jack Churchill was already on Vis. There was a plan to reinforce the island with more commandos in the near future. On the island at present there was just one section of a Light Field Ambulance unit, and this consisted of a medical officer and ten men in support. The colonel to whom I spoke had no idea of the medical requirements needed to set up a hospital unit; nor were there any official recommendations regarding equipment. He appeared to be under the misconception that if you could provide a surgeon with a little black bag, then all would be well. In short, he had absolutely no idea of the set-up out there and the problems I would face.

He took me along to the mess, where there was a further collection of men and women, refreshingly civilian both in their speech and outlook, and introduced me as the new surgeon for Vis. They immediately broke out in loud guffaws of laughter. I found out later that the reason for the laughter was pure sarcasm, as the island was certain to be attacked at any moment. As a result, everyone was extremely anxious to get me and as much equipment as possible over there PDQ.

---

1   The First Aid Nursing Yeomanry or FANY was established prior to the First World War. Originally they were conceived as volunteer field ambulance medics. See Appendix B.

He introduced me to Johnnie Forster, who would act as an adviser and facilitator for me. Forster was a well-known character, fearless and quite unconventional. He dressed in such a manner, that unless you knew, it was impossible to find out his rank. He was in fact a major, but he might have been much higher up the scale had he not caused an almost continuous series of problems. He wore a black beret with the crown of the Indian Army, which made him look as if he were a full colonel. Apart from this, he wore no badges of rank or unit. He wore an Indian pattern grey shirt, as issued to the troops, and denim trousers, the whole covered by a very ragged and disreputable sheepskin coat. He had already been on Vis and the other islands before the Germans had decided to recapture them. His autocratic character had made him unpopular with Tito's staff, with whom he had little sympathy. His way with senior officers was most amusing. He started off with a punctilious salute and then sat himself down. At first deferential and polite, he gradually lost this thin veneer and became chatty and friendly. He would end up giving his advice without fear or favour and would often finish the interview with his feet on the table.

Johnnie Forster was wonderfully helpful and, being an experienced hand with all the various departments, took me round at whirlwind speed, all in one afternoon. First we went to base medical stores, then on to the blood transfusion depot and other stores. I was able to get all I could in the way of blood plasma and transfusion equipment. His experience was invaluable in deciding what to take. He was leaving for Cairo by plane the next morning, so I had to make what use I could of him in the short time available.

We could take no blood, as this requires refrigeration for storage and, even when kept cool, has a shelf life of only a month. Plasma would have to be used as a blood substitute. It has a much longer shelf life. However, it contains no haemoglobin and therefore can only be used in very limited amounts without causing profound anaemia and other circulatory problems. Any blood used would have to be provided from donors on site and then cross-matched before transfusion.

We had to consider our needs for surgical dressings, drapes for use in the theatre, and intravenous fluids. Then there were drugs, including morphine and antibiotics[2], and anaesthetic requirements. We were to be given a folding operating table, instruments, and sterilizing equipment. At the time I had no knowledge of what, if any, energy source for lighting and heating would be provided.

Having made an initial somewhat exhaustive tour of the base stores, I went straight back to see Brigadier Cameron. I had to sort out the supporting staff. This was going to be absolutely crucial. I would need first and foremost an experienced and reliable anaesthetist. Next on the list was a theatre orderly. I had already given the matter considerable thought. This meeting was therefore extremely important, so I was glad Forster was still with me. With his help I was able to get Brigadier Cameron to agree to my having Frank Clinic, whom I knew to be a very sound anaesthetist, and he also sanctioned me to have Dawson, who had been one of the theatre orderlies at my old 76 General Hospital. There and then he wrote out a posting order and gave me his car to go and fetch him. Frank Clinic was, at the time, on an anti-malarial course in Bari and was delighted to hear of my proposition.

With these two men, I knew we could form the basis of an effective surgical unit. As an anaesthetist, Frank would be an ideal colleague and companion. He was a cheerful, small, chubby boy, blue-eyed and pretty, with wavy fair hair. He was a born potterer and had no idea of

---

2   Sulphonamides had just become available, but not penicillin

time. Most important, he was unperturbed by stress, would rise to any occasion, and was extremely capable in his job.

No. 76 General Hospital was not pleased to let me have either Frank or, for that matter, Dawson. In particular, they regarded Dawson as their own private property. Some unkind and somewhat sarcastic remarks were made, begging me not to be shy in asking for anything else I might care for, and I got profuse thanks that I had left at least some of the staff. These remarks were also accompanied by genuine regret that they could not come with us and join in what was obviously going to be an exciting exercise. Dawson was out when I arrived at the hospital, so I took the posting order to the hospital office, where I saw Major Jones. He was a bit scathing, in that the order had neither the service number nor any initials, and my old CO, Black Jack, was inclined to be indignant at first about losing one of the best orderlies that either of us had met in the Army. However he soon entered into the spirit of the thing and became quite amenable to Dawson's coming with me.

Dawson was aged about 28, married, and came from the Midlands. He was to become the mainspring of our team. My experience of his work so far was that he was without equal as an assistant in the operating theatre. He was an enthusiast about anything that he tackled, and he flung his heart into the job in hand without reserve. He became the key of our unit. He was thin, of medium height, and his black hair was plastered firmly down. Before the war he had held several jobs, and he might have seemed, to anyone who did not know him, a bit of a rolling stone. This I must emphatically deny. A jack of all trades might perhaps be nearer the mark. He was a wonderful fixer. He had at one time been a bricklayer, and subsequently had a number of other jobs, including at one time being a roller-skating instructor. I personally knew him only as an extremely hard-working and enthusiastic man. He was capable of an infinite amount of work and was restless in his efforts in making improvements to our set-up, which was, at least in the early stages, parlous to say the least. He would work all hours to bring the theatre up to scratch. He had an inventive mind and spared himself no trouble. Like so many enthusiasts, he was intolerant of obstruction and was inclined to be a bit moody when things did not go so well. Had I not been lucky enough to get him, I could never have made even a moderate success of the job we had to tackle.

When I eventually found Dawson, he received my news with no outward sign of enthusiasm. I know that he was pleased, but he was as sceptical as everyone becomes after a few months of army life. He packed his immediate belongings, and in an hour we were on our way back to Bari in Cameron's staff car. That night I shared a room with Johnnie Forster, who had to start at 3 a.m. in order to catch his plane to Cairo which left at dawn. For Dawson I found a billet in the pool drivers' mess. This would not be like Buckingham Palace for him, but I had learned from experience that to send anyone to the alternative, which would have been a transit camp, would be mistaken. To stay in such a camp would have meant getting embroiled in the slow-turning military machine and endless red tape. For us, this could have meant that vital opportunities to obtain his advice about getting essential equipment would have been missed.

The next morning I went again to the base medical stores and added many things that I had omitted on the previous visit. I met Frank Clinic, who was now released from his malaria course. He stated his needs for anaesthetics. We decided we should not take anything complicated like the standard anaesthetic machine that was used in hospitals. This machine would have required regular back-up supplies of oxygen and nitrous oxide, the supplies of which would most certainly be unavailable on the island. After that we would have to rely entirely on the old rag-and-bottle methods. It would be better to use these basic methods from the start. We would use ether and chloroform for serious abdominal wounds and major amputations, and intravenous Pentothal for the more superficial wounds.

In making up our supplies, it was very difficult to imagine the topography of the island or even the facilities in the area where we would find ourselves. In fact, the only information we had was that there were two small towns, or rather large villages, on the island, both of which had electricity. However, to avoid the regular bombing of the towns, we felt and were advised that the best site for our unit would be well away from either. For lighting we would therefore have to rely on paraffin lamps until we could get hold of a generator. Then there would be the blackout to consider so that we could continue working at night.

All supplies were still very short. Such things as primus stoves were almost unobtainable, and we were able to get just one at the base medical stores. Obviously we were going to be very much in a "make do" situation. Lighting was a particular difficulty; as there were no acetylene lamps available, our total lighting consisted of three hurricane lamps and the Tilley that we had been given by Black Jack Donnelly. There was a vague suggestion that a generator might be supplied at some future and unspecified time, but heaven knows when we might expect that!

The officer in charge of the stores was as helpful as he could be, but it was here that I found that the sergeant could get us things that the officer, through fear of the consequences of ignoring guidelines and codes of practice, had refused. In general, however, we were well treated, especially as all these stores were, as far as the War Office was concerned, written off. They were later, apparently, to be paid for by the Foreign Office. This habit of one government department paying the other for stores or for work done amused me. Was this bureaucracy gone mad?

So eventually the whole of our kit—all ten tons of it-was crated up and packed into two three-ton trucks, ready for loading on the following day.

The plan was to embark at Monopoli, a town some twenty miles south of Bari. We had seen the people of Force 133 at Torre a Mare. They appeared to be in rather a high-powered state of confusion. We were told they had made the necessary arrangements for us to load our two three-tonners with all our kit, and so we motored down to the port, planning to embark after dark. When we got there, the embarkation officer told me there was no room on the LCI [Landing Craft Infantry] and that my gear would have to go on a schooner. I told him that in that case I would also go on the schooner, as I was useless without my kit. I knew that once we were separated, we would almost certainly lose the lot. He was somewhat apathetic about the whole affair and seemed unable to make a firm decision, and I could see that he was to be no further help. The best thing to do would be to take matters into our own hands and get right down to the quay, locate the LCI, and then persuade those responsible for loading of the need to get our stuff on board.

Accordingly, I found the way down and identified the LCI. I had taken the opportunity to bring a sack full of food for the journey. I had also managed to get a few boxes of that blessed "compote ration", which provided everything a man could want, even down to cigarettes, matches, and toilet paper. I have to confess I obtained a good store of NAAFI supplies by telling lies about the size of the unit. I secured *enough cigarettes to last us some time, along with two bottles of whisky and three bottles of brandy as medical comforts. It is an old joke in the Army that the RAMC lives off the medical comforts meant for the patients, and I have to say that in practice most of our patients were either too ill or not ill enough to be given the brandy treatment!*

At the dock-side it was raining in torrents, and there was confusion. I found the man who was organising the loading and persuaded him of the need to get our stuff on board. Loading then continued at high pressure in the dark. We simply had to get our stuff on board somehow. I found some Italian labourers and set them to work. I got our gear stored on the upper deck in the only available area, which was on top of ammunition and guns of all kinds. This was hardly the ideal place, but at least it did get loaded. Having got it all aboard, we found our way below and into the aft accommodation quarters, such as they were.

For those who have never travelled by LCI, my advice is the same as for plagues, and that is at all costs to avoid them. They are small and smelly, and although I am normally a reasonably good sailor, these craft invariably make me sick. As the wind was howling outside, I knew that the crossing would likely test even seasoned sailors. It was with no pleasure, therefore, that we received into our quarters a gang of young RSRs [Raiding Support Regiment], all of whom had enjoyed the most monumental party before coming on board. They came in and immediately dumped their piles of kit everywhere. Then they sat about holding their heads, making the cramped room even smaller. To make matters worse, there soon developed a highly acrimonious argument as to whose fault it was that they were travelling without any rations.

Following a difficult night, during which we made very poor progress as we battled against a gale force head wind that threw us about like dice in a shaker, we found ourselves on Sunday morning in

John Rickett

Bari harbour, just twenty-five miles up the coast. The flat-bottomed LCI rode every wave like a cork; deep-draught vessels cleave a passage through them, and consequently the motion is not nearly as violent. I had been sick but was beginning to feel better, when we tied up alongside the harbour wall in Bari. The decision to put into Bari was taken in order to avoid making the crossing over to Vis during daylight. We were all grateful for the delay, especially poor Dawson who had been lying almost unconscious in the acute misery of seasickness.

I could make out the Hotel Imperial Officers' Club standing out on the waterfront, and the thought came to me of the possibility of one more comfortable dinner before starting off. It also gave us a wonderful opportunity to augment our meagre supplies.

Ashore at HQ, we secured the loan of the brigadier's car once more and went round to various stores that we had had no time to visit before. Amongst these was the BRCS (British Red Cross Society). In spite of it being Sunday, the stores were thrown open for us and every help given. Amongst our many finds were two more primus stoves. These just made the difference between being able to do a job and failing miserably.

Full of good cheer, we loaded these extras on board and repaired to the Officers' Club for dinner. We had an excellent meal, and it was a pleasant surprise to find some of the sisters from the old 76 General Hospital that we had just left. This was luck indeed. We sent messages to friends, and I wrote to Dorothy to say that I hoped that small boats would not make me sick. I learnt later that from this remark, together with an announcement on the wireless that we had occupied an island in the Adriatic under its Italian name of Lissa, she was able to guess where I had gone.

The weather, which had been foul all that day, improved towards the evening, and by the time we had wined and dined well at the Imperial, the wind had dropped and a better day was promised for tomorrow's crossing. When we reached the mole where our little ship was tied, we met up with the RSRs and I found that one of them had got into trouble. He was a big Glaswegian boy with an almost unintelligible accent, and he had got mixed up with some Italians. In the scrap, he had sustained a nasty cut on his wrist. On examination, I found he had divided one or perhaps even two tendons to the fingers, and so there was no alternative except to leave him behind and get him into the 98th General Hospital locally.

On board, the RSRs had got over their hangovers and were subdued, possibly in anticipation of another night like the last. Our mess deck was altogether quieter, and we all got some sleep. Washing and cleaning in a large crowd with no arrangements at all for accommodation was bound to be a bit of a scrum. We were under way by seven in the morning, and although the wind was less, the swell had not gone down. The Adriatic was as choppy as one very often finds in our own English Channel. We had a bouncy trip! Dawson and I both suffered as we ran up the east coast of Italy. Then in gathering dusk we turned east and headed across the Adriatic towards Vis, the wind easing as we did so.

We arrived at Vis under a starlit sky in the flat calm of the dead of night. As we motored slowly into the harbour, the atmosphere was electric. It was a moment I shall not forget.

CHAPTER 2

All this seemed a million miles away from Jim's work at the outbreak of war as a GP in a country practice near Portsmouth. Before telling the Vis story one should go back to that time. The Blitz German bombing campaign was just beginning.

The start of the war had not gone at all well. Within nine months of the declaration of war in September 1939, the country was faced with the first major disaster, which was the retreat of the British Expeditionary Force in Flanders and the evacuation at Dunkirk. The country went into a state of shock. What was Hitler's next move going to be? The British Expeditionary Force was thought by the country to be invincible. The Army, poorly equipped against the Panzers' superior weaponry and air support, was driven back and had to evacuate under the most difficult conditions and with the loss of thousands of lives. England was poorly prepared for war. Soldiers were young and inexperienced and had not seen action in the First World War. Germany had shown its superiority. We were running scared. Many families had evacuated to escape the inevitable bombing of London and other large towns and cities. Jim Rickett's family went to Scotland.

Portsmouth, with its large naval base, was clearly going to be a prime target for German raids. The harbour was their main objective, and it was under constant threat. This was clear to the local defence team, whose camouflage concealed the dock relatively well by day, and by night the blackout was rigidly enforced and highly successful.

So effective was this that the docks were not badly hit during the raids, which were mainly at night when bombs would be dropped by pilot guesswork, As a consequence, the local area and the surrounding population suffered badly.

GPs were thrown in at the deep end, so to speak. Most of the senior medical specialists were called up to serve in the forces abroad, leaving the local population in the hands of doctors with basic medical degrees and without specialist training to deal with those who were injured in the raids. Qualifying as he had in 1929, Jim had been lucky enough to have a few years' surgical experience behind him. Although he had never taken any formal specialist surgical training and had no higher degree, he had picked up the trade, learning as he went, as was usual for those who settled into general practice as the local GP surgeon.

Jim operated on a regular basis at the Victoria Cottage Hospital at Emsworth. He would do the straightforward surgery, orthopaedics, and midwifery. This would include some relatively minor surgery, the removal of lumps and bumps, and the repair of hernias. He reduced fractures and in addition was often required to do what is now considered major surgery—abdominal surgery, including the appendix but also bowel resections, gall bladder removal, and so forth. His anaesthetist was a local colleague GP. If help was needed, he would call on the local specialists of Portsmouth or Chichester for advice and assistance. The midwifery would include occasional forceps deliveries and caesarean sections. The shortage of specialists caused by the call-up meant that he was kept very busy and was under some pressure to get on and do whatever he thought he could.

Late in June, Jim Rickett wrote this letter to Dorothy, whom he affectionately called Doo. She was with the children in Scotland. He wanted to put her mind at ease, as she would have heard about the raids

John Rickett

on the news and in the papers. Hitler's plan was an invasion to take place after an intensive bombing campaign had weakened the nation's resolve.

>30 June 1940, 11.55 p.m.
>21, East St., Havant

>My darling Doo,
>I was so glad to hear your voice today and was sorry I could not get through on Saturday night. I think we must always do our telephoning in the early morning as the lines are so bad at night, and I am unavailable and busy during the day.
>You will be interested to hear that three salvos of bombs were dropped between Compton and Marden last night. Luckily they landed in the woods. There was also machine gunning, probably aimed at a search light. This seemed to have been a completely haphazard affair and quite indiscriminate. No damage was done except to the local pheasant population.
>Tonight, Sunday, I went with Matron to dinner with the Dymoke White's. They were very friendly, but I had a phone call and had to leave to do an operation immediately after we had eaten. I have only just got home, having taken Matron back after the operation and then seen another patient on the way.
>It has been very busy since getting back down here from Scotland. Most people seem to have saved themselves up to see me, rather than going to see a doctor they do not know.
>Ring me up again soon. I like to hear about you all, and it makes me feel much closer. I wish you were on the phone now so I could talk to you direct.

Give my love to the children. I am tired and must go to bed now to face the deluge tomorrow.

Love from your

James

The Battle of Britain started in July 1940 and continued until October of the same year. During July there were heavy attacks on dockyards, convoys, and the ports along the English Channel. At this stage the RAF was quite depleted, with only 600 aircraft, of which a mere 400 were available for action. Lord Beaverbrook was appointed Minister for Aircraft Production, and under his influence the output of aircraft increased from 256 to nearly 500 per month.

The main offensive came in August, when Goering's coded messages about it were deciphered by the enigma machines. This gave Hugh Dowding, Head of Fighter Command, some warning. At the outbreak, serious losses were sustained by a convoy and its escort in the Channel. Damage was also done to some airfields and radar stations. In the main attack, which started on 13 August, the Luftwaffe made 1,485 sorties. Goering then decided to make 15 August what he called "Eagle Day". On that day there were 1,786 sorties, with attacks mainly targeting airfields. The Luftwaffe lost seventy-six aircraft, against the RAF's thirty-five fighting planes. The attacks were kept up, and on 18 August we lost a further thirty-three aircraft. At that time fighter pilots were under very severe strain due to tiredness and lack of sleep. There were mounting casualties, with many pilots lost. It was on 20 August that Churchill made the famous speech about the Battle of Britain, saying, "Never in the field of human conflict was so much owed by so many to so few."

John Rickett

This letter was sent to Dorothy in Scotland by her great friend Margot Campbell. Margot and her husband Alan, a captain in the Navy, lived close by in Emsworth. They had planned to visit her. The house in which they were all staying in Argyllshire was close to Alan's family home.

18 August
Saxtead House
Emsworth

Dearest Doo,

Alan really thinks he may be able to get away on Friday! So I am packing feverishly.

If all goes according to plan, we shall arrive by the Saturday boat. I wanted to write and tell you to make whatever arrangements you feel necessary about extra help, with which I'll share of course. We had quite an exciting time yesterday after a day's hell on Saturday. Just after lunch Alan was changing—Jimmy came to lunch and was in the garden with John Hamilton, when suddenly Alan shouted down, "Into the shelter quick—a dive bombing attack on Thorney," and things started happening. Alan saw five planes come down before he got to the shelter. It only lasted a few minutes, but was pretty noisy—machine gun fire, AA fire and bombs, and the noise of diving planes made the shelter vibrate, but it was soon over, and we went out to look. There was a huge column of black smoke over Thorney—in the same place as on Friday. The raid went on for about an hour and a half with pretty loud explosions Portsmouth way, and we had to keep on taking cover because of the danger of hits from the shells. When it was all over, I'm sorry to say we went off to see what we could see! We found a German plane in Chidham

Lane—burnt out. We got quite close to it and were presented with a huge bit of the engine by an LDV man[3]. Really, Doo, it seemed awfully cold-blooded, but when you've been attacked, you can't help feeling thrilled to see the plane a burning wreck in spite of what it cost some poor wretch. There was a crowd of course, and a general feeling of bonhomie prevailed. The LDV man was killingly funny but revoltingly bloodthirsty in giving us all the details.

The reactions of the people were very interesting. The plane landed a few yards from a farmhouse and buildings, but no one seemed at all disturbed, except one good lady, who was a bit wrought up and angry that the plane had crashed over her garden and knocked all the plums off her trees! There was another plane just off the main road and another near Chichester, as well as others all around.

When we got back, Jimmy had to go to the hospital for five casualties brought in from Thorney Aerodrome. We imagined he'd be away for hours, and I kept seeing all the awful things he'd have to cope with in my mind. So we were surprised to see him back an hour later. The two bombs had hit an air-raid shelter, and the worst casualty was a badly bruised knee! Isn't that amazing? So we decided to celebrate by going out to hear a good bit of peace and quiet and having dinner later at Midhurst.

I wish you'd been with us, Doo—even for the air raid!

Best love to Clare, the children and to you,

Margot

---

[3] The British Secretary of State for War was Anthony Eden. In May 1940 he set up the Local Defence Volunteer (LDV) organisation. Initially 250,000 volunteers came forward and by the end of July no less that 1,250,000 had come forward. At this stage Churchill decided that this force should be known as the Home Guard.

John Rickett

It was in late August 1940 that the first bombs were dropped on central London, though it was learned later this had in fact been unintentional. This was the start of the Blitz and marked the onset of the RAF retaliation that culminated in the Battle of Britain. Hitler had drawn up an invasion plan which was called Operation Sealion. This was timed for September. The decision whether to go ahead or not would depend on winning air supremacy by the end of August.

The London bombing provoked an immediate retaliation to bomb Berlin, but the damage inflicted on the city at that time was only slight. The serious and intentional bombing of England's capital started on 6 September. This provided the airfields, hitherto the target of the bombers, with welcome relief and gave Fighter Command a little breathing space. Fighter aircraft were put on full production to replace those lost. On 15 September a major sortie of 1,300 Luftwaffe fighters was launched against 170 British planes. On that day fifty-eight German aircraft were shot down, against just twenty-six of our own. Goering and Hitler came to realise that their aim of air supremacy had not been achieved, and as a result of the severe losses the Luftwaffe had sustained, Hitler decided on 17 September to postpone Sealion.

The fear of an invasion was very real, and warnings were issued to everyone. Dorothy, in fear of the invasion wanted to hide bottled fruit and other food she had stored in the house. She had some high shelves on which she kept these storage jars. Except to a very tall person, they were hidden from view. She climbed up and set a row of mouse traps on the edge of the shelf on which they were stored. If a German was curious and was looking for food, he might want to explore what was on the top shelf, and to save himself the trouble of getting a chair on which he would have to stand, he might feel with his fingers. The unpleasant surprise of getting his fingers caught in the mouse traps might put him off exploring further. After the war the family was unkind enough to make the mouse trap idea a family joke.

The bombing of Portsmouth and the neighbourhood around the city was heavy. The siren to warn of an enemy attack was constantly going, and people would eventually go to bed, often to the sound of aircraft and of bombs falling nearby. If the attack was close, the official advice was to go to the nearest air-raid shelter. People were reluctant to do this, as they were crowded, cold, and a breeding ground for flu germs and worse. They were also at some distance from the house. Frequently, people would stay at home and hope all would be well. If there was immediate danger to the house, the government's advice was to shelter under the stairs or even to sit under a strong table in one of the downstairs rooms such as the kitchen. If the house had a basement, that was also a good place for shelter, but stairs were often narrow and wooden, and in that case evacuation would be difficult or even impossible if the house collapsed or had been hit by an incendiary bomb. Helmets and gas masks were issued to everyone, including children. For them, masks had funny faces like Mickey Mouse and other Disney characters.

This letter, written on the eve of the Battle of Britain, was full of reassurances.

>10 September 1940
>21 East St
>Havant
>
>My darling Doo,
>I am afraid this letter will take ages because communications are a bit upset in London. It must be difficult for you to

visualise the situation down here. I will try and visualise it for you. Portsmouth was supposed to have been heavily damaged, but actually you have to look hard to see any difference. Many windows have gone around Portsmouth Road, but life continues just the same. Morants', the outfitters, lost half the building, and the Midland Bank must have had a direct hit, and as much as seven-eighths is destroyed.

Here in Havant you can't see where they have been, so it is all fairly reasonable and undamaged and not as exciting as it sounds.

Hayling keeps having a few bombs, which usually means Miss West, our secretary, is either absent or late.

It is such a bore that Alan has to sleep at Whale Island until this new scare of invasion is over. I saw him yesterday. He remains frightfully well and is likewise full of beans. Everyone is saying how well we both look. I had old Bertie B. (a friend) to dinner tonight to enjoy the grouse. He did it full justice and appreciated my Scottish holiday in a liquid form enormously.

There is a new game here called "potting the red". Thorney air field has a red landing light, and, naturally, it is very attractive to the German night bombers. The RAF decided to move it each night to avoid themselves being constantly picked out for German favours. Sometimes it is placed here, sometimes there, with the result that when it was put in Stansted Park, the bomb blasts broke all Lady Bessborough's windows. Then they had one outside the Carr's at Walderton, which burnt a shed to the ground. Hambrook and Woodmancote have also suffered. Naturally the residents are getting a bit resentful when this light is left close by their house. Are they being stupid and narrow-minded? Protection of Thorney is, after all, such a good cause![4]

My love again,

James

The first day of September was the start of the season for partridge shooting. Jim Rickett's practice was in the heart of the West Sussex/Hampshire border. This was excellent farm land for rough shooting, as both partridges and pheasants were plentiful. These were a particularly useful supplement to the meat coupons as they did not come under the rationing restrictions. Jim Rickett's love of country pursuits went back to his childhood, when he enjoyed the hunting behind hounds in Northamptonshire.

With the Battle of Britain at its height, Jim Rickett wrote to Dorothy.

> 16 September 1940
> 21 East St
> Havant
>
> Dear Doo,
> We are all well here. Norah Galbraith is a good girl, and she works well for us in the surgery. We are sweeping lots of old things clean with one broom. I am doing away with those awful ledgers and starting a new card index system which I think will be much more satisfactory. It is also pleasant to have one's

---

[4] The comment is intentional sarcasm. Thorney Island with its air field was low lying, surrounded by mud flats, otherwise very marshy and unsightly, and the water was plagued by mosquitos.

letters typed again, provided Miss West can dodge the bombs and escape from Hayling.

It was a very quiet night last night. Now three nights in succession have been quiet, so we are beginning to feel perhaps we are in a relatively safe area. If our air force continue to destroy German planes as they did yesterday, it must make the war shorter. I feel there are grounds for more optimism. Moreover, we are now already getting used to shortages of odds and ends, though it is frustrating that one is not able to order supplies from London as we did previously.

I have just got over a tummy upset. I can't think why it should have let me down, but there seems to be a prevailing epidemic. I have had a great deal of treatment with brandy from Matron, port and brandy from Miss Dunning, White Horse whisky from Alan, ground rice from Mrs Whitbread, and a nice dose of *mist pot cit aromat cum opio* by my own prescription. Amazingly, all this has effected a miraculous cure. The various prescribers are now crowing, so I think I shall probably have a relapse quite soon, but I will limit the treatment to the first three prescriptions.

My love to you and all the children,

James

A day or two later this letter (undated) was sent. At that time Jennifer Gault, aged nine, the daughter of Dorothy's sister Iris, was staying in Havant with Jim Rickett. The bombing remained heavy.

Sunday
21 East St
Havant

Darling,

I have had quite a good day, having worked all the morning. Joe Briggs came this afternoon or rather to lunch. We slept in the afternoon and then went to Stoughton to tea, had a short walk, supper with Winifred, and then home, seeing patients on the way. I have just finished writing up my diary for twenty visits tomorrow, Monday, already, so I shall be nicely occupied.

Joe is tired. He has had no nights in bed before 4.00 a.m. due to raids. It is odd that the very first day you left, they started. The night I wrote to you, Jennifer came to stay, and we went to bed fairly early. At 2.30 a.m. they dropped a big something which woke me up. The house rocked and the gun fire was considerable, so I reluctantly (as you may guess) got up (the lights were off, so I fumbled for torches and candles) and went in to see Jennifer. Mrs W. produced tea, and I was really rather scared: it felt as if one bomb had arrived on the front door step and one on the back, another on Miss Chandler, and one on the International Stores. I turned in with Jennifer in the spare room, and she dropped off to sleep after a bit when things got quieter, so I went back to bed about 4.00 a.m.

Judge my astonishment the next morning to find that the nearest bomb was two miles away in Farlington. It must have been a really beautiful bomb, as they sometimes have been described. It destroyed 120 houses. The blast a) opened our kitchen windows, b) broke the co-op windows in North St., and c) blew open doors and brought down ceilings even in Warblington and Denvilles.

Miss Pratt, Miss Chandler, and Mr Outen were unscathed. I decided then that Jennifer had better go back, so Iris came for her on Friday. Jennifer had been a very pleasant companion, and I missed her after she had gone.

Last night was quiet. It is cloudy and quiet tonight, so I think I shall go to bed in good time.

I'm a bit worried about Libya. I hope they stop at Tobruk[5] and don't sail straight in to Alex. I also hope we hold them by Mount Olympus.

I had to give my patient Mrs Jackson a sharp talk yesterday. She was being thoroughly negative about everything and everybody. One might call it a typical puerperal anti-climax depression. She said she hated bottles, hated nappies, hated babies, loathed the guns at night, and incredibly(!) had only one maid. I thought about this and decided to attempt my mark-1 "psychological" approach. I painted a worst case war picture, with England becoming a fortress island and Winston heading the Government remotely from across the Atlantic. She was rather taken aback and asked me, "You think I'm making a fuss?"

---

5   Italian forces invaded Egypt from Italian-held Libya. They took Sidi Barani, which was sixty miles across the border. General Sir Archibald Wavell, after receiving tank reinforcements, made a counter attack and drove into Libya, capturing Tobruk, which was an important Italian naval base. Mussolini understood he was outnumbered and did not fight back, turning his attention to Greece, which he intended to invade through Albania.
Despite the small success at Tobruk, the war in North Africa and the Balkan States was not looking good. After the failure of the Tripartite Pact, which was Hitler's attempt to recruit the support of Russia and the Balkan States, he was planning to overrun Yugoslavia. The Allies had a large naval base in Alexandria, which, along with Malta and Gibraltar, was crucial to us in the Mediterranean.

"Yes," I said, "you have been comfortably isolated by pregnancy, and now you are not feeling too fit, so you let your own molehill obscure the mountain that is the war situation". Amazing to say, she took it well. Perhaps now she may improve. You know the moralizing humbug that I am! At least on this occasion I got away with it.

I shall go to bed Doo. Love,

James

Dorothy returned to Havant from Scotland, leaving the children behind. She was to stay for about three weeks and then return to Scotland.

Alan and Margot Campbell

CHAPTER 3

The diary starts

26 September 1940

I had to operate in Southampton this morning, so I arranged for Dorothy and self to have lunch with my good friend and fellow GP Bill Sears and his wife Helen, who live nearby in Lyndhurst.

Before I left, I was summoned to see Wing Commander Knocker, who had just returned from London where he had an unpleasant experience. Having finished his day's work at the Air Ministry, he was sitting in the lounge of a small private hotel in Earls Court, when the house received a direct hit. It collapsed like a pack of cards, and Knocker was buried in the debris. Incendiary bombs set the ruins alight, and the bombers then returned and used the beacon as a target so that bombs fell in the neighbourhood about every quarter of an hour. He managed to speak to the rescue party quite early in the night and so was assured they knew of his presence. As he expresses it, "It was a most restless night, with a large piece of hard rubble piercing my buttock, and hearing the flames crackling overhead." However by ten o'clock next morning they managed to extricate him. He was suffering from a broken rib, but otherwise no more than slightly bruised.

His sister, who was in a nearby room, was killed at the same time. He was clearly deeply upset but was anxious to return to London, as her affairs needed sorting out. I persuaded him, however, to take a few days off to get over the shock.

He expressed enormous admiration for a young civil servant who was pinned beneath him, who had a broken leg and a badly crushed foot. This boy was eighteen hours before they got him out and, although conscious, he uttered not even the mildest complaint during the entire rescue procedure.

There have been frequent warnings today, but no aircraft have been overhead until this evening, when the customary intermittent barrage started.

Nell McDowell, my partner's wife, came to supper. She has just heard from her husband Toby, who is with the Navy and still in Malta. He recently received a batch of twenty letters from her, so at times they both must feel really quite isolated from each other.

27th September

I heard today some other details from Knocker, who was in the hotel in London when a bomb landed. He was able to talk to his sister throughout the night. She suffered severely; she was continuously sick and in great pain. Presumably, she had severe abdominal injuries. Added to her sufferings, she had a severely injured dog pinned on top of her, which died early in the night, and later she complained of its unpleasant smell. Presumably the wretched animal had also sustained abdominal injuries. Her body has not yet been recovered from the wreckage, now four days later.

Knocker's comments mentioned how useful a torch would have been, as he found it was difficult to assess his plight with accuracy in *total darkness. Having a penknife however, he was able to cut a hole in an overhanging carpet and so obtain a free supply of air. He remarked on his extreme alertness throughout and his complete faith in his rescue, although he was resigned to the fact that it might take days. There was a small shaft of light and air between the debris and a remaining wall, he judged, and about ten feet of debris on top of him. Every time a bomb exploded, this settled a little, and his available space became correspondingly smaller. He looks better today and is resting in bed. His work at the Air Ministry is not of paramount importance, so he has agreed not to go back immediately.*

The next day I had an amusing conversation with a young serving colonial officer's wife who has a nasty boil on her cheek. This certainly can be a most serious condition[6], but it is responding nicely to treatment. She, for her part, however, is showing extreme resentment that it had not cleared up in twenty-four hours and is rebellious. I encouraged her with the notion that it was subsiding and should be settled in a week. Her horror at this length of time led me to gently point out that one's body cannot be expected to always carry on in perfect health. Impatience tends to retard rather than hurry the process. This smug homily obviously annoyed her, and she replied that she neither needed nor wanted a lecture from me, apparently having already had several from her family. You don't always get away with it do you? Despite the rebuke, somehow we remained in communication, and the conversation then took a general turn. She has a quick mind—not very accurate, but she has a way of firing questions without waiting for a reply. Hence the conversation started to run in a series of darting movements in many directions, reaching no great distance in any one.

---

[6] In those days prior to antibiotics, an infection on the face could be very serious and lead to a "cavernous sinus thrombosis"—a complication which could lead to a fulminating and often fatal meningitis.

Alan Campbell arrived home from Whale Island at seven o'clock in the evening, and so to celebrate we went to enjoy a drink with Peter Jopling. When we did get home, we were more than ever ready for a late supper. As we drove in the dark, we noticed that the Thorney Island red Luftwaffe decoy light was now on Westbourne Common. This seems a little hard on the rabbits there, but at least the local people aren't complaining. It is moved about every two nights.

Everyone is rather depressed about Dakar[7]. It seems the least said about it the better.

30th September

A busy day. Old farmer Arthur Bray of Compton scratched his finger while thrashing and has been running a temperature of 104 degrees. I was a little alarmed, but I found him slightly better to-day and responding to sulphonamide. He is an extremely busy man, who farms over two thousand acres of rather poor land, but by dint of the scientific application of artificial manure, his crops are as good as farmers with the best land. He uses the most up-to-date machinery, and he told me to-day he had seven tractors all at work ploughing. He also uses a cutting and thrashing combination. He is also lucky in having an excellent landlord, who keeps all the buildings in excellent repair.

I was sent for urgently to see Mrs McKay, whom I found unconscious, having shattering epileptic fits every five minutes[8]. Apart from general

---

7   Dakar, which is in Senegal, was a part of French West Africa and was under Vichy control. It had considerable potential strategic importance, as it was situated on the Atlantic coast. It was a possible landing place for the Allies into North Africa. De Gaulle hoped to win it over to Free French control, but the Vichy French refused to surrender and damaged two British battleships, *HMS Barham* and the *Resolution*, which were then forced to withdraw.

8   Prolonged epileptic attacks amounted to a condition called *status epilepticus*. This was, at that time, a lethal condition. Nowadays it is extremely rare owing to modern drug treatment.

measures, there was little I could do medically, and I immediately ordered the ambulance to admit her to hospital. I stayed with her while we waited for the ambulance, but a sudden and more severe fit just before it arrived finished her. These terrible attacks had never been properly controlled by any of the many treatments we tried, so her life had recently become unbearable. This was the time, I thought, for a philosophical approach.

My lunch, taken at teatime, was more than usually welcome.

Before I went to Scotland, I operated on a patient whom I summed up in my mind before the operation as a pathetic old dear, doubled up and acutely ill with bowel obstruction. At that time she was very sick, but after I operated to form a colostomy, exteriorizing the bowel to relieve the blockage, she rallied well. I surmised she must have a malignant constriction in the lower part of the pelvic colon. This was the most likely diagnosis. Because of her poor state, I was not able to explore the cause of the obstruction. When she recovered, I sent her home and, on my return from Scotland, went to visit her. I was astonished to find she was six feet tall and only about fifty-five, whereas when I had seen her previously, she looked like a woman twenty years older. In the course of conversation, I found that she had been a chauffeuse in 1908 and had driven all over England for twenty years. Today I gave her a spinal anaesthetic and was prepared to do whatever was necessary, even a major bowel resection, but I was delighted to find that what I thought must be a malignant constriction was actually massive adhesions from a previous abdominal operation. I was able to do an anastomosis to join her transverse and pelvic colons together, which by-passed the obstructed area. This was a most satisfactory alternative. I went out to see her late tonight to find that she had stood the operation extremely well.

While sitting with Matron later, the hospital was shaken by two very loud explosions—presumably bombs dropping fairly close. This cannot be very pleasant for Matron, who sleeps in the hospital all the time.

1st October

Farmer Bray has had a very bad night. His scratched finger is still swollen, though thankfully it is not getting any worse. He is a wiry, active man who sets a very high standard, both for himself and his men. He works for twenty-five hours out of the twenty-four. I noticed that both he and his wife had become very anxious, so I telephoned and arranged for Dr Hern (consultant physician in Portsmouth) to come and see him this afternoon. He had had a lot of muscular pain recently and laid stress on this, so that I suspected they were thinking that tetanus might possibly the problem. Reports of tetanus were appearing fairly regularly in the farming world.

It is curious how intolerant of illness the active people can be and how soon the morale is undermined, giving way to introspection and apprehension—especially if one's livelihood might be affected. This is the only time Bray has experienced a septic fever since he was a lad. It shook him severely.

I managed to get a couple of pleasant half days rough shooting recently. The first one was at Fishbourne, where Hallett and I took Dorothy, who agreed to help as a beater to try to get the birds to fly. We were delayed at our start by examining a Junkers 88 which had been shot down and had landed in one of the fields. This is the first time that I had examined anything but a total wreck close up. The intricacies of its electrical system particularly impressed me—also the quality of the interior finish. We then had a bit of sport, finishing up with a whisky and cake with Katie in the farm house.

Katie is the surviving member of three spinsters who have continued to live as they did eighty years ago. The house is dark, dirty, and full of red velvet and plush curtaining; the carpets are threadbare. They have no electricity. The very dim oil lamps hardly pierce the gloom. The fire and food, however, are past criticism. The cooking is performed by Annie, a young thing of some sixty summers who has been with them since she left school. It is done in front of an open fire. Usually after shooting we "take a little tea". This starts with whisky to help our appetite. Then, suitably revived, we are able to sit down to tea, consisting of ham, brawn, cold sausages, hard-boiled eggs, celery, and tomatoes as a first course. Jelly is always served in narrow glasses, so that the spoons provided will not reach the bottom because of the conical shape. The jelly is so good that it is permissible to use the spoon handle for the last mouthful. Cake is then served. This is made with ten eggs and all the trimmings of the old farm-house recipe. Before rising to leave, we are pressed with chocolate to "fill the corners".

Then attention is turned to the dogs, who, muddy, tired, and wet, have lain steaming and smelly in front of the roaring fire. They are fed with the best sweet biscuits and bread and butter, after which Tigger usually gallops round the rooms, rolls, and scrabbles up the heavy draped curtains. Then he embarrasses us by making loud reports, as he unashamedly farts—his favourite way of showing appreciation.

I learnt that Katie, together with Evelyn and Annie, the two housemaids, sit up all night until all gunfire has ceased. Katie tells me that Annie frequently gets nervous, which Katie treats with a liberal helping of whisky. Evelyn then also becomes frightened, but she is given sherry, as it is considered wiser not to take spirits until you pass the age of thirty. There is, of course, brandy nearby in case any one of the three gets really faint.

The other pleasant day was with Peter Jopling, of which more later.

Then the diary relates the story of a serious accident that occurred at Thorney airfield, a small nearby unfenced airstrip used by the RAF. In those days, the modern emergency service did not exist, and ambulance crews were under instruction to take casualties from road accidents and other emergencies to the nearest hospital. This might even be a GP-managed cottage hospital with no resident doctors. On their arrival there and after assessment and resuscitation by the GP, if they were considered serious enough, they were then sent on to a larger hospital. Only in exceptional circumstances would the ambulance crew go straight to a major hospital. In this particular case, the ambulance crew might have thought the casualty was so seriously injured that he might not have survived the longer journey.

Here Dorothy interrupted with a call on the telephone. Matron from Emsworth Hospital says would I come as soon as possible as they were expecting an ambulance bringing a man from Thorney airfield who had both an arm and a leg cut off in an accident involving a plane that was landing on the airstrip at the time. I put off two people in the surgery and overheard one of them remonstrating that he was a new patient. I saw him for a moment and could not stop myself from being rather cold. I think he felt that a new patient was worth catching. At the hospital I phoned for a blood donor who lived near, deciding to get a group O[9] patient to attend. In the circumstances this was better than having to wait for the official cross match. Kent, my GP anaesthetist, arrived soon after and immediately got ready to give the anaesthetic.

---

9   Blood group O rhesus negative patients were then known as universal donors. A blood incompatibility reaction was then extremely unlikely. In an emergency it was justifiable to take the small risk of incompatibility against the greater need to save a life.

The ambulance then arrived with the casualty in a state of severe shock. He was extremely collapsed and bloodless, so I was glad I had the blood already for immediate transfusion.

Such was the state of his circulation that his pulse was barely palpable, and I could not obtain any blood-pressure reading. There was no tourniquet on the severed limbs, and yet despite this there was no bleeding.

Kent gave gas and oxygen, while I attempted to clean up the lacerated stumps. During this procedure, however, he stopped breathing, and in spite of our vigorous efforts, he died. The story was that he had been driving a tractor across Thorney airfield when a Blenheim bomber was coming in to land. It failed to clear him. It severed his leg below the knee and his arm above the elbow.

Dorothy and I then left for Hayling Island where we had been invited to dine, arriving an hour late. Despite our protests, they had waited for us without starting the meal. Alan, also a guest, with a couple of drinks inside him was in excellent form and recounted the following telephone conversation. In my absence, he had picked up the surgery phone to answer an incoming call.

Voice (female) on the telephone (VOT): "Is that the doctor?"

Alan: "No."

VOT: "Well, perhaps you can help me. My husband is having eight teeth pulled out at the hospital tomorrow. Should he take his pyjamas?"

Alan: "I should think so."

VOT: "Will he have to stay the night?"

Alan: "I will just try and find out."

VOT: "You see, if he does, I should like to get someone in to spend the night with me."

Alan (surprised): "I see, but I expect you would like to have him home with all this gunfire."

VOT: "Of course, but I don't want him home if he is not going to be any good."

Alan (still more surprised): "Oh!"

Farmer Bray with his septicaemia is a little better, but still feels very low, chiefly due to the effect of M & B 693[10]. It does make one feel depressed and ill.

Last night a most distressing incident occurred. I had dozed off in my chair, when I was wakened about midnight to see Sheba in the middle of a very severe fit, with her head right in the fire. The fire had sunk rather low but was hot enough to seriously burn her nose and mouth. I pulled her away from the fire, and when she came round from the fit, she was in great distress, scratching, whining pitifully, and rushing about the room. I was quite powerless to do anything to make her more comfortable, and there was nothing I could think of that might soothe the raw mucous surface to quieten her. I was in a quandary. We had never been able to control her fits. I felt the time had come that I should put an end to her life and put her out of her misery here and now. Vets were, by now, all tucked up in bed. Leaving it all until tomorrow seemed simply prolonging the agony. I reached for my syringe and stock of morphia. I prepared a dose of 11 grains (over half a gram)[11] and added a fiftieth of a grain of hyoscine as an enhancer, mixed it in a syringe, and gave it to her, hating the whole business intensely. She appeared unaffected for twenty minutes, then gradually sank, first on her haunches, then onto her paws, only after being violently sick. By 1.30 a.m. she was still alive and whining periodically. I thought this

---

10   One of the first sulphonamides which was used before penicillin was discovered
11   The adult dose to relieve pain is just a quarter of a grain—15 mg.

was amazing, as the same dose would have made a man unconscious within five minutes and killed him within an hour.

I decided to repeat the dose, this time into the heart to make it more rapid in action. Her respirations then became quite quiet, but still she lived. I curled her up in her basket on the kitchen floor, cleaned up the mess, and decided to leave her. So at 2.30 a.m. when eventually I went to bed, I wrote a note to Dorothy, saying, "Wake me before you go down," and went, very miserably, upstairs. This morning to my astonishment, Sheba was up and awake. She was rather restless but in less pain. Animal tolerance to some drugs is astonishing. She was only asleep for five hours despite the huge doses of morphia I had given. She has a nasty burn on her nose and lip but has this morning taken some milk and pheasant stock, so I have decided (to my intense relief) to await developments and see how she gets on. She is much quieter tonight but was restless during the day, following Dorothy from room to room. She has a most pathetic look in her eyes and has lost all her wild and joyous spirit.

Margot Campbell telephoned from Scotland to say the children are all well. Considerable domestic details are being discussed, with the idea of our friend Molly Atkinson joining up with the Scottish contingent.

Last night Alan again answered the telephone and listened to an anxious voice saying that a little boy had tied himself in knots, and could he help? Alan admits he thoroughly enjoys getting these titbits. He suggested that perhaps she had better talk to the doctor. I then gathered that a small child, a Slovak evacuee, had very deftly tied a piece of string round his penis. This had caused a constriction, and intense swelling had resulted. I went to visit him and found the string was cutting deeply into the flesh. This poor little chap, who wore powerfully refractive glasses, had a sad and frightened face. He was obviously terrified at what he had done and what might happen to him, but at the same time he showed remarkable courage. I got him to lie down on a couch and very carefully, though not without pain and much difficulty, managed to remove the ligature. He bore the pain and discomfort with what I have come to regard as Slovakian stoicism. Compared to many English children, he was considerably more controlled. I talked later to his foster mother and came to admire her for taking an evacuated and orphaned child into her household when she already had three of her own. I wondered how she could possibly cope with all the feeding and clothing. He was obviously being well looked after, and I wondered if she had received any help. Before I could do this, clutching her purse, she asked my fee. I then enquired how her expenses were met. She replied that she had clothed and fed him for a year and had received nothing. In the circumstances it was obviously quite inappropriate for me to make a charge.

Today I attended the inquest on the Thorney airfield fatality. The RAF was represented, and I was struck by their laudable lack of formality in comparison with that in both the Navy and the Army. One would expect that it might lower efficiency, in that the free and easy atmosphere which pervades the RAF might suggest slackness in discipline. Their combat results, however, speak for themselves, as illustrated by the numbers of RAF planes shot down compared with the loss of German aircraft. Despite being heavily outnumbered, their masterly air tactical fighting is proof that there is absolutely nothing wrong with their methods.

I have just heard the reason why the little Slovak boy tied himself up. Apparently he caused a good deal of annoyance to the occupants of the air-raid shelter by running up and down the garden path to spend a *penny every quarter of an hour. Hating to cause all this inconvenience, he tied a piece of string around the offending organ.*

6th October
Today I found Farmer Bray much better. His temperature has fallen, the finger is better, and he has reached that stage after an illness when, relieved of its pain and discomforts, he is still glad to rest in bed. Having been off of his job for a fortnight, he is no longer fretting as to how things on the farm are going. It is in this stage that it is so pleasant to spend half an hour talking, when the veiling cloak of reserve is readily shed, and he is only too glad to see someone from outside the house to relieve his boredom. He has that mental relaxation when he is prepared to talk about his work, his attitude towards life, politics, and so on. This was the case today. He talked of the inevitable social reform which we must face both during, and more especially, after the war. This will probably involve the state control of banks, of railways, and of medicine. There could even be state influence in foreign trade. Indeed, even nationalisation of land might be embraced as a socialist ideal.

At the present time, the voluntary hospitals are magnificently run. The standards are excellent, but the problem is that financially they are on a hopelessly unstable basis. The various hospitals that are now run by local government give an indication of efficiency, but they lack that team spirit amongst the medical staff and the nurses that is found in voluntary hospitals.

Medicine is very much a personal business. Diagnosis is an art and is based on the knowledge of the family, the background, and the temperament. The GP must always be the key and must use it to open the various social welfare doors. A recent example of how the state failed is provided by a problem I experienced at the height of a bitter cold spell last winter. Mrs H. was expecting a baby. Her husband, an officer in the RAF, had been killed in a flying accident. She was terribly upset but had been wonderfully brave and was most thankful that the baby was on the way, so to speak. When she started labour, she was suffering from the first uncomfortable day of German measles, which was rampant in the district. She was a big strong athletic girl, but I had been a little apprehensive, as the foetal head was still high when labour commenced. Labour went slowly and with very little advance for twenty-four hours. Then about 2 a.m. on the coldest night possible, it became evident that the likelihood of a live child without a caesarean section was small. Emsworth Hospital was full to overflowing, the County Medical Officer comfortably in bed. (His office closes at 4 p.m.) The municipal hospital in Portsmouth, to which all difficult cases have to be admitted, refused her on account of the history of German measles. The only alternative was the Hospital for Infectious Diseases, which was full of scarlet fever and meningitis patients, and no one would think of a caesarean in such a place. In any case, the senior medical officer, who I eventually managed to contact, was adamant. They had no operating theatre.

I got back to Marion Reece, matron at Emsworth, whose reaction was magnificent. She told me that despite the hospital being full she would move out of her office to make an extra bed. She decided that to operate in the theatre would contaminate it and result in spreading the infection into future open surgical wounds. So her office was cleared and the dining room would be used as an operating theatre. Supporting her, the whole staff rose to the occasion. They rushed around providing nurses, instruments, and sterile drums. They turned up the radiators, got extra heaters, and warmed up the freezing cold room. They brought down spotlights and suction equipment from the theatre, and the *operation was carried out under anaesthesia on the dining-room table. Both mother and the baby were saved, to the delight of all.*

In the evening, I was called to see Peter's mother, Mrs Jopling, at Aldsworth. In the dark and under the blackout restrictions, she and Peter had driven their unlit car into a lorry without lights and smashed up their rather nice MG. Fortunately, apart from a shaking up and a grazed lip, they were well. They had with them two undergraduates who had recently joined up in the Navy and were stationed at St Vincent in Portsmouth preparatory to joining the Fleet Air Arm. They were quite badly shaken, so I phoned Alan, who contacted St Vincent and was able to get them a leave extension.

CHAPTER 4

<u>10th October</u>

Just recently, a young and recently married wife consulted me about her problems which I attributed, after talking with her for some time, to a nervous state. She appeared happily married, she had a job, and there were no immediate financial worries. At that time they were anxious not to have children, which they could ill afford. I found nothing amiss medically, so I prescribed a little sedative. I saw her again later, and I found her to be no better. When she came back, I wondered if there could possibly be something more to it that I had not uncovered with my original talk. Certainly nothing obvious was apparent. I thought I had better speak to her husband. He came to see me. He appeared to be a very caring young man and was most concerned for her. After talking generally to him, I enquired about sexual relations, remembering that they were trying to avoid starting a family. So I asked him what form of contraception he was using. "Yes," he said and, after a little thought, added, "I get out at Fratton." For a moment I wondered what he meant by this, and then I remembered that the last stop of the train from London to Portsmouth is Fratton Park. "Get a condom," I said, "and stay on the train." He did, and after that she had no further problems.

A wet sleepy afternoon in front of the fire after a surfeit of pheasant. Thank goodness they aren't rationed!

<u>14th October</u>

What's in a diagnosis? The answer is "everything". I went to see Warner at Farlington. He is off work and is confined to bed with acute lumbago. Today he asked me what I had written on his medical certificate. I could not remember for certain, but I suggested to him that I had written fibrositis. He said, "But I thought I had lumbago?"

I then decided on a gentle tease. I pointed out that the head of his department might well react quite differently to the two diagnoses. In fact, each was equally correct, as the conditions are synonymous. To the lumbago he would say, "Why the deuce doesn't Warner come back? He has only a touch of lumbago." To fibrositis he would say, "Poor Warner! He has been on night work with the ARP, besides doing his ordinary day's work. He is obviously overdoing it and is now crocked up with fibrositis. I must ease off his work a little."

This seemed to satisfy him, and we then returned to discussing his pain. His wife had completely covered his back with Elastoplast. He made an anxious enquiry about this. I replied with great emphasis and solemnity that this must on no account be removed. He expostulated, "It doesn't seem to have cured me, and it irritates frightfully."

"Yes," I admitted, "but it keeps your wife happy." Flippant remarks don't always work and are often intensely irritating, but fortunately on this occasion it pleased him, and we both laughed together.

On Tuesday morning, who should arrive but an old friend, Molly Atkinson? Her parents have been bombed out of Beckenham and have joined her in her house in Westbourne. Saying what I thought at the time she might want to hear, I told her how quiet it was in this area, except for the regular nightly bombardment against what we thought were just single planes on their way to London. The words had hardly left my mouth when, with impeccable timing, we were all startled by a flight of daylight raiders, including bombers, flying low just over the housetops, machine-gunning Bedhampton, Havant, and Emsworth. Poor Mrs Luff was killed while gardening in Bedhampton. A bomb in Meadowlands brought tiles off our roof, and one in Denvilles demolished about six houses, killing the people inside. There was an immediate local reaction, and the locals are quite amusing. Stuart Hallett described it graphically and admitted to lying full length on the path outside his house during the raid. George Orr, as usual roaring with laughter, said the pilot who machine-gunned the Downs villages around Compton and Fernbanks must have been drunk, while Mr S. said, "They actually came over my house and put a bullet through the window—bloody sauce!" The general air seems to be a mixture of indignation and amusement rather than fear.

Dorothy engaged Miss Tofts as nursery governess for the children. Poor soul, I know she's destined to become "Toffee". Although she has no experience of teaching, she seems keen and willing to turn her hand to anything.

Dorothy goes back to Scotland tomorrow, but I am consoling myself with the thought of going up there myself, hopefully near the end of November.

Yesterday I cut my work to a minimum, as I wanted to take Dorothy to see her father. He is aged eighty, alert and active. True he is rather deaf, but today he had an electrical gadget with the aid of which it was possible to converse at ordinary levels of speech. He is a most admirable man. He is absolutely upright in mind as well as body and has that strong, simple, single-mindedness that results from about sixty years of army-induced self-discipline. He is a widower who lives alone, loves a glass of port, and appreciates good food. He does not allow himself port unless he has a guest, which, of course, nowadays is very rare.

He occupies his days with church finance and church warden duties. He also acts as an air-raid warden and goes patrolling, complete with boiler suit and tin hat. Then, for a little relaxation and leisure, he plays bowls and snooker at the club in Milford-on-Sea. He has become an institution in the district and is an inspiration to all, including myself. Recently he bought himself a new bicycle and so can now ride down to the club.

Gerald, his son and my brother-in-law, was also there. He is now an enthusiastic Home Guard member. On his beat the other night, he found a car apparently abandoned at 2 a.m. He approached it and shone a light inside, to find two rather startled occupants. "I must see your identity cards," he told them.

The male occupant nervously asked, "Why? Have we done anything wrong?"

"That," said Gerald severely, "I must leave to your conscience."

In its short life, the Home Guard has rapidly become an institution. Taking part are old retired soldiers, old seamen, farm labourers, retired admirals, country gentlemen, and others. They are of all political hues and made up of intolerant Tories together with Labour Party supporters, enthusiastic undergraduates, and those with no politics at all. They work together, happily, give up their sleep, and do ordinary jobs in the day time. Retired commanders-in-chief might be in the ranks and on equal terms with their gardener or odd-job man.

We went to see a crashed German plane not long ago. An enthusiastic Home Guard member was in charge. When he learned that one of our party was a naval officer in mufti, he took us to the front line and gave lurid details of the anatomical parts of the German pilot that were scattered over the countryside. He was happily giving us enormous pieces of fuselage as mementoes when, becoming mysterious, he promised to show us his own particular find. Walking away, and with frequent glances over his shoulder to see he was not observed, he thrust his hand into the depths of a nearby haystack and pulled out a cylindrical piece of metal, eighteen inches long and three inches in diameter. "See that?" he said. "Incendiary bomb." Then quite happily he thrust it back into its hiding place—the middle of the haystack. We kept our distance after that.

Dorothy and I went to the cottage today and arranged with Phillips, the local builder, to talk about the alterations. He is a character who works himself alongside his men. He will tackle more or less any job. He is constantly at loggerheads with the local council, whom he regards as a body of men specially got together for his annoyance. He is quite unscrupulous about evading the various restrictions. At one point we had considerable difficulty with the plans for our drainage system. The local springs of the valley called the Lavants rise up in the winter and flood the cess pit. This he neatly overcame by putting in an overflow pipe and leading it off into the neighbour's ditch!

On Tuesday, 15 October Dorothy returned to Scotland. To avoid sleeping close to the Portsmouth bombs, Jim Rickett accepted an invitation to stay the night with Alan and Margot Campbell, now renting a house in Stoughton close to Jeremy's, which is still not quite ready.

21st October

I have written nothing for days, and it seems a shame to let this opportunity slip by, despite the late hour, as it is nearly midnight.

Ronnie Hornby phoned me a day or two ago to say he was quite alarmed by his wife Margot's nervous state, which had been brought *on by her realising she was pregnant. Caring for the future baby, along with the pressures of the school, was clearly weighing heavily on her. I thought the only possible way to help her to calm down would be to get her away, and the only answer would be for her to come to stay with us for a few days. So this was then agreed.*

She was brought down by car. However, twenty-four hours later she suddenly said that she thought she might be starting a miscarriage. This very much affected the plan. I thought she would be better off back at the school with some help and the advice of her local doctor, who could keep an eye on her. So I returned poor Margot to her own home at Amersham and, being intensely pragmatic, I felt that her nervous state would be relieved if she did in fact miscarry.

Eileen T. (an old friend) turned up tonight from London. It was good to see her, but she was really shattered by it all, jumping at the slightest noise. She was in a pretty awful state and, I thought, on the verge of a nervous breakdown. She was on her way to Shanklin on the Isle of Wight to take up a permanent job. She has not slept in a proper bed for a month on account of the constant air-raid warnings. She has spent most nights in the local shelter waiting for the all-clear. She starts at every bang and is exhausted and weepy. She looks older and is quite subdued. She sobbed uncontrollably on Margot's shoulder when they were left alone. I would not let her go to Mrs Weekes', which was the original plan, but insisted on her staying the night here. I rang up the Shanklin place to say she could not get over today. Then I gave her a hefty dose of Medinal[12] and sent her to bed. I sincerely hope that a long night's rest might make her fit to take up her new appointment, particularly as the Isle of Wight should be a lot quieter than London. It is now after midnight. I must go to the post and get my letters off.

---

12   Contains phenobarbitone—used as a night sedative.

John Rickett

22nd October

I was prepared for a very heavy day today. I had fixed up for all sorts of minor operations and consultations in the morning, so when I met Nurse Anderson on the doorstep at 7.30 a.m. saying that Mrs Pearce was well into labour I had to sit at the telephone and alter all the arrangements.

I then had breakfast and saw some of the waiting patients in the surgery, when the expected message came that I was wanted for Mrs Pearce. When I had seen her originally at the ante-natal clinic, I had written myself a reminder that the baby was at the time a breech. At the next consultation, I had to decide what should be done if it remained a breech. After confirming the diagnosis by X-ray, I endeavoured unsuccessfully to turn it under a general anaesthetic. Then I was faced with the knotty problem of how to manage the delivery. As they are sensible people, I put the problem to both husband and wife. The risk of going ahead with a natural delivery—which would mean a small risk of losing the child with which a difficult breech delivery can occasionally be associated—must be weighed against the slightly increased risk to the mother of a caesarean. They asked my advice, and after some hesitation I cast my vote in favour of leaving the baby to deliver naturally. Of course I was anxious, but in the event it proved to be perfectly straightforward. This can so often happen when anticipating trouble. The whole thing was easy and gave no cause for anxiety. She delivered herself in record time, with only a little manipulation on the extended legs and to the after-coming head. I left them all happy and well at 10 a.m., with the resulting slack day lying ahead. As a consequence, I dawdled round chatting to people until I found I was getting behind with my other arranged work.

Here writing my diary has been interrupted by an irritation and the great satisfaction of giving my foot a good scratch. Having suffered on and off for many years with epidermophytosis or, as it is usually called, Chinese toe rot, the physical enjoyment of a good scratch is usually denied me. As Dorothy says, it is unseemly, and anyway I drop patches of skin on the carpet. Alone now in the surgery, I can indulge myself to my heart's content. It is a most satisfying indulgence and well worth the slight inconvenience of perpetuating the toe plague.

To resume my story of Sunday, I motored up to Amersham with the miscarrying Margot Hornby. It happened to be a glorious October day. There are always a few days when beech trees seem to change colour all at once. These spells are usually associated with night frosts, misty mornings, and sunny days. All the autumnal colours are brought out by sunlight, particularly in patches of light and shade. Woodrow High House, in such a setting, was the home of Margot Campbell's parents, Sir Nigel and Lady Eileen Campbell, and was rented to Ronnie and Margot Hornby to accommodate their evacuated school. The school looked tranquil and restful as we drove into the drive. It is astonishing, however, I have to say, just how rapidly one can be transported from one atmosphere to another. We approached the house relaxed and in good humour, but as we crossed the doorstep, Margot immediately locked into her role as the headmaster's wife.

"There," said Margot "that wretched boy should have swept the floor at 7.30 this morning, not just before lunch." Ronnie greeted us with a wan smile and a nervous laugh. The small boys, whose school has been evacuated to this peaceful spot, scampered about banging doors, falling on the stairs, and making an infernal racket. In the drawing room Sir Nigel was smoking, but he got up at once and button-holed me, asking me to have a serious talk with Margot C. I went in search of her,

John Rickett

only to be caught by Ronnie, who wanted to clear up one or two points concerning management of the possible miscarriage, and suggested to me that I have a word with their local doctor. I agreed to this and decided straightaway to go and phone for an appointment. While going to the phone, however, Lady Eileen appeared and announced to me that she wanted to have a few moments chat all alone. The hall in this house has been well christened the Brenner Pass, as it is the intersection of so many paths and as a consequence is the scene of often highly important consultations.

Finally, with two glasses of sherry inside my stomach and so many viewpoints in my brain, I joined the lunch party in the oak-panelled dining room. Here the pandemonium of fifty small people eating and talking did little to clear my now quite befuddled state of mind. I remember a remark recently made by the Chinese writer and academic Lin Yutang: "It is only when the bottomless pit has been filled that one can think clearly." I soon came to realise that the only clear-thinking and utterly sane person in the house was Lady Eileen, or Mopsey as everyone calls her. She is practically stone deaf, but lip-reads with uncanny accuracy. She has developed an extraordinary common-sense approach, apparently as a result of this deafness, and partly from her amazing empathy and grasp of the situation. She has reached that stage of peace with the world by a clear definition of her ideals and philosophy. This is, after all, what we all seek but few of us find. In this house, along with the responsibility of caring for the children in the absence of their parents, and compounded by the war situation, there is a fraught domestic atmosphere. Through this, Mopsey alone remains beautifully unperturbed, a true friend and a pillar on which all could lean. Even I, a relative stranger, leant, I hope without her noticing, and then went off fortified to talk to the doctor.

He, poor man, has had no holiday since the war started and has just risen from his bed after recovering from a feverish cold. I thought he looked tired and ill. If he starts the winter like this, I shudder to think whether he will survive it himself. In spite of this dilemma, I had to burden him with the household troubles, medical, domestic, and otherwise. I then suggested a firm line for him to take, to avoid an implosion with the various impending crises of nervous breakdowns, miscarriages, and staffing difficulties.

At this stage in the war the German U boats were attacking the convoys in the Atlantic from the French Atlantic ports and were causing heavy Allied losses. In September the Italian Army invaded Libya and captured Tobruk. General Wavell made a counter attack in late September, recapturing it and driving the Italians back into Egypt. Rather than reinforce the African campaign, the Italian Army turned their attention to Greece and in October invaded through Albania. Meanwhile, back at home the blitz continued.

25th October

Colonel and Mrs Young came over from Hambledon for dinner, which was very courageous in the blackout. Unfortunately, they were caught on the way in Havant for not having complied with the lighting regulations.

I must now tell you about Mrs Hickson. She is nearly forty, and after fifteen years of childless married life, she sent for me to come and see her some months ago, saying she could not understand why she had persistent indigestion. She had tried Carters Pills for the liver, Bile Beans for her bile, and MacLeans for her stomach, and all with no success. When I came to examine her, I found, to both my surprise and her horror, that she was three months pregnant. Yesterday, now a fortnight before her "expected" date, the waters broke and she started labour, so I arranged for a nurse to call. She was an elderly patient, and this was her first pregnancy. I had put off making a final decision as to how to conduct the labour until this last month.

When I went this morning, I found the baby's head very high, well above the pelvic brim. She is a large, athletic person who plays a great deal of tennis. Her muscles are like iron. With the membranes having ruptured early and the head not yet engaged in the pelvis, it was clear that labour would, at best, be long and difficult. With the high head, one could only guess where the placenta was sited, and heaven only knows where the umbilical cord was lying. It could well be lying deep in the pelvis, in which case it would get compressed as the baby's head engaged. Close foetal heart monitoring would be vital[13]. Even a successful vaginal delivery could require, at the end, a tricky forceps delivery. As a live child was particularly important in one of her age, I advised a caesarean section forthwith. This plan was readily accepted, and I moved her to the cottage hospital and did the operation this afternoon, and I am glad to say all went well. When I went in late tonight, I found she was very comfortable and her strappingly healthy baby girl was keeping the whole place awake with screaming.

Mrs Hickson has appeared to be forty ever since I met her ten years ago. She got married quite young to a large man who has never quite grown up. He is still mentally hardly more than about twelve, and unfortunately the difficulties of life terrify him so much that now he has slightly hunched shoulders and a permanent expression of anxious enquiry.

---

13   In those days foetal heart monitoring was at best spasmodic and performed by an attending midwife or the doctor, who would use an ear tube against the abdominal wall.

Having married this strong, energetic young woman, he has sheltered behind her skirts and has been protected against the wicked world. She is full of character and has clearly made the most of what must have been a very difficult marriage. She talks endlessly and laughs immoderately, having a great sense of humour to which a sound common sense is applied. After coming round from the anaesthetic, she was in a highly excitable state. She was so stimulated that she could not sleep, chattering without stopping to take breath. I gave her morphine earlier in the evening but had to supplement this with bromide and even chloral before she settled for the night.

<u>26th October</u>

I found when I went to see her that, despite my powerful medication, Mrs Hickson had a bad night, is demanding visitors, and is talking endlessly. On medical grounds I refused. She has only just undergone a caesarean operation. She is in a highly excited state and must have rest and a quiet time rather than the stimulation of relatives and friends. Unfortunately, this did not stop the flow of words, and I eventually had to walk out of the room to be able to get on with my other work.

This morning when I visited her, Mr Hickson was at the bedside, and I was amused by his appearance. He had rather the hangdog look of a naughty boy. There was a subtle mixture of paternal pride, acute anxiety, and utter astonishment that this should have happened to him of all people. He reminded me of a recent anxious father who, after a long and difficult labour, was informed that his wife had given birth to a daughter. He said with great relief, "Thank God it's a girl! I should hate to think of a son of mine having to go through what I have been through tonight."

John Rickett

The Hickson daughter weighs nine and a half pounds, so I am more than thankful that decided upon a caesarean. Just before the operation, I had changed into a green suit which I use in the theatre. Mrs Hickson was most impressed by its startling colour and said, "Well I should call you Dr Robin Hood." I replied, insisting that I was just looking for the babes in the wood.

CHAPTER 5

The following is a letter from Margot Campbell to Dorothy. It is undated but was probably sent from Jeremy's cottage on 26 October. There had been a raid with reports of parachutists, and a bomb fell near the house in Scotland.

> Jeremy's
>
> Darling Doo,
> We all had a marvellous night and no bombs or guns, so we were all the more horrified to hear of the bombardment you have had up at Rhu. It must have been a shock and not at all pleasant! I wonder where they fell. I feel bad, as you seem to have had all the difficulties to cope with up there—the change of staff and bombs dropping, and then the parachute scare. That must have been extraordinary. Did it seem real? Poor Margot Hornby has a problem. Her threatened miscarriage has settled down, but she remains very low and seems to feel hopeless about everything. It's odd, but when you talk to her, it seems hard to get through to the true Margot and get beyond all the servant worries, etc. As soon as you clear up one worry for her, she digs out another! It's hard to know how to help her. She seems to be living in quite the wrong direction, and she won't feel differently till she tackles life differently. And it's so awfully easy when you

start feeling like that to lose sight of real things completely. It's so hard on Ronnie—I'm afraid this threatened miscarriage only unsettled her more.

Best love to the rabble,

Margot

28th October

Mrs Blore came up to the surgery to see me. She is a pathetic middle-aged soul with a ghastly complexion and a contrastingly brilliant red and bulbous nose, wherein lurked her problem. After I told her once again that she must face an operation to remove these polypi, she moaned that this was the sixth time that it had been done. Friends of hers had told her that normally for this condition only one operation was needed. She then volunteered the thought that, rather like natural things that grow in the garden, her polypi might be of both sexes. In that way they might reproduce. Or perhaps, I reflected, she was thinking that her nose had become a hotbed of wickedness.

Letter from Jim Rickett dated 31 October:

Jeremy's

Stoughton

My car's brakes have got badly, worn so I have had to borrow Mrs Glanville's *[senior partner's wife]* car whilst mine is in dock. This reminds me, there is a second-hand Standard SS 20 h.p. car in Twine's Garage going for £35. I am offering my Vauxhall 14 in exchange. To make the deal I may have to give way slightly on the price of the Vauxhall.

I shall lay it up or rather not license it just now. It will make it a second car, which will be a standby if the other Standard breaks up. The old Standard is showing its age, having done some 30,000 miles now, but apart from brakes, it appears in reasonably good nick.

1 November

My plans for shooting straight have gone astray. I slipped into the surgery to look at my letters and make arrangements about my work. The second letter I opened was the following :

Surgeon Rear Admiral R. J. McKeown OBE, RN.,(Retd.)
Flat 50 Southsea Terrace
Southsea
30/10/1940

Dear Dr Rickett,

At a meeting of the Local Medical War Committee yesterday, it was decided to recommend you for a Specialist Commission in reply to an urgent letter from the Central Medical War Committee. This has been done. The next move will be that you may shortly receive a letter from the War Office directing you to attend at Salisbury to be examined by the RAMC. Kindly let me know when you are granted a commission, i.e. of Major.

Best wishes.

Yours sincerely,

R.J. McKeown

Hon. Sec. Local Medical War Committee, Portsmouth

John Rickett

PS, Please show this letter to Drs Soames and Glanville

Although I have been on the list for possible call up since the spring of this year, this came as a bit of a shock. I had been told that the Army was so well supplied that I should be required more as a GP here. I suspect it heralds an offensive in the Near East. So I spent the day with my mind filled with one hundred and one arrangements which would have to be made, not only for my practice, my partners, my patients, but also for the family in Argyll.

I had a day shooting which started at Up Marden, where there was quite a nice show of birds. Ordinarily, I would have thrown off all my worries and enjoyed the day, but I found myself unable to get my mind away from McKeown's letter, the implications of which will cause a considerable upheaval.

After the first two drives, there came the sound of aircraft overhead, and soon there was the incessant drone of planes. The path of each could be traced by the exhaust tracing white streaks across the blue of the sky. From the varying pitch and from the twisting exhaust trail, it was obvious that a brisk fight was going on what seemed like about five miles above our heads. I found it a little difficult to keep my attention on the job in hand; it tended to wander skywards to see how the fight was progressing. This was to the detriment of accuracy and to the benefit of the birds flying over me. During the last drive, I saw a plane crash. It must have fallen quite close to Stoughton, so at the end of the day I motored that way home. I found Margot in the cottage, pink and excited, as the plane had crashed a very short distance from the house. Unfortunately, it was a hurricane with a Polish pilot.

4th November

Today I went to see old Mrs Gardiner, aged ninety-four years, a funny and rather fierce old lady, with a piercing eye and a hawk-like nose. Her daughter Sophie, a widow of some sixty-odd years, is a charming woman, but it is easy to see that she is completely dominated by this old lady. She told me of a conversation with her mother soon after I had started seeing her. The old lady told her, "Sophie, I am really no better, and if that young man (and she must have been referring to me) doesn't take me in hand seriously, I shall turn into an old woman." This was said in all sincerity.

Today she was talking about old Mr Peel, whom she knew when she was a child, and recounting how he used to hunt over her father's land. "Show the doctor John's horn, my dear," she said, whereupon Sophie disappeared and brought back the old hunting horn given to her by John Peel.

These close family ties and relationships remind me of a visit I made recently to a boy called Barrett. After examination, I found he had an inguinal hernia and recommended an operation. His mother said, "Well, I must ask his father." His father had, at that moment, walked in for lunch and, on being consulted, said, "Yes, but I must ask my father." It so happened that I was going to pass the garage at which he works, so I took him in the car, and we went into the office to talk about it and hear his verdict. The old man of seventy standing behind the desk was the grandfather of the lad. After a little pondering, he said, "Well, perhaps I had better have a word with Dad." So we then moved back to the kitchen, where the grand old man of the family was sitting by the fire. The talkative little bearded figure, aged ninety-eight, who was sitting in a high-backed chair, gave his verdict: "Certainly, if the doctor advises it." All matters to do with the family are eventually referred back through the consultative chain of dads and back to this wonderful old man, who treats the whole lot of them like a pack of children.

I went to fit my new plus fours on today. They were hastily ordered before the purchase tax, as my old suit is full of holes, and its blemishes can no longer be hidden by leather patches. The new one is a nice quiet check from Mackintyre of Inverary, but I am afraid it will not be ready for Friday when I shoot at Littlegreen. I saw Sir Phillip today and enquired about the Saturday shoot which I missed. I immediately realised all was not well. Apparently, there was a first-class scene with the old head gamekeeper, Snook. There has been quiet warfare which has gone on all the season. Which way should the birds be driven to give the best presentation to the line of standing guns? Snook insists on driving them up wind in order to keep them on his ground. Sir Phillip says drive them down wind, and if they go over the boundary "at least let us have a little shooting." On Saturday after lunch, having Snook's agreement that the birds were to be driven down wind, the guns took up their stands, when an under-keeper was sent to alter their positions, as Snook had decided to take the drive the other way. Sir Phillip stood his ground, and at one moment the drive was going on from behind the guns in the opposite direction! After a "slight" altercation, Snook announced that he was going home, and home he went, leaving the party to arrange their own drives. Today, however, he and Sir Phillip made up their quarrel and almost wept on each other's necks.

On leaving Southsea this afternoon, the sirens started, and when we reached Portsdown Hill, a raid was in progress. We decided to stop and watch it. It was really a most magnificent sight. Portsmouth was half shrouded in a dark grey mist. The Isle of Wight stood out *clearly beyond. The sun was low, and the sky shone brilliantly with Turneresque colouring. We watched the flight of German planes, which appeared as luminous dots in the clear sky over our heads, as they were only visible when the sun caught them. Bursts of anti-aircraft fire appeared and were extraordinarily accurate, at first behind, but then in line, and then each successive burst getting nearer the planes until they appeared to be amongst the flight. Twenty yards from the car, a small shell fired by one of the planes fell and exploded. There have been many warnings today, and the drone of planes high overhead has been incessant. Tonight again they were very active, with two very loud explosions whilst we were having our dinner.*

Ronnie H. writes today to say that as a result of my invitation, Margot, still in a nervous state, will come after all to Jeremy's, this time together with the children and nannie. I hate the thought of losing the cottage again, but I feel that it cannot fail to help her to straighten out her sadly twisted ideas, and in view of this, it will be a worthwhile sacrifice.

Greece was invaded yesterday. We, as usual, are giving our full support, and they appear to be resisting the advancing forces to the full. I expect this heralds the announcement of another "brilliant" evacuation and "glorious" retreat. We are, of course, preserving a policy of defence until we are really ready and fully armed, but the regularity of the evacuations becomes a little monotonous.

Jim Rickett's sarcastic comments were brought on by the news announcements, which always gave an over-optimistic interpretation of events. At the time the news from the Atlantic was bad, with German U-boats attacking the British convoys and ships, and the Italian Air Force attacking in the Mediterranean, where Malta, strategically placed as it was, was under heavy bombardment. In addition, there was continuing heavy bombing at home, and morale was not good. On 6 November another armed merchant cruiser, the *Jervis Bay*, was sunk in the Atlantic. Mussolini planned to invade neutral Greece, the timing of which angered Hitler. He went ahead despite advice that the mountainous area would prove difficult so late in the year. Churchill offered Greek General Metaxas help, but this was turned down. In the event, the Italians were overcome and forced to retreat back into Albania early in 1941. In November the Italian fleet was attacked and badly damaged by Swordfish aircraft in Taranto Harbour. Supplies were then able to get through to Malta.

But November was not a good month, as both Hungary and Romania joined the mutually supportive Tripartite Pact with Hitler. This ensured the security of his oil supply.

The diary continues.

6th November

On the way over, I left Margot Campbell at Jeremy's, where she had lunch with Margot Hornby. I am thankful to say that M.H. has already greatly improved and seems to have been influenced by the happy atmosphere at the cottage. She is now looking forward to the infant more or less philosophically, instead of the absolute horror as of a few weeks ago.

Norah, our secretary, made me laugh when she was writing up my diary. She described my shooting Littlegreen birds as "little green birds". Later, when going through the bills—gas, electric light, etc.—we came to the wine merchant's account, at which she made the acid comment, "I am not surprised they appeared to be little green birds."

Letter of 6 November 1940:

21, East St., Havant

Darling,

Lots of conflicting thoughts today. Liston, a surgeon in Southsea, contacted me and said "I hear your name has been sent up for calling up. I understand that as your practice is under pressure at the moment, you are reluctant to leave. I am willing to take your place although my name is lower on the list."

This is the quandary. I shall not try to interfere but leave it to the powers that be to decide. No news at present, so I am sinking back into that state which I reached last time of not expecting it. I can't help feeling, however, that if I eventually have got to go, I might as well go now. However, all is in the lap of the gods, so I shan't worry.

My dear old Mrs Wilders' nose is bleeding, so I must go and plug it. Hell!

Letter of 7 November 1940:

My darling Doo,

I think I will probably ring you up tomorrow morning as you will have by then heard my news. I'm definitely starting to think that by now I should have heard something if they wanted me.

Today I went to Iris' for lunch. The General was there and was in very good form. He is coming to stay the night on Tuesday and is going to have his birthday dinner here. I must get him a present. We are going to get a special dinner for him.

Anyhow, I come up on Wednesday week. Isn't that marvellous?

I went to see Margot Hornby today. She is already in better form. She is at last settling to the idea that having the baby is at least a bearable trauma.

We had a noisy night last night, but I did not stay awake. This morning there was some more machine gunning, but I was safely tucked away having a bath.

Lots of love,

James

The diary continues:

8th November

We were machine-gunned again yesterday morning. The dentist next door got a bullet through his window. Quite frankly, it is a very fruitless form of warfare, as it is too quickly over to frighten anyone, and only very seldom does anyone get killed.

I saw old Colonel Sands on my way out to go on home visits. He now looks even more like the typical local retired "red admirals" than before. His small eyes are set deeper in his now almost purple countenance. I am afraid his love of the Spirit of the Glen does not seem to have suffered from the new war prices. For us mortal folk it is now prohibitive.

21, East St., Havant
Saturday, 9/11/1940

My darling,

I was so thrilled with your Wednesday's letter. It was such a good one after hearing about the Medical Corporation's moves. I have still heard "double nuffin'"!

Now I am afraid I have to confess to you I have been a very naughty boy. I have changed the old Vauxhall 14 for the second-hand 20 h.p. SS, with a bonnet stretching from here to Bedhampton. The Andrews call it a "tart's parlour". Greedy on petrol, but thankfully for medical use, that is accepted, and it will allow me to do my rounds quicker.

Don't come down, I'll come up instead. If I am called up for army service, I will have a lot to do.

My special love,

James

CHAPTER 6

Jim Rickett took a week's holiday to visit the family in Argyllshire.

20 November, 2 p.m.
I am sitting in a first-class compartment on my way to Scotland, and this makes me expansive enough to write some diary. For the last week, what with all the innumerable arrangements to be made for even a week away, coupled with several evenings when I was dining out, I have written nothing. There have been many alterations to the plans. Alan found that he must attend a conference on Friday so, nothing daunted, he decided to delay the trip and go on to Scotland from Bath after his meeting. He will either come by night train or be able to obtain a service plane to fly him up. Margot at first had decided to stay with him, but the fates had ordained otherwise, as her father, Sir Nigel, is going to be in Glasgow tonight. These arrangements suggested it would be best if Margot came with me, for which I must confess I am grateful, as a long train journey with a congenial companion is much more interesting.
We left Havant at 6 a.m. and drove the SS through pouring rain in the dark. We made very poor time, having had to make a long detour to avoid a bomb on Butser Hill. At Esher the roads were better, and it began to get light. We finally reached Euston at 8.45. I had wired Bobby Plowright yesterday that we were coming up, and

he met us there for breakfast. He looks astonishingly well and has, I think, put on a little weight. He sleeps peacefully in his own bed in London and is undisturbed, except by bombs when they fall in the very near vicinity. There have been two within a hundred yards of the house, but, thankfully, no damage was done to his home at 9a Church Row.

We ran it rather close for catching our train and nearly missed it. When I went to the garage where I had planned to leave the car, I found that it longer existed but was just a heap of ruins, so I had to enlist the help of a taxi man to find another close to Euston, where I could leave the car while we were in Scotland. He piloted us through all that remains of Woburn Square, which seems to have suffered heavily, and he eventually found us a garage which previously had a glass roof. It was now open to the sky with debris everywhere. "Can I leave my car here?" I said. "If you like," he replied with a rueful smile. I purposely came up in the SS instead of the small Standard, as the capital loss will be less if it is destroyed by a bomb.

A week ago I had assisted a young Miss Swift into the world. She was, one might possibly say, lucky enough to have her birth saluted by a salvo of guns. This is a privilege that is normally only accorded to royalty. That these were fairly close seemed, apparently, to be of no consequence to her. When I heard that bombs had been dropped in Havant's Mulberry Avenue, I called to see how Miss Swift and her mother had fared. I found that six bombs had fallen within one hundred yards of the house, two of them not more than twenty yards away. Mrs Swift was composed, the nurse rather irritable as the noise had awoken the baby, and the mother-in-law, who is running the house, apologetic because the customary standard of cleanliness was temporarily abandoned. Many tiles had come off the roof, and this had allowed rain to soak the ceilings, while the vibration had sent plaster everywhere. I called again yesterday, and all was quite restored to normal. A large piece of paving stone from the drive had to be removed from the roof and had been autographed by all and kept as a memento.

It is remarkable how people have already given up the idea that it is the wrong time to produce children, and for the most part they are content and happy to be pregnant. One such person recently came to see me at the third month for a routine examination. "Let me see," I said, trying to remember her dates, "May, isn't it?" "No," she replied coyly, "Phyllis."

Friday, 22nd November

It was so extraordinarily dark this morning that we were all late rising and were nearly late for our appointment for a day to be spent shooting at Glenakil. We went by way of the glen to meet the shooting party. It was a crisp, frosty morning with a clear sky. Standing in the shadows of the hills for the first two drives was rather cold, but as the sun found its way through, it turned out a wonderful day, and the birds, though not very high, made great sport. Margot was shooting conspicuously well. An exhibition of over-indulgence was in evidence at the lunch at Glenakil House. Lady Eileen and Colonel Campbell were our hosts, and they plied us with masses of excellent food. A delicious leg of lamb, brawn, cold roast duck, cheese, and shrimp paste, with more cream and butter than I have seen since the war began. The brawn must be eaten with a concoction of sugar, mustard, and vinegar. Although a little conservative about messy sauces, I was astonished what a fine art the food has become in this house. Rounded off with port, it was a meal to fortify against any eventuality. This all had an excellent effect, in that immediately afterwards I shot five pheasants in quick succession. "You will have to have port for breakfast on shooting days," was Dorothy's comment. Of course I agreed with her, but sadly it never happened. It was a happy party, and although I was a cuckoo in the nest of Campbells, they all made me feel like one of the family.

23rd November

I was looking forward to another day of planned sport. However trying to live in a house full of children complicates the morning routine. No bath is possible, as the only bathroom in the house is full of children, who seem to be partying and in various stages of dress or the lack of it. Children of all ages enthroned on each of the available seats. There they sit, singing or talking through the open door with anyone who happens to pass, swinging legs, kicking the pan just to make sure the background noise level never drops too low. All attempts I made to make the necessary visit had to be aborted. I realised today that one must rise early!

We met at Rhu Bay and having lined out ready for the birds enjoyed what turned out to be the best drive of the day. From one wooded hilltop to another, the birds flew fast in the wind and rising sharply. They were high by the time they broke cover; when they reached the guns they were even higher and curling—a shot to try the very best though I was unlucky enough not to be put to the test. The wind turned my birds the wrong way. We also beat out the woods round the house, Rhu. This was much to the delight of the six children who were all watching from the bathroom window.

John Rickett

"Bath time at Rhu"

(by Margot Campbell)

25th November

It started a wet day with rain pouring down, so we lined the children up in mackintoshes, gum boots, and sou'westers and drove out a wood near Rhu. Early on I organised a walk through the oat stubble to drive about fifty birds into the wood. Then the children, making the most fiendish noise, attempted to drive the birds back out of the wood so that we could get a shot at them. Not to be outdone the birds decided to lie low. Despite excessive noise and enthusiasm on the part of the children they refused to fly, burying themselves in the thick bracken. Not one single shot was fired. The beaters were not in the least disappointed. In fact, Philippa was quite openly delighted, as she strongly disapproves of blood sports. John, on the other hand, has no such finer feelings. When he was three and Dorothy was tucking him up after singing a lullaby, she said, "Listen to the pigeons calling." She thought this was a nice soothing sound and he would go quietly off to sleep. He, however, reacted quite differently. He woke up straight away, sat bolt upright, and said firmly, "They must be shot."

<u>27th November</u>
Today I returned south with Dorothy, Alan, and Margot. We spent a poor morning, trying to drive grouse in a direction to which they had absolutely no intention of flying, and then we had to leave the Glenakil party to start heading back. First we saw Kenneth Atkinson off on the boat at Tarbert and picked up Molly to give her a lift home. We were then already very late for lunch, but Alan could not resist the sight of seven cock pheasants sunning themselves in a small grass field beside the road. This was too much for him, so we were bundled out of the car spurred with his enormous energy and, full of strategy, we endeavoured to surround them. They were disturbed, however, by a passing cyclist. However we did manage to shoot one unfortunate bird. This wasted another twenty minutes, so lunch was not until two o'clock. Consequently, our departure for Glasgow was delayed, and we had a most trying run in the rain and failing light. Finally it was pitch dark. One hundred miles under these conditions proved such a strain that Alan and I had to resuscitate ourselves in the bar, where we met acquaintances from all over England! Glasgow seems to be the centre of the social circle, and the Central Hotel seems to be the general rendezvous.

As an extraordinary coincidence, Alan's brother Lorne was there. This was very much to Alan's delight, particularly as he has just been

John Rickett

awarded the DSO for leading two hundred men through German lines to Le Havre at the time of the evacuation of Dunkirk[14].

Then we got onto the train, a comfortable four-berth sleeper, arriving in Euston for a late breakfast.

The car, I found having dodged the bombs and falling debris, was intact. After a long day which included some Christmas shopping in Harrods, we were glad to reach Havant at 6.00 p.m. Mrs W. gave us a pleasant welcome and had laid on a special birthday dinner for Dorothy.

<u>5th December</u>

Dorothy is out reading a book for poor old Grainger, who, having saved his money all his life, has got a house of his own at last. He has always looked forward to retirement, but soon afterwards, he developed glaucoma and then a cataract. As a consequence he is now nearly blind. He can get no one to come in to look after him but, thankfully, still manages to cook for himself.

<u>Later</u>

I have just operated on Mrs Brady, aged seventy, doing a hysterectomy for cancer of the uterus. Unfortunately, there was one secondary deposit which could not be removed. The operation went well, so I hope she will have five years of comfortable life. Just as we were finishing the operation, a very heavy bombardment started. Bombs and guns were really very noisy tonight, rocking the house. I have just heard

---

14 The 51st Highland Division had been cut off by the advancing German Army at Dunkirk, unable to be evacuated. They retreated with a part of the French Army to St Valery, where the majority of the division was forced to surrender. Some troops under Lorne managed to escape through the German lines to Le Havre, where they were picked up by Alan Campbell's ship, which by coincidence happened to be there. Lorne was later awarded a further DSO and also a VC for other exploits.

that there is a large unexploded bomb in the garden of a nursing home at Warblington. Rankin McIlroy, who runs it, decided to take all the patients to his own house. I call this a truly Christian act, especially knowing the patients are bedridden old dears and mostly senile.

This made me wonder if the Carlills needed help. I phoned Stephen and told him the news of the dangerous bomb quite near his house. It cannot be more than one hundred yards away. He told me that he planned to leave with Hilla, his wife, and their boy Michael at 6 a.m. tomorrow. I arranged to fetch them at midnight, when they have finished their packing, to come and stay overnight with us. We have fixed up one bed in the consulting room and two in my dressing room.

There was a good lively fire following a bomb north of Havant, but we have had no news as to where or what damage was done.

I went to the cottage myself today and was delighted with the builder's alterations. The new kitchen will eventually be a great success.

6th December

I had a letter today from the Central War Committee declining my services in the capacity of a surgeon, so the doubt and uncertainty has now been removed, and I can settle to the idea that I shall be stuck here for the rest of the war, or until I am possibly called up as a MO. This has been naturally both disappointing and all very unsettling. I am now determined to stay and instead of a "blooming hero" be a "blooming martyr".

Dorothy and I went up together to Stoughton to the cottage today while Phillips is hard at work converting the garage into a kitchen. The effect will be to make the whole house much larger; it will also provide a really adequate larder and increase all cupboard space. One can never have too many kitchen cupboards.

Last night the raid was heavy, and a good many bombs were dropped indiscriminately. Just now another raid is starting. I suppose we may expect an attack like that recently launched on Southampton where the damage was serious. Let us hope not.

The Greeks still continue magnificently to fight off invasion, and my gloomy forebodings were thoroughly unwarranted.

8th December

Nothing more came out of Thursday's raid, though a delayed action from the night before went off and rocked the house. I learnt today that, sadly, Mrs Ripley was killed by a bomb which landed on her house, which was close to the nursing home. She had just started work after a serious operation. Poor soul and such bad luck! Philosophically and cynically, I feel that my time might have been better employed! At the time of her operation I had been very worried about her and had expended a great deal of energy and anxiety in looking after her. Finally she recovered. Now they can't even find her body. That makes two of my patients killed on Thursday, and neither body has been found. I wonder how such a death is registered. There is no death certificate. The statistics of home casualties, I am afraid, must be pure guesswork.

I was distressed today by finding poor old Miss Hancock with a strangulated hernia. During the ten years I have attended her, she has had a gall bladder full of stones removed, then had a gangrenous appendix removed, She has been ill with a bad heart, and then developed a thrombosis of the right axillary artery (the main artery to the arm), with which she was ill for weeks. After this she had a cerebral thrombosis, which affected her speech and gave her a facial paralysis.

Now she has to return to the hospital once more. I operated on her this afternoon. She stood it well and was comfortable when I visited her late tonight.

I took Dorothy with me when I called in to see her and we went on after the operation to see the Halletts. There we simply listened to them. Everyone was rather agitated as a result of the recent frequent raids. They were all talking at once. Paul, E.P.H.'s son, has had his house in Southampton destroyed by bombs and spent a very uncomfortable night in their Anderson shelter.

The conversation was difficult. There was Paul describing his experiences, E.P.H. tired of talks of the war and very anxious to describe his day's shooting at Fishbourne, and Paul's wife with photographs of her youngest son Morris, who is now in the Irish Guards. It ran something like this:

"I saw the flames, so hurried her into the shelter . . ."

". . . up by the elms I got into the ditch."

"It's very like him, but the mouth isn't quite right . . ."

". . . a beautiful covey. I got one with my first shot, but . . ."

". . . then they started. Six people were killed in the shelter next door . . ."

"I could see Lucky had a pheasant in front of him . . ."

". . . then one dropped right on the house."

". . . don't you like his moustache?"

"His old tail was going, then up he got. I missed him with the first but got him with the second."

"Now he is coming on leave . . ."

"I'm afraid they've completely messed up the car."

John Rickett

10th December

With the great shortage of doctors, my days consist of busy surgeries which are followed by the problem of finding the time to fit in all the home visits. Interviews with patients have, of necessity, to be brief and to the point. Avoiding waffle and vague ramblings, I prefer to get to the point as quickly as possible. However some patients have the greatest difficulty expressing themselves, and they can even be evasive and awkward in describing their symptoms.

It never fails to irritate me on entering a sick room and asking "What is wrong?" to get the reply "Ah, doctor, that's what we want you to tell us." When this happens, a fit of uncontrolled facetiousness is prone to well up inside me, and I reply, "Well have you a broken leg, or are you going to have a baby?"

I have been attending old Mitchell, who prefaces any reply with "not to say". He was lying in bed complaining of a chill on the stomach following his ARP warden duties at night. The conversation was like this:

"Have you had any pain?" "No, not to say pain."

"Have you had any sickness?" "Yes, doctor, terrible sick."

"Have you been feverish?" "No, not to say feverish."

"How many times have you been sick since yesterday?" "A good few times."

"Are you bringing up a lot?" "Not to say a lot."

"What was it like?" "I can't say I've taken that much notice."

"Was it bile?" "No, not to say really bile."

"Was it dark?" "No, not to say really dark."

"Was it colourless, like water?" "No, not to say like that."

After several days, I put him in hospital for observation and found that his vomit was typical of "coffee ground" vomit, with the tarry black stools of melaena. In fact, if he had been in the least helpful, I could have told at once that he was bleeding from a gastric ulcer.

Another woman I went to see today reported to me that she was "losing terrible". On examination I found nothing amiss in the gynaecological area, but there was a large palpable swelling in the abdomen. I placed a catheter into her bladder and drained down two pints of deeply blood-stained urine. The swelling then vanished. She had urinary retention with overflow from the bladder. She seemed to have confused her pelvic compartments.

This reminds me of the story of the two Mrs Harrises. I saw Mrs Harris of North Street, Havant and recommended her for admission to nearby Emsworth hospital for a routine examination under anaesthetic. I gave her name to Matron, who in due course wrote a letter but addressed it to Mrs Harris, North Street, Emsworth. So I was confronted by an entirely strange woman who answered the summons to the hospital, despite the fact she was not my patient and had had nothing wrong, not having consulted any doctor in years. The extraordinary thing was she did not think it peculiar that she should suddenly be summoned for an examination under an anaesthetic! Such is the implicit trust placed in our profession!

And, talking of irritating habits, some patients either don't listen or don't believe what one says. After explaining to the patient at considerable length all about the illness, including the diagnosis, the complications, and what steps you propose to take to remedy the problem, one gets the question, "Yes, doctor, but what do you think is really wrong?" There lurks a suspicion that there is something more that is being withheld. To be kind, I think they are probably distracted and are thinking of something else the whole time one is talking. This is especially noticeable when giving bad news. I find one has to go *very slowly and be prepared to repeat all one has said over and over again.*

With reference to breaking bad news, I have never regretted telling a patient, when necessary, that they are suffering from an incurable cancer[15].

---

15 At that time the standard teaching and practice of the medical schools was that it was best to conceal the truth of certain really serious illness—cancer, tuberculosis, and syphilis, in particular. It was thought that the patient's morale would suffer as a result, and this would be likely to have a deleterious effect on the disease itself. There was a stigma attached to these illnesses that was likely to cause serious depression. Language existed so that these diagnoses could be avoided when discussions took place between doctors in the presence of the patient. "Neoplasm" was the word used for cancer, "Koch's disease" was the term used to refer to tuberculosis, and "the spirochete" or "spirochetal illness" for syphilis.

Chapter 7

21st December

I don't know whether to ascribe my lack of writing to a very heavy cold or to Dorothy's departure on Wednesday back to Scotland. The plan was that I should drive up with her together with Jeremy Atkinson, Molly's son, stay overnight in Scotland, and then return back the next day.

We left at 6 a.m. on a cold Wednesday morning. As so often happens, it was bright moonlight, but there was freezing mist and fog patches. With steadily increasing fog, our pace got slower and slower until just short of Petersfield the car went completely out of control on a patch of ice, and visibility was reduced to only a few yards. I therefore decided to change the plan and put them both on the train at Petersfield instead of risking the journey by road.

Other things have disturbed my mind lately. The Central War Committee, having originally decided two weeks ago that my services as a surgical specialist are not required, then changed their mind and decided after all that I was needed, but as an ordinary medical officer rather than as a surgeon. This was not ideal from my point of view, so I phoned the secretary of the local committee yesterday and discussed the situation. I pointed out that I was willing to go where I would be of most value. The local committee then suggested I should volunteer for surgical work.

Currently, here at home, half my time is spent on surgery. I told them I would be happy to sacrifice my work here if there was a shortage of army surgeons. With the high incidence of air-raid casualties, there would then be a continuing need for local civilian surgical cover. They must understand the position fairly clearly, so now it is up to them to decide. I expect I shall soon find myself inspecting latrines. Should I be conscripted in the ordinary way, I think I shall likely endeavour to get in the Navy where I may be at least amongst some local friends.

The next disturbing thing, though disturbing in a different way, was the death of my mother's sister, poor Aunt Mary. She was an elderly "Quaker by adoption", a spinster who warmed her poor thin self over inadequate gas fires, eating frugally and reading the Church Times and the Daily Herald. The periods of moderate health were few and were filled with frantic writings to such newspapers as would accept her strangely expressed criticisms of modern decadence, the military training of the young, and like topics. The lulls between orgies of asthma, attacks of myocarditis, and inflamed ovarian cysts all culminated in her mentally throwing in the sponge and wading off into a semi-conscious world of her own. Singing, talking, and dreaming, she gradually slipped away. This, I confess, was at the end none other than a good thing. She, relieved of the very unequal fight against the horrors of war, has relieved me of a very unequal fight against an unsympathetic bank manager, who was responsible for her financial affairs. It will not have quietened him for good, but I am sure he will feel mollified for the present.

Kiki White, Sir Dymoke's daughter, is getting married early in January. She is only nineteen, which is early to be embarking on wedlock, but seems happily set on her future. Margot and I went to Chichester this afternoon to buy wedding presents, and we had a very entertaining afternoon—or at least, perhaps I should say I was very entertained. We went to an antique shop that caters for wealthy

Americans. Automatically I would assume that, though everything is in good taste, it is fabulously expensive. M. happily beat down and bargained in such a brazen way that I left feeling we had robbed the poor woman shop owner shamelessly. I told M. that as an exhibition of "honour among thieves" it left me painfully disillusioned. The result, however, was excellent. A Swiss oil lamp of about 1870 converted to an attractive electric lamp priced at five guineas, I got for three pounds; a Swiss milk bucket as a present for Dorothy, originally at four pounds, I got for three pounds; and a forty-five shilling set of table mats was procured for thirty shillings.

We went up to the White's late, took the presents and stayed for an hour drinking Lady White's potent cocktails. She told us that on a cruise she became so renowned for enjoyment of the cocktail White Ladies that they became generally known to the ships company as Lady White's.

This letter was written the same day, and Jim Rickett was wondering if by chance anything had happened to Dorothy on her way back to Scotland.

>21 December 1940
>21 East St
>Havant

>My darling Doo,
>I was so glad to get your wire. Though I remained quite calm, I did begin to wonder when it got to Friday lunchtime if you had really got back all right.
>There is a Budapest Orchestra playing tonight, and a sudden break occurred in the very nice music and a voice on the wireless

said "Germany calling". This completely destroyed my happy line of thought.

Haw Haw's broadcasts[16] are very distracting when they interrupt programmes like that. Again, there are times when I do wish Alan didn't have the wireless on quite so much! Haw Haw's voice has now given way to two women talking awful rot, which I'm not sure isn't worse.

This afternoon Margot and I went to Chichester. I bought a very nice lamp at Alysia for Kiki's wedding.

I phoned Iris today and fixed up my Christmas Day lunch with her, also to let her have the pony Minnie for the holidays. She is delighted, and we are having her shod tomorrow. This will give Jen a great thrill.

Guns a bit noisy tonight, but not too bad. We seem to be getting used to them. Jeremy's kitchen is looking marvellous. I have told Winifred she can stay till we come down in February or early March.

It may be the White's cocktails, but tonight I am feeling quite optimistic and harbour views of you coming home and the war to be soon over. We will then be back to the old ways of a peaceful Stoughton—everything back to normal. The war has done something in making me feel that things do happen in

---

16   Lord Haw Haw was the nickname of William Joyce, a man born in 1906 of an Irish Catholic father and an English mother who had moved to New York and taken US citizenship. He became a fascist, attending Birbeck College in London and joined Oswald Moseley's British Union of Fascists. He became an anti-Semite and went on to form the National Socialist League. In 1939 he fled to Germany to escape arrest and worked in 1940 for German radio's English service. His broadcasts started: "Germany calling, Germany calling," which interrupted English programmes. His voice came over in a jeering and at times sarcastic and menacing tone, with propaganda that caused considerable resentment and increased antagonism in England towards the fascist cause.

Havant and life is certainly not dull. I just want peace and to be with my family.

I heard from my brother Dick, or rather from his wife, and hope he will come over tomorrow for lunch. I was sure he would turn up as soon as he had heard Aunt Mary died. He will be asking about her will, so I phoned Earls Barton. Apparently the entitled bit all goes to our Mother for life—about £12,000. She then left various small legacies and the residue for us four children. The bit not entailed is £11,000 so we shall get about £1,500. Dick's bit is tied up. My brother, Jack, and I are trustees and will not be in a very enviable position, as he will do his utmost to untie it. I shall make no move without a solicitor.

My special love to you,

James

23rd December

Rather disturbingly, Sheba, who made a very good recovery after her severe burn of two months ago, has continued to have occasional fits, and last night she had three. She was in season a month ago and has had none since, up until now. I noticed yesterday that Margot's corgi Rob was showing undue affection towards her, and today our other dog, the spaniel Tigger, seemed to be interested. I wonder if this is what triggered the fits. Female reproductive organs, either human or animal, certainly seem to govern one's life! We should get her spayed, though with the shortages of vets these days I even thought[17] of doing a hysterectomy myself on her, combining the operation with removing

---

17 At that time a doctor was legally allowed to advise and if necessary treat animals as well as humans.

both ovaries. However, on reflection it would be simpler to get someone to give her a few doses of X-Ray.

Margot's dog Rob swallowed a sheep vertebra last month, and this lodged halfway down his gullet. Palpating his neck, one could feel the bone lodged there. Margot consulted me. She must have thought that, qualified as I was for human beings, then surely all other species would be simple, and therefore I could advise and, if needs be, operate. She supposed the anatomy of the dog cannot be very different from the human! So, undaunted, I took him to the cottage hospital, had a word with Matron, gave him an anaesthetic, and endeavoured to pull it out, but with no success. He was very troublesome under the anaesthetic. He alternately struggled and succeeded in biting my finger. In the end he became somewhat collapsed and moribund, and I was sure he was dead. After an hour of struggling, I decided to cut down on his oesophagus at the point I could feel the bone in his neck. The operation proved more difficult than I had anticipated, but after a bit of a struggle I succeeded. I then sewed him up as best I could and sent him home from the hospital to be nursed. As he got better from the operation, a troublesome fistula developed, so we had to reduce his food and fluid for about ten days, but eventually it all healed and he is now a very normal, though a highly oversexed, dog. In Scotland he disgraced himself by having an affair with his mother, who had just given birth to a fine litter. I am sure it is his presence in the house that has brought Sheba on heat prematurely. This is in addition to her fits. Perhaps, after all, it is on Rob that I should operate rather than Sheba.

Brother Dick's new wife sent a telegraph today. Brother Dick is the thorn in the family flesh. He gallantly joined up at the outbreak of war, leaving a good solicitor practice and an incredible pile of personal debts. He has bluffed his way from private to lieutenant, and up to date he has not been cashiered. I do not doubt that if he ever sees active service, he will be up to some exploit and—knowing him and his devil-may-care attitude to life—may get up to heroics and then get covered with glory.

However, I predict with some confidence that, having so irritated his seniors by complete disregard of red tape, army discipline, and tradition, just as soon as the war ends he will be discharged from his unit. At that point he will be returned once more to be a burden to his long suffering family. He is an incredible mixture of suave dishonesty, disarming candour, and complete irresponsibility. Having said that, I have to admit he was marvellous to his first wife who died soon after the marriage. She was a victim of disseminated sclerosis—in the latter stages of which he cared for her in every possible way, nursing her, managing even bedpan duties. Although he is a complete atheist, he took her to Lourdes. He did this with a mixture of cynicism and bravado, but underlying was great sympathy and affection. There is some good in him deep down somewhere.

Soon after joining the Army, as was his custom, he turned up to borrow money. He confessed to me then that he had thoughts of marrying again. "Why do you want to marry this girl? You can't keep her."

"She is an asset not a liability. She keeps herself."

"Why not live with her?"

"I have."

"Well, why marry?"

"She's frightfully keen."

I heard no more until today, when the telegraph came from Eve to ask if I would come to see them. I understood they had no car. I wired back: "Short of petrol. Both of you come to lunch tomorrow. Please reply." No answer. Will his desire to know more of Aunt Mary's will stir him into coming ten miles by bus? I shall be interested to see what happens tomorrow.

The following letter was written two days later and was sent at that time, just before Christmas, when Jim was missing the family and feeling quite low in spirits. Staying in Havant, he felt very close to the regular nightly bombing and very much on his own.

23/12/1940, Monday
Havant

Dear Doo,

I was so pleased to hear you on the phone today. Funnily enough, yesterday I had a bad day. I was fed up with being nice to people, considerate to Campbells, thoughtful about Winifred. It all arose out of whether we should have tea here or there-some silly thing in which I suddenly felt "to Hell with everybody" and got all silent and cross as you have seen me and know so well. I wanted you very badly. Still, it's all better now, and I realised that a little sacrifice on my part is in fact so good for me. No complaints darling, but I felt at that time damn lonely.

I am doing very well in the Xmas dinner line. The first with Iris on Xmas Day, then with Winifred on Xmas evening, Dymokes for a "Christmas lunch" on Boxing Day, and then there's shooting, and on our own on Boxing Day night.

You know, Doo, that with all my friends—and I suppose I have many—there is only one person in the world with whom I could live. When I think about it, the only time misunderstandings occur between us is when you get low because you want to be someone other than yourself. This is usually my fault. I want to be social or go gadding about and force you to be a gadder too. But in truth, I think, as I'm growing older, I'm more inclined to stay at home. Anyhow, don't ever be anyone but yourself. You must not change, because I can't possibly do without you, and you can't possibly do without me. So there we are. Maybe I am not considerate enough. I go gently off on my own tack or sometimes violently down my own way, grasping things I consider important and procrastinating about what does not appear important to me personally.

Enough of this. These thoughts do not need answering, and they are only the maudlin wanderings of a sentimentalist. I strongly suspect it was brought on by the enclosed letter[18], which at first struck me as pathetic, too. I'm afraid I thought he wanted to borrow some money. I feel ashamed of this thought, which made me maudlin again. In my case, this not due to an overdose of good Scotch liquor as I'm afraid it is so often with Dick.

The cottage thrilled me yesterday and at the same time contributed to my temporary depression by seeing the Andrews in it. The family looked so nice gathered round the log fire along with a lot of children—Colin, John, two Gilmans, and two Wallaces.

The invasion scare is still on, but there is not sufficient concern for the Army to stop Christmas leave, so I suppose it is only a relatively minor crisis. I am afraid the shopping situation is much more acute, especially as the supply of meat has dried up in Havant and we are told no more will be available until

---

18   This letter from brother Dick has been lost.

after Christmas. There are no sweets of any sort obtainable anywhere. We are commencing the tightening of the belt scene, the process of which we have talked about so long, but about which we have so far had to do so little. I really feel that the war is progressing and soon it will gallop off, hopefully into its final debacle.

Unless situations are constantly on the move, we tend to drift into apathy. I suppose that is why a dictator must constantly whip up the masses with hysterical harangues, speeches, and specacular coups. Apathy also creeps into my own life in my acceptance of things like secretarial muddles. General slackness slides in; then suddenly a frenzy of energy assails me and I clear up the surgery, sack the secretary, and pull myself together to do more conscientious work. This makes me envious of the Percy Levicks *[his senior partner]*—of their life and their slow and methodical conscientiousness and thoroughness on all occasions—though as a result, I suppose on the whole they have less fun.

Margot took Minnie over to Harting, much to Jen's delight. This was wonderful for her, as she loves riding, and Jen had been saving her Christmas money to buy enough food to have Minnie over for a week. David Gault has grown inches, and Christopher is a much nicer child, having been thoroughly squashed by the young Beddard, who is sufficiently large to knock him about.

Somewhat as I expected, Dick did not turn up yesterday. He has no doubt decided to have Aunt Mary's will looked up at Somerset House and will then try to find some legal flaw whereby he can get his hands on what little capital there is.

I need to be off to bed. The Campbells have gone up ages ago, and I'm with Tigger in the surgery. He is getting restless and he should be let out. I had better be off.

Goodnight, my darling, and keep remembering me.

Your James

Chapter 8

There was no further diary. After Christmas and in the first months of 1941, the damage caused by the Blitz, both in Portsmouth and in the surrounding area, resulted in some extremely heavy work, which Jim described in letters to Dorothy in Scotland.

This letter was undated but was almost certainly written on 5 January.

> Darling,
>
> It has been a very big day. First of all, there was Lady Mary with an acute ear, and then lots of visits. Amongst these was poor Doris, who was thoroughly bored with her sciatica and needed jollying along. I then saw a six-month expectant mother with a degenerating fibroid. I had to admit her to hospital [of which more later].
>
> I went on to do some surgical operations which were interesting. First there was Brigden. I had been watching him with a curious acute abdominal inflammation which we had hoped would settle. I decided I could wait no more as he was not getting any better. So I opened him up. He proved not to have a gall stone as had been suggested on the X-ray, but an enormous swelling forming a mass. This on investigation proved to be an old intususception[19] gone all funny peculiar.

---

19 An intususception is a rarity. It is an invagination of one part of the bowel into another. Peristalsis, the natural method of moving food down the alimentary tract, then complicates the invagination by working overtime, thereby resulting in a blockage.

It measured the most fantastic size and was ashen white and tense. I swooped upon it and separated it from all its surroundings, to which it had formed considerable attachment.

Having removed it, I investigated and found it lined with white stuff rather like toothpaste, and then in the middle a thick glutinous stuff which stuck to the fingers and behaved very like treacle. I sent the whole show off to the Radcliffe to analyse. Such a specimen was really a museum piece, but we are at war and it is only shrapnel and pieces of bomb splinter which really count now.

The next patient had a breast lump which happily proved to be just a cyst.

After this I dealt with the girl I had seen earlier who had abdominal pain in pregnancy at twenty-four weeks. I knew she was very keen to have the baby, particularly so in view of the fact that fibroids mitigate against pregnancy. The problem was that I felt sure that it could well be more than just some degeneration in a fibroid. It was mischief lurking in her abdomen. I had to open her up to deal with it.

On opening the abdomen very carefully, I found on the anterior surface of the uterus acutely inflamed giving already local peritonitis. I incised round the fibroid growth, only to run into excessive haemorrhage. I decided I must push ahead and separate it so that the bleeding could be controlled. This went well, but the haemorrhage was worrying. It is as well to remember that the pregnant uterus is a most vascular organ. Each time I put in a needle to close the exposed surface, the catgut cut through and fresh bleeding occurred. However, by dint of severe perseverance and that nice mixture of firmness and care that is so essential, I stopped the flow and closed the abdomen. I have been to see her tonight. She is still well and has fortunately not started labour. However, I feel that this situation is unstable, and the trump card is firmly in her own hand or she could keep it up her sleeve. At any time she could have a haemorrhage, a miscarriage, or worse—even (heaven forbid) an eclamptic fit—hopefully she could just go on and produce a normal infant. We shall see.

I then went on to give an arranged St John's Ambulance lecture. I have broken away from all set rules for lectures. I now work up a theme before going and then describe imaginary emergency situations and talk about the practicalities of dealing with them. I enjoy it better like that and only hope they do the same and will not need to put into practice the advice I give. Though in this situation, who knows?

I am sitting here writing and listening to a violin on the wireless playing "Kiss Me Goodnight, Sergeant Major". Personally, I'd prefer you to him.

My love,

James

On the night of January 11 1941, Portsmouth received a severe bombing attack. This was the most serious raid on the city so far. Three hundred bombers attacked the city and dropped an estimated 25,000 bombs. These were high-explosive incendiary bombs and land mines, many of which were parachute mines. Their whole charge was disseminated at ground level and had, therefore, the greatest impact of all.

Extensive damage was caused to the city centre. Kings Road, Palmerston Road, and Commercial Road were flattened. Six churches were hit, and an incendiary bomb lodged in the roof of the Guildhall. The resulting fire could not be put out for twelve hours so that this night became known as the night of the fire blitz.

The Eye and Ear Hospital was hit, and the Royal Hospital as well. The official figures estimated 171 people killed, 430 injured, and 3,000 rendered homeless. These figures must be a considerable underestimate.

Very early in the raid, the electricity generating station was hit, so the whole city was in darkness. There was also damage to the water mains, making fire control impossible.

That night Jim Rickett was motoring back from London down the A3. As he came past Petersfield over Butser Hill some thirteen miles away, he saw the city on fire. He wrote to Dorothy describing the scene. He started this letter wanting to reassure Dorothy in Scotland in case she had heard on the news about the blitz.

21 East St., Havant
Sunday, 12th January 1941

My darling D,

I feel all rested and good tonight because another phase in the war has developed. We have just had the Portsmouth blitz, and are now more settled again—at least partially.

I went to London on Friday to see McN. and others. Margot came with me to have her hair done and to go shopping. On the way back at the top of the Butser Hill and overlooking Portsmouth, an AR warden flagged us down and told us to turn off our head lights as Portsmouth was getting hell. By this time, there was an enormous glow in the sky—7.30 p.m. When we got to Havant, you could see flames shooting to the sky from many points. At home the house was in darkness due to a power cut. Margot was, not unnaturally, very worried about Alan, but she remained fairly calm. Mrs Whitbread was a bit shattered, but we decided there was nothing to be done. I phoned up the Eye and Ear Hospital but got no reply, which was not surprising as it was in flames. I phoned Ridout. He told me there didn't seem to be many casualties but the destruction is awful. There was a lull about 8.30, then at midnight it started again. We had gun fire, but out here in Havant there were no local bombs. The net result in Portsmouth was that Commercial Road from halfway down to the station and beyond is a heap of ruins. Palmerston Road and Osborne Road are burnt out, Handleys, Morants, and all of them just flattened. The Guildhall has been burnt out and knocked down. Eye and Ear [Hospital] are completely gutted, the Royal [Hospital] evacuated because the nurses home has been demolished. The Hippodrome, etc., is all finished, and Portsmouth station has been hit and we are sitting by candle light, which is a bore. The Landport Drapery Bazaar [large department store] has gone. Poor Horace Parkhouse is bewildered—his whole life job gone in one big puff of smoke. Next thing was Pop Ridout. Having lost his hospital and unable to carry on his work, he felt lonely and quite lost, so I said, "Why don't you move out and do the country work outside—Petersfield, Midhurst, Chichester, etc.?" The result was he came over this afternoon. He saw Saxtead [Margot and Alan's house in Emsworth] and has taken it for nine months.

Margot was delighted and said it's an ill Blitz that occasionally blows good.

Portsmouth is still a shambles with no light, no gas, and no water. There are streams of refugees evacuated from the demolished houses in the town and great miseries all round. I'm afraid this will increase the food shortages. The power failure is a bore, as it extends from Fareham up to and including Petersfield, Chichester, and even Bognor.

On top of all this, we went on Saturday to Kiki White's wedding. There was champagne galore and a rather forced gaiety. The Bishop was tut-tutting about the damage to morale, and Mrs Edwards was twittering nervously. They were all asking after you and saying how wise and how relieved you must feel to be safely distant. Little do they know the personal costs in terms of missing the family, but I do feel just now glad you all are comfortably away.

Yesterday on my rounds, I found every single woman patient I saw to be in a thoroughly miserable state. I was ticked off for rudeness, wooed, and just ignored, all because the women were feeling the emotional turmoil about the Blitz. The main street in Havant was a continuous procession of fire engines by the hundred. This made the traffic like a pre-war bank holiday. There were engines and fire brigades from Brighton, Tonbridge, and even Guildford, all muddled up with Kiki's guest's cars. This resulted in the sort of crush we know so well.

Alan is still down there in Whale Island, and now we are waiting for him for dinner. We heard the whole of the Whale Island team were out helping to clear up the surrounding mess.

Well, darling, I must write lots more letters. I feel a bit content that we are dealing with the crises in a nice British manner and that the war is progressing. It isn't like that damnable last winter when we had suffered so little and so much that was unknown and only pure speculation lay ahead.

Special love to you and to all, James[20]

In April there were more severe raids, and on 17 April Hayling Island was targeted. The reason for this was that the air-raid authorities had deliberately lit decoy lights on the island in order to simulate the lights of the dockyard. After the raid had started, they also lit decoy oil-drum flares to give the impression of burning houses and factories, in order to lure the bombing away from the dockyard. Naturally, the local people were somewhat indignant, but they were overruled in the greater public interest. The Portsmouth Dockyard was largely spared.

On 17 April, Jim Rickett wrote this letter to Dorothy in Scotland. The letter was started in the evening before the raid had started.

21 East St., Havant

My darling,

I have just received your Monday letter. I have not been able to write much, because I have been busy—in point of fact it has been hectic. I believe I wrote after Jenifer had come to stay. We had a very noisy night, and I had to send Jen back post-haste the next day. Last night there was another severe raid, and again it was very noisy—it even woke me!

---

[20] A graphic eye witness account of the night of January 10th is presented in Appendix D.

Tonight they are at it again, with flares over Portsmouth, continuous droning engines, and terrific barrages of shelling. I suspect it's Portsmouth tonight. The gun fire has got almost laughable. This has been bigger and better, and on a fireworks scale, the shells are even more beautiful each time. This poor old house will be shaken down soon, I feel sure.

Bill the builder is coming tomorrow to be vetted. He is anaemic, which I diagnosed on my first sight of him. He is such a nice chap.

I have just been interrupted by a lady who lives opposite here. The guns shake her all to pieces. She was brought over by an AR Warden, who has been carrying out his duties conscientiously "comforting the nervous civilian population". Perhaps his comfort was not to her liking, so she came to me full of hope or despair. She has left me armed with a sedative pill!

I am gratified by your remark about expecting me to kick over the traces, though at the moment there is nothing very tempting here. Still, you never know. Well, darling, I am hoping to see you soon. I went up to Stoughton this afternoon. Compared with Havant it is a haven of peace.

Lots of love to you,

James

The letter was then continued on the same date, 17 April (Thursday). This part was added later and speaks for itself.

The noise tonight is phenomenal. It is useless to try to go to bed, so I may as well write. I have stood in the arch of the front door, complete in my tin hat. It is as safe there as anywhere, and one can watch the blinding flashes. These must be land mines. Some look close enough and might be on Thorney. After each explosion, the blast reaches Havant thirty seconds later, accompanied by the tinkle of falling glass as the larger shop windows go. The larger guns are silent, but there are bursts of our machine gun fire which are very clearly heard and show that the anti-aircraft fighters are now busy.

The people walking by in the street are few, but the odd soldier returning and AR Warden pause to comment on the size of that one or the blast of this one.

"If the shaking that old back door is getting continues," Mrs Whitbread warned, "there won't be any door left by the time they are finished."

With all this going on, it makes me very restless. Should I ring up Thorney to see if they want help? I would be called to Emsworth hospital if there were any casualties, and to gallivant about the countryside searching for incidents is hardly fair to Mrs Whitbread (who would have to try to find me in an emergency).

It is now 5.30 a.m., and I have just returned from operating. What a night! I've had my hand inside a chest and felt the beating heart, seen lungs blasted by a nearby bomb, amputated a leg, and repaired multiple wounds of intestine—all accompanied by the music of shattering explosions. What a night! I sweated at the palms in anticipation of the work on which I had to embark, but when I started I was too occupied to think about it. There is a mobile machine gun close to our doorstep, and the noise it makes when it is fired is worse than the bombs.

Shall now go to bed.

21 East St., Havant
Saturday, 19 April 1941

Darling Doo,

What a night Thursday was. The gun fire was terrific. The blast shook all the windows and even the houses. They were grander and larger guns which appeared from all accounts to have been so close that they seemed in a local garden. However the reality is that they are few in number.

After the first part of this letter after a major explosion I phoned the hospital. Matron told me the windows had gone and there was moderate chaos. The phone conversation to Matron was something like this.

"Hello, how's things?"

"Oh, rather noisy as all the windows have gone."

"Oh well."

"My God,"—indecipherable remark-"My God."

Rings off.

Relieved for an excuse to see the scene, I went over. The police stopped me and warned of masses of broken glass, so I had to drive slowly. The last thing I needed was a puncture.

When I got there, I found Emsworth busy. Two land mines had dropped on the foreshore just at the end of South Street. I inspected the patients huddled in the hospital theatre anaesthetic pre-op room. They were a little inclined to giggle at my light-hearted remarks about the smell of sweaty bodies, but emotionally they were well controlled. All this went on to the accompaniment of terrific explosions and blasts outside.

As I am writing this, the telephone went. Mrs Whitbread was on the phone. Speaking to her during the last half an hour has just about destroyed my line of thought.

The guns are now at it again—but only occasionally and with no flares.

The telephone again. This time it was Dr Southam, who had sent along a girl who he said had evisceration of her intestines. It is difficult to describe the night, but it was a complete nightmare. Incessant bangs with the drone of aircraft all the time.

Later

Dr Southam's casualty was removed with some difficulty from the car which brought her up in the dark. The rescuers were tripping over stretchers whilst muttering curses. The ARP people were thinking because it was dark that "bloody hell" would sound less blasphemous than in daylight! We got her to the theatre and found her stomach, spleen, and intestine under her rather dirty vest. She was an ARP worker from Lovedean and was also wearing trousers and dirty undergarments. We cut these all off to find that her diaphragm had also gone, so that when I put my hand upwards from the abdomen inside the wound, I could feel a 'curious' organ pulsating in my hand. Then I realised I was holding the heart! I pushed back the viscera, but in the absence of bleeding I could do little except close the wound. (She died the next day.)

Then I went across to the FAP to find people had turned out in tin hats and were all busy. There was Dr Glanville in shirt sleeves and a tin hat, patching up minor casualties from the land mine in South Street. Granny Kennett, aged eighty-seven, had a fracture, and Granddad Kennett from the cottage at the end of Margot's garden was shaken and white, but he was standing and using his usual missionary voice with which he addresses the Hermitage Mission : "The Lord is with me. Therefore I shall lack nothing." Considering he had just lost his house, one had to admire his positive approach.

Mary Soames [Dr Ralph Soames' wife] is still like a rather intellectual mouse, with serious large eyes trotting hither and thither until Ralph himself appeared in a Mackintosh with hair very dishevelled. Mary, with a giggle, then straightened his hair and suggested that they go and see how if their house was still standing. Considering all the neighbours windows and doors had gone, I thought it pretty good of her to be busying about.

Tea at the hospital was liberally laced with whisky and was interrupted by the telephone. It was Dr Dewhurst at Havant to say that there was a man with a perforating wound of the abdomen who was very shocked, Please would I come. I got into the car and called in on the way to Mrs W. to find her calm but shaken, so I went on to Havant hospital and started on this chap. He had multiple lacerations of his intestine, and the abdomen was full of blood coming from a main vessel in the abdominal cavity. Clearly this man was another who was mortally wounded, and there was no possibility that he could survive. I hesitated whether to simply close the abdomen and do nothing, but I decided to give him the benefit of any doubt. So I went ahead and excised two feet of jejunum, closed a rent in the descending colon, packed the bleeding vessel off, and closed him up.

While I was doing this, Mrs W. phoned to say someone died in his sleep at Up Marden. Would I go? No, I said. The phone then went again. There are ten seriously injured marines from Hayling Island. Emsworth hospital can't take them because their lights have gone. Could we take them at Havant? Send them in, says we.

Well, altogether, we dealt with about thirty seriously injured, amputated a leg, stitched up intestines, treated multiple injuries, and had what I had only read about but had never seen—blast-injured lungs. The patient comes white, shocked and collapsed. There is intense pain in the chest and the coughing of blood-stained froth. The blast itself ruptures vessels and damages lung tissue, which then become acutely inflamed. It is a lethal condition.

All this went on to the accompaniment of the most infernal racket outside.

Four a.m., and we had dealt with them all and just had to watch the seriously injured. We phoned and evacuated to Chichester all those who were not desperately ill—luckily the lights stayed on in Havant so we could see what we were doing.

I then went back to Emsworth to see how they were getting on. All was quieter, and after a final visit to Havant, I came back to bed and to sleep.

Margot's house looks awful. All the window frames and doors have been blown out. The garage is half down, and the old kitchen is half flat. There was debris everywhere. The roof has kept intact except for one corner where a boulder hit it. The masonry above the kitchen window is all out. Inside I have seen little trouble, but there are ghastly cracks between the ceiling and walls, plaster is off, and dirt and chaos abounds everywhere. The Ridouts, at the time of the bomb, were lying flat on the drawing-room floor and were fortunately unhurt.

Last night Ma and Pa Ridout slept with the Glanvilles. Their two children were with Dr Arnold. One son, who had a temperature of 104, was somewhere else, and another son was with me.

Ann Morris was smoking a cigarette the next morning in Tower Street with slates, tiles, and glass around her. She was looking white and shaken but was being all very relaxed and airy about it all, saying she was going to stay with the old G.'s in future.

The trail of seventy-five children I saw during the raid last night along with the ashen faced lady who was leading them all slept in the school. Where they will go from there heaven knows.

Last night it rained, so we had a really quiet night and I feel rested. Today has been frightfully busy with work till 8.15 and then infinite phonings and a great deal of arrangements to fix.

Old Mrs W. has stood it all well. Father Mion came from Hayling. He is still as talkative as ever. He chatted to Mrs W. incessantly as the surgery waiting room was full to overflowing—they all enjoyed him. He waited his turn like a good old panel patient and went home quite happy.

Hayling had the brunt of it. They killed many at the Sinah Battery and hit the Sunshine Camp several times. Thinking about it now, distressed as I was by the very elderly civilian casualties, to see the young army boys in the prime of life shattered and blasted to hell was even more distressing.

I myself was very frightened at the time, but I felt composed when in front of others and content, as soon as there was work to do.

John Rickett

From a military point of view, it was a pointless raid. There was damage at Hayling, Denvilles, Emsworth, Westbourne, Waterlooville, and Denmead, but little in Portsmouth. I suppose we should be thanking the Civil Defence.

My love,

James

Chapter 9

It was in February 1941 that Rommel landed at Tripoli and made a sensational advance east through Libya, getting as far as Tobruk by April. He then drove on past Tobruk, which became isolated though remaining in Allied hands. He got as far as the Egyptian border. While Rommel was waiting for panzer reinforcements, Generals Auchinleck and Cunningham were planning a counteroffensive and the relief of Tobruk. Later in the year the tables were turned; Tobruk was relieved and Rommel forced to retire west out of Cyrenaica and back to Tripoli.

Meanwhile, the German army was invading east into Russia and making rapid progress, so that in December 1941 they were within nineteen miles of Moscow. The bitter cold (-35 degrees Celsius) halted the German tanks. The situation in the Pacific at that time was getting worse, with Japan siding with Hitler and signing the Tripartite Pact in September. They had developed opportunistic plans in the Far East to invade China and the Dutch East Indies to secure oil and other raw materials they lacked. The famous Pearl Harbour attack was in December, and this immediately brought a hesitant United States fully into the war. At that point, Churchill conferred with Roosevelt at the Arcadia Conference in Washington. Roosevelt was concerned about a Japanese invasion of his west coast, but Churchill persuaded him that Europe presented the greatest threat, and he agreed to supply American support for a landing in North Africa in 1942. To Stalin's relief, this also took some pressure off Russia. This became known as Operation

John Rickett

Torch. It was to be headed by General Eisenhower. There was a massive troop recruitment in England, and Jim Rickett was a part of this.

The following account was written in 1946.

It was a year later in the spring of 1942 that the question of my joining the forces again came up. I had just had the cartilage of my knee removed in the Middlesex Hospital, and during the time of my convalescence, the war situation for England looked worse and was deteriorating in the Far East and Pacific. Finally, in the early summer came the news that the three services required 2,000 more doctors. In my district, this meant every fit medic under the age of forty.

This last demand persuaded me of the need to sign up. I had virtually got to that point already, having come to the conclusion that the time had come when I could and should go into the service. The provision of cover in my absence was important. I talked this over with my partners and made arrangements for a woman doctor to do the midwifery and a local surgeon to do the operating at the local hospital. Bomb damage was no longer a problem, and I could therefore leave with a clear conscience. In spite of this, one of my patients told me that to go into the army was to run away from my responsibilities! Resigned to the inevitable, I told the local committee that I was ready to go.

I went first to the Central Medical War Committee to ask them to explain the exact situation. I was told that the War Office was clamouring for more doctors. I asked them about the likelihood of overseas service if I went in. The reply was that this was fairly certain and would come within three months. I discussed the question of joining the Navy but was assured that it was for the Army that the need was really acute.

It was obvious that the war must eventually be won on land and that therefore army casualties would constitute the greatest need.

Having made this decision, I wrote to the secretary of the war committee, and at that point the dye for me was cast. Before I went abroad, I would have to go through a training course.

On August 1st (1942), in my new uniform, I went to Kings Cross and took the train to Leeds to join No. 11 RAMC Training Depot. Coming out of the station, the scene was bleak and depressing. I found someone to ask the way and then took a tram to Becket's Park. The sentry on the gate gave a smart salute as I went in. I immediately felt uneasy. How should one respond? I had a lot to learn about army methods, etiquette, drill, and so on. Inside the barracks I was completely lost and rapidly became inured to the routines.

However, after a few days of getting the hang of the system, the naughty boy in me crept out. I knew that salutes should always be acknowledged or returned, and without having been taught the correct procedure, I would deliberately leave my cap behind so that I need not bother with saluting. I had the utmost difficulty in detecting rank. I walked on grass, often finding that certain lawns were sacrosanct. The weeks spent here, however, proved thoroughly enjoyable, as it was the first time for years that I was without any personal responsibility. It was good to be able to make the most of it.

Drill parades were, of course, a part of the initial training. In the end I found them easy and even faintly amusing. One soon got used to obeying the new orders and the new way of moving about in formation in threes instead of forming fours as I had learnt in the old cadet days. It was quaint to see a collection of doctors, some of whom were well into middle age, being marched about like packs of school boys.

I quickly made a friend of Bill Ling, who had his wings from the last war, and so he knew his way about. His home was near Leeds, and he very kindly invited me home for the weekend. His wife was also a qualified doctor but had not used her qualifications since her marriage some twenty years earlier. She was coping with just that part of his practice that she could. She had given the day off to their little maid, so Bill and I decided to undertake the cooking. The result was that we had a terrific supper that night, but it was not ready until close on 10 p.m. When it did arrive, it was a meal worth waiting for! Soup, grouse done to a turn, dressed crab, and a chocolate soufflé, followed by cheese and coffee. We found some Chateau Margaux in the cellar and a very drinkable port. It was rather late when the meal was finished, and so a democratic decision was taken to leave the washing up. I remember we were a little horrified in the morning at the enormous heap we had left. The greasy cooking pots and pans were not attractive in the cold morning light, especially with a head that felt like a ton of bricks.

After the preliminary training period at the depot, we were sent off to do a sanitation course at Mytchett. I found this dull in the extreme. I dozed in the lectures, wrote letters, and read novels. At the end of it all came the posting to units. Mine was to a general hospital that was mobilizing in Scotland, at Peebles. I went home for the weekend and then travelled up from King's Cross on Monday. I was not yet used to the fact that time seems to be of very little account in the Army. Postings marked as immediate need not be taken as such. They may have been lying for days in some office awaiting a signature, so that these orders can always be adapted to suit one's own convenience. With my lack of experience, I arrived rather breathlessly in Scotland on Monday to find, of course, that in fact it seemed that I was not expected and had apparently never been heard of. The unit was new and was very young in terms of army service, except for the commanding officer, who was a colonel and happened to be a regular of the worst sort. In fact he has since died. He was killed in an unpleasant accident when a jeep left the *road and plunged into the deep canal alongside the Naples to Rome highway. In spite of this sad fact, I have no hesitation in saying that he was quite the worst officer it was my privilege to meet! He was cruel to the men, and his method of discipline was nagging and petty. He trusted no one and consequently led a very unhappy unit.*

My time in Scotland was therefore never happy in the mess. I had, however, a fairly good time outside the unit, as I managed to meet some local people with whom I had some very pleasant days on the hills.

The unpleasant colonel took a keen delight in ridiculing and making the most of the understandable ignorance about service matters of his junior officers. Naturally, since some of these officers were of some standing in their profession, they resented being treated as if they were children. Quite soon after I joined the unit, he tried to get me to take on the duties of messing officer for the unit. I had no wish to do messing, and I had not been consulted as to my views. I was, however, sent on a messing course near Edinburgh. I received considerable disapprobation, and not a little umbrage was taken when I returned having failed in the examination at the end of the course.

Then suddenly an order came through that all future leave was to stop, so I hurriedly applied for mine as it was evident that embarkation leave would not be granted. This was to help the secrecy of the North Africa landings, which I learned later was known as Operation Torch.

The following letter was written on November 8 1942 from Peebles, Scotland. This was the day of the first North Africa landings. The news about it was not released in England. Nor were the troops themselves told in case information should leak out. Jim Rickett's letter conveys more than a hint of emotion.

John Rickett

My darling,

For the last two days I have known we are off tomorrow for embarkation. I don't know where we will be headed but have a shrewd idea. Anyhow, I could not see you, so that, sadly, is that. I was told in strict secrecy. I had to promise I would not even tell you.

Never, Doo, have we had a better time together. We recently have been much more harmonious (harmonious is not quite the right word, but at a time like this I think it is accurate) than we were even in idyllic Budapest or any other holiday we have ever had.

My address at the moment is Lt JR Rickett 241092 RAMC Army Post Office. When we get on the boat we will be given a more specific address which I will write to you at the earliest opportunity. You must not put 95th General Hospital any longer. Apparently it would help Hitler to know the 95th was in action!

My feelings are so mixed—sentimental to a degree, but thank God these are swamped by a thankfulness that the war is improving and if I can help by fighting for my country, I should do so because I am a fit man.

We are probably fighting in one of the most momentous epochs in history. In spite of the shocking start in 1940, we, who will have lived through it, will have our faith restored at the time that good eventually triumphs. This does not say I am disillusioned by our current political situation. As we now stand, our social conditions in particular are far from ideal. We have, however, a higher and more Godly, principle guiding us than the brutality of the Hun.

Keep up on top of the world, and in times of stress stay level headed. Never get cross with yourself. Remember that you are the best mother of three of the best children. No one else's opinion of you matters a fig, because I alone know your goodness, conscience, love, and worth.

God keep you very well, safe, and happy till I see you very presently. Give my love to the Stoughton gang.

Your husband,

James

Churchill and Roosevelt decided against a repeat of the French West Africa landing at Dakar in 1940. French West Africa had remained under Vichy control ever since the unfortunate incident when an Allied attempt to take it had failed. French North Africa was also under Vichy control, and though their support for Germany had weakened. There was still anger and resentment against the British for the bombing of the French fleet with the loss of 1,000 lives, when the Bretagne was sunk.[21]

Instead they went for a bold Mediterranean landing on the French North African coast in Algeria. This was Operation Torch.

Three separate areas were chosen for the Operation Torch landings. A total of 110,000 troops would land in Casablanca, Oran, and Algiers. There would then be a further landing of 15,000 solely British troops in Algiers, where Jim Rickett's ship was headed.

On 8 November the landings took place. Some remaining loyal Vichy French, under Petain, inflicted some damage to the Allies at all

---

[21] The thinking behind this was that the French fleet would otherwise have been taken over into enemy hands and used against the Allies.

John Rickett

the landing sites, and Axis aircraft and submarines also damaged a number of ships off Algiers.

Further fighting took place around Algiers, Oran, and Casablanca, but this was not serious, and on 10 November all Vichy resistance against the Allies in North Africa ceased. On 22 November Darlan signed an Armistice Treaty putting French North Africa at the disposition of the Allies. A month later on 24 December, Darlan was assassinated, allegedly by a French royalist acting on his own.

The account continues.

The trip out to North Africa was a series of contrasts. We left under the heavy cloud of the Clyde, with seagulls circling and screeching at our departure. This contrasted vividly with the entrance into Algiers harbour several days later on a flat, calm, and brilliant sunny morning.

The misery of army travel was immediately evident in this troop transporter, which had been converted from a luxury liner. The quarters for the men were no better than shocking. They were all crammed on the mess decks so thickly that it was impossible to find a space anywhere. There were hammocks slung over the tables, which were also used for sleeping accommodation, as was the floor space under the tables as well. It seemed impossible that this poor state of affairs had actually been planned! Presumably, some officer had walked round the decks and, finding there was no alternative, had resorted to arranging a thoroughly unsatisfactory state of affairs. Morale-wise this was a poor introduction to army life.

That first night was rough, with a strong wind and a sea to match. The effect below deck was chaotic. As an officer, I was lucky enough to have a small cabin, but to venture onto the deck on that first morning and see the squalor was an eye opener. The decks were covered in dirt, orange peel, paper, and cigarette ends, all swimming around in vomit. The stench was mediaeval. The task of cleaning it all up was a nightmare. The comparison between officers' and men's quarters was disgraceful. I have always had the greatest admiration for the British Tommy, who with philosophical calm accepts any and every situation in which he finds himself and will make the most of it. Despite the slow start we made in France in 1940, during this war he has shown himself to be better disciplined than his counterpart in either the Navy or the Air Force. Admittedly, his behaviour has been at times rough and even drunken when off duty, but that is only natural. In army service and altogether on the whole, he has behaved with dignity and decorum. This has, anyway, been his characteristic while serving abroad.

There were US troops with the convoy, in fact some in every ship. The whole convoy was dry. This was without doubt a good thing, because with so little room for exercise, it was difficult enough to keep fit, and the effects of alcohol would have been disastrous.

As we sailed south the weather improved, and gradually some sort of order was restored. The monotony of the cruise was relieved by the daily announcement on the wireless that the convoys approaching North Africa were awaited by "packs of submarines numbering as many as fifty in a pack". Whether this was a piece of propaganda put out with some ulterior motive by our side we never found out, but a hollow laugh greeted this so-often-repeated warning. We felt that it was not the most tactful form of broadcast for our unfortunate relatives who, by this time, must have guessed the theatre of the war for which we were heading.

In actual fact, except for a few depth charges being dropped by our escort, we had a voyage that, right up to our entrance into Algiers harbour, was peaceful in the extreme. The sight of the convoy entering the harbour was one that I shall not easily forget. The surface of the sea was like a mirror, the weather was exquisite, and the calmness of the water accentuated the size of the eleven transport ships as they majestically followed us in. The town which straggled up the mountain side showed vividly white against the varied greens of the countryside foliage beyond. It seemed unreal to consider that this was all part of a particularly unpleasant war.

The adjutant brought us sharply back to reality, when he gathered us together in the saloon and told us that Algiers was the number one target for an air attack. His words were amply confirmed almost at once by the familiar wail of the sirens and the sending up of a smoke screen. We were to spend two fairly agonising days and nights in the harbour before we got ashore. I need hardly say that these were not enjoyable. For the whole day we simply lay around on the top deck, watching the more fortunate ships unloading, and most of us took the opportunity of getting our heads down during the afternoon, for which we might be glad later in the night. The sirens started up at sundown, and the sound of our own gunfire for the rest of the night made sleep impossible. We were unable to find out what was going on, as we were all at action stations the entire night.

For me this meant a dull post with a section of men in the bowels of the ship. It was F deck, if I remember correctly, with little hope of getting out if we were hit. We could hear nothing but a series of crashes, bangs, and bumps. This included the rattle of machine guns when low aircraft came in. My impression was that the gunners shut both eyes and pressed the button. The next morning many of the decks were punctured, sometimes even with bullets from the deck below.

The behaviour of the men was excellent. They saw that nothing could be done to improve the situation, so they just sat resigned and *waited patiently for the morning, as indeed civilians sat throughout the long nights of bombing in London and in the large naval ports at home. In fact, only one ship was hit during this time, though there were many hits on the quayside and some dock installations were destroyed.*

The next day was another lovely day. It was inactive for us, but unloading was being speeded up. I think that the military experts were getting a bit sick of seeing so many transports lying about in the bay with the risk of having bombs thrown at them all night. At about 5 p.m. our turn came at last, and we slowly made our way into the harbour. Just then the old familiar wail started up, and we were in that tricky position, with tugs fore and aft trying to get us alongside a difficult piece of jetty. Immediately both the tugs, which were manned by Arabs who were terrified by the bombing, cast themselves off and made for home very quickly. This left us swinging, with about 20,000 tons of shipping, alone in the harbour. How it was all solved I don't know, but we finished tied up fore and aft with long warps, one to a quay and another to a buoy in the harbour.

That night was noisier but less uncomfortable, since they allowed troops anywhere on the ship as long as they stayed under cover. Personally, I went to my cabin and dozed on and off between the bangs and bumps. On one occasion the ship rolled violently in reaction to a near miss, and I was thrown out of my bunk.

The next day, unscathed except for damage from some of our own and our neighbours guns, we got alongside and unloaded.

The scene of a busy port unloading troops has to be seen to be appreciated. There were Arab men with stores, some shouting, some pushing, and some simply just sitting and resting themselves. There was little we could do to speed things up; most of us took a leaf out of the Arab book and simply sat and contemplated the situation. We sat

John Rickett

until 3.00 in the afternoon. Then at last news came that orders had been given. We were fallen in with full kit and marched off. I think I shall always remember that march. After a fortnight on the boat, we were very unfit. So I, knowing how cold the nights were and certain in my own mind that we should not see our kit again for many a long day, loaded up with three blankets and a greatcoat and all the rest of the full kit, with as many extras as I could carry. I was to curse the decision after four hours of mainly uphill marching! At dusk we reached our camping ground—a bare field, not even a bivouac. It had a great advantage in that it was nice and high. Having marched all the way up the hill from the harbour, we were able to look down and see the port and to watch with some satisfaction the start-up of another raid.

The gunfire flashes later became strikingly vivid and the gun reports rather more rolling, and then I realised that this was more than an air raid. It turned into a real old-fashioned Mediterranean thunderstorm. The sound effects continued all night, and the fair weather having broken in earnest. It went on to rain incessantly for three days. This was not just a gentle and refreshing rain from heaven, but a downright tropical deluge. Needless to say, we all got absolutely soaked. It took days to get cleaned up, dry, and morale restored.

Marching as a unit, we were all pretty inexperienced in those days about what was necessary and what was not. After our sparse training in Peebles, it was a rude awakening for us all.

General Anderson was put in charge of the troops, which consisted only of two infantry brigades and two commandos. His orders were to make a dash for Tunisia, but his intelligence was poor, and communications and air support were lacking. Some progress was eventually made, but Hitler sent reinforcements. The Allied forces failed to take Tunis. Hitler then decided to make Tunis the base for a counter offensive against the British First and Eighth Armies. This diverted a part of the German Army away from the Russian campaign and was precisely what Stalin had asked for when Operation Torch had been planned. Rommel had been in North Africa for eighteen months. The Torch landings marked the prelude of his defeat.

Jim Rickett was with a General Hospital unit behind the front lines, receiving casualties on transfer from the front line, where the immediate needs had been met and dealt with. The letters he sent home were strictly censored. Information about the work of the unit, the personnel, and place could not be divulged. No diary was kept, nor was any later account written. During 1943, progress was made in Tunisia in the African campaign, though the fighting was intense. In May that year, the Axis troops were finally evacuated from the north-east tip, Cape Bon, and Bizerte. We had won the African campaign. At the same time, in the Atlantic the turning point was reached in favour of our Allied shipping. The Sicily landings followed in July, with the island falling to Allied forces in August. Clearly, Italy would be the next target, and at that point negotiations were under way for an Italian armistice. On learning this, German troops under Rommel were rushed into Italy.

An armistice with the Italians was eventually signed on 8 September, and the Allied landings took place at Salerno a day later. The Germans had expected this and provided a substantial Luftwaffe welcome. A beachhead was established, but there was a fierce German counter attack. This was resisted, and the Allies went on to make good progress up through Italy, stopping at the Gustav Line some sixty miles south of Rome.

In January 1944, the Allies then landed north of the Gustav line and only about forty miles from Rome, at Anzio. Later in January, Jim Rickett was posted from North Africa to Italy. He worked there briefly

John Rickett

with 95 General Hospital. At that time the British 5th and 8th Armies were making progress north towards Rome.

The posting to Vis came through a month later in February.

The following letter to Dorothy from Italy was dated 10 February 1944.

76 GH CMF

My darling,

Such a good letter from Iris in her telegraphic style, as one must be in these days of airmail letters, but full of bright wisecracks. Her letter was so good it stimulated me to write an airmail back—hopefully also capturing the same style. I was able to use airmail, as I have sneaked quite a few from Bussey, which he got out of Pills so that he could write to distant relations. I also added condolences to Bill for his brother dying in Italy.

Pills—rumour has it that he is off to a new job. I suspect this is the reason for his better humour of late. A grand hospital full of middle-aged GPs and specialists is no place for a man who might have been the result of a wild night spent by Dick Turpin with Emma Hamilton!

The weather here—let me disillusion you—is not blue skies, wine, and black-haired girls with mimosa in their hair. It is alternating days of April—happy warmth promising everything on one day with bathing in the clear Adriatic, and then the next is likely to be an extremely good imitation of the Steppes of Russia. A howling NE wind with driven snow. After Africa—damn me, sir—it freezes the blood. A good example of this comes in my operating list tomorrow. I am keeping quite happy, because on each day I manage to concoct such an operating list. Tomorrow:

two hernias, a couple of fingers to be chopped off, and a plaster to be put on a wounded leg. One of the finger patients is a boy who was lost in a blizzard and got quite badly frostbitten. His left hand is all right, but his right sadly will lose three fingers. He also will need to lose the big toes of both his feet, but he was just incredibly lucky not to have lost his life from hypothermia. The other amputation lad is a Bechuanan boy who was embroiled in a civilian disturbance with some Italians. He smashed up his finger. He is under close arrest, which adds to the difficulty of hospital administration. He speaks no English, and his name is Archangel! As a messenger of God he would leave much to be desired.

Old Fen (my anaesthetist) is a great joy. He sees eye to eye with me. He is kind, with great sympathy, and has a deal of sentiment, so we can talk openly of all our doings and of all the folks around.

My love, Doo. I am with you in thought so often.

James

PART TWO
CHAPTER 10

Following the Italian armistice in September 1943, the Allied forces landed at Salerno in January. Hitler, determined to maintain the Adriatic Sea route, responded by reinforcing the Yugoslav occupation and giving instructions to take reprisals against the local population should they be caught cooperating with the Allied forces.

Vis was a large island strategically placed between Italy and the Yugoslav mainland. It had two harbours which provided good shelter. It immediately became the key to the Adriatic, the holding of which could give the Allies control of the sea. A Royal Marine commando force occupied it in late in 1943. They mounted a garrison on the island, and it was used as a base for the Royal Naval Coastal Forces under Captain M. Morgan Giles. A fleet of motor torpedo boats (MTBs) and motor gunboats (MGBs) was established. These small fighting boats were used very successfully in the Channel in the early war. They were built of wood and were fitted with three Vosper Thorneycroft 1,000 horse-power petrol engines. They were capable of thirty-five knots.

These boats were used to attack the German supply ships going north. Hiding up by day to avoid the Luftwaffe, they would wait for enemy ship movement at night and carry out surprise attacks. This became a major nuisance to the German supplies.

The partisans on the Yugoslav mainland, working undercover, were also making life difficult for the German occupying forces. They were actively sabotaging the roads and bridges on the mainland and were destroying the German supply transports, communications, and rail links. As a result the Axis forces were being forced to use the sea for transport and supply. To protect this route, the Germans were patrolling the waters and had set up garrisons on the islands to ensure safety of the coastal traffic. They lacked the resources to occupy all the islands of the Dalmatian archipelago, and on those that were unoccupied small groups of partisans remained. These small units were able to provide intelligence concerning the strength of the Germans positions and the movements of the coastal supply boats. This greatly helped in the planning of the commando raids from Vis.

Hitler's forces already occupied the southern Yugoslav harbour of Split, which he had taken in December, and after this they went on to garrison the islands of Hvar, Brac, and Korcula. He would then be well placed for the invasion of Vis in February. He devised a plan, which was to take place during the last week of the month. It was given the code name Operation Freischutz. (Freischutz was a folklore marksman with magic bullets.) A substantial naval force was to be used, along with the German crack Jaeger 118th Rifle Division. There were to be other forces and a squadron of supportive dive bombers. The plan was to land on the southeast side, and this is precisely where the commandos had anticipated and had set up a watch.

We return to the account of the landing on the island of Vis in January 1944.

Stretchers Not Available

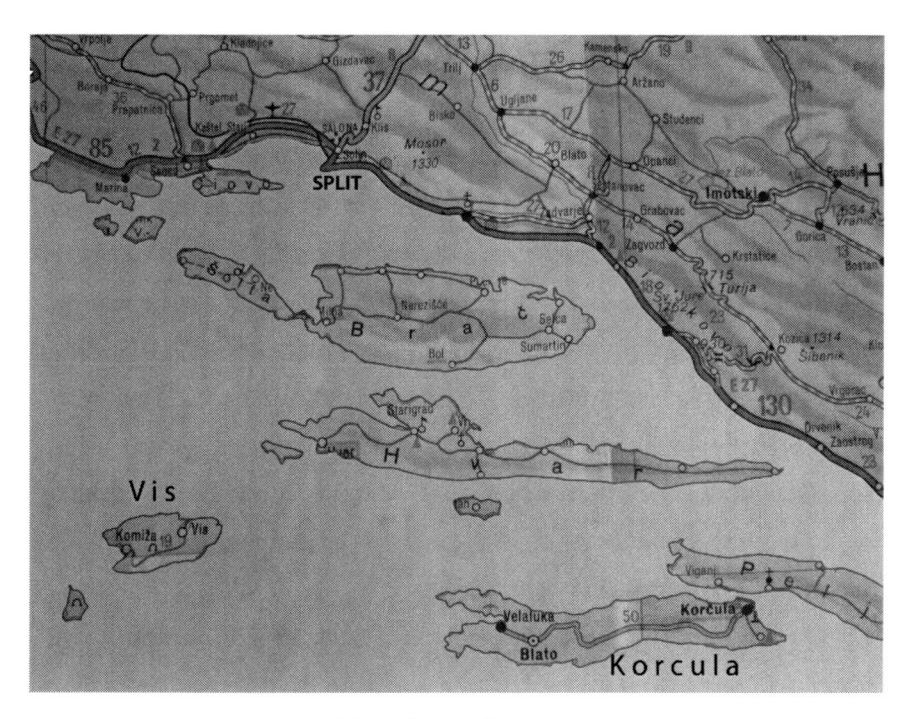

Vis and Yugoslav coast

The wind had dropped by the time the LCI arrived, and it was midnight on a beautiful clear starlit night, but bitterly cold.

As we nosed our way slowly into the harbour in the complete darkness of the blackout, we were just about able to make out large towering masses of the land behind showing up darkly against the night sky. Suddenly a shout of "Stoi" echoed out of the darkness as we approached the jetty. Pandemonium then broke out, with the crackle of machine-gun fire. They must think we could be a part of the planned German invasion. Indeed to the partisan force on harbour guard duty that night, a boat arriving by night would likely be a German invasion. They would best assume this was the case and make an armed challenge. Communications between the partisans and the British command were at best uncertain, at worst parlous.

Gradually the indiscriminate machine-gun fire died down, and the LCI was permitted to berth on the quay with loss of neither life nor limb. Then there started a scramble to get unloaded and to get the LCI turned round and back across the Adriatic before daylight. Unloading in the dark, with an unknown quantity of medical stores piled on top of arms and ammo, caused a few rather acid comments about health and safety. On the whole the work went off without any serious disagreements, though I had some trouble in holding onto a drum of industrial methylated spirit, which nearly got thrown in the sea. The only casualty was a carboy of more meths, which was dropped onto the quay and shattered. With concerns about continuing supplies from Italy, this was a little worrying.

On the quay we were greeted by Lieutenant LeBosquet, a SOE Force 133 parachute trained officer and now the self-appointed i/c of embarkation, who, though appearing slightly intoxicated, was doing marvellous work. Working with him was an English-speaking female partisan. She was dressed in English battle dress, with flowing hair tumbling over her shoulders and a troop cap on the side of her head. Unused as I was to women in battle dress, she cut a somewhat curious figure.

Eventually we managed to get our stuff unloaded into a truck and were taken to a small nearby house which had once been a butcher's shop. On being assured that any partisan touching our kit would be shot, we left it until daylight and followed Le Bosquet, who suggested that for what remained of the night we could use his billet right on the quay. Captain Heron said he would take us there. He was head of the field ambulance and the very man I had to contact on arrival. He and LeBosquet had been helping each other to overcome the stress of the expected German invasion by keeping up their spirits to maintain morale—with a little help from the local vineyard. This was particularly unnerving, as he drove very fast on the waterfront quay, with the mudguard of the vehicle catching on each of the stone pillars that guarded the edge of the quay, giving a curious xylophone effect.

The billet resembled all the other houses on the island in that the ground floor was given up to the making and storing of wine. A venomous-looking machine gun was mounted on a tripod and faced us as we went in. We went upstairs, where we helped ourselves to the leftovers from a large litter of dirty plates on the kitchen table.

If green flares were lit, Heron explained, this meant that the German invasion had actually started. Should this happen, we should use the Sten guns which were kept by the open window. These were the only instructions. I therefore assumed we were to fight an open house retreat if the invasion started. So, fortified by a swig of whisky—I had taken care to have a bottle with me—we settled down and slept till 7 a.m. with no disturbances, despite almost continuous bursts of machine-gun fire from excited partisans, who would fire off at anything.

After this short but uneventful night, when daylight broke I looked around to get my bearings. The house was in chaos. People were sleeping all over the place. The tables were heaped with dirty plates and glasses. An old woman was starting the overwhelming task of clearing up the mess. I decided to go outside to explore.

As I stepped out that morning, the sun was still low behind the mountain. The soft light picked out rock pinnacles on either side of the harbour entrance, and in the distance haze obscured the horizon, promising a day of spring sunshine. The harbour was littered with a motley collection of small untidy fishing boats tied up against the quay. The naval boats were concealed and heavily camouflaged.

John Rickett

It was just a small fishing town which hosted the local community. There were probably no more than 2,000 inhabitants. The houses were no bigger than small cottages and built of heavy stone, somewhat similar to those of a Cornish fishing village. They were clustered at the foot of the tall mountain which ran straight down to the sea. The quay was wide enough, but all the streets were so narrow that a jeep could barely get through. This made passing at best difficult and at worst impossible, involving complicated reversing manoeuvres.

The only building of any size was a block of modern flats, which the Navy had taken over. Apart from these flats, there was nothing of any size that could possibly be turned into a hospital. Indeed, the flats themselves were not suitable, so I immediately decided we must be outside and possibly up on the mountain. A farm house would be ideal, but failing that we would need to resort to tents. This plan fitted with an earlier thought that in the event of the island being attacked, it would be better to have the hospital away from the target area, which the harbour would undoubtedly become. Elsewhere on the island there would not be any electricity, but hopefully we could borrow a generator from somewhere until the promised Force 133 generator arrived. We were told that even in the small towns of Komisa and Vis, the electricity supply was dubious and unreliable and would need the back-up of kerosene lamps and even candles. At the time of any bombing raid, electricity was usually the first service to fail. This might be disastrous if it happened during a surgical operation.

The mountain called Hum (pronounced Hoom) came down to the water's edge, with Komisa, the harbour where we had landed, clinging to its foot. As I walked about, I drank in the wonderful scenery of that lovely morning. The colours were intense. There was a clarity that made everything stand out vividly with sharp, cut edges, giving the whole *scene a rather theatrical atmosphere like a stage set. One could not imagine that this particular set was that of a brutal war. This theatrical effect lasted throughout our stay. The stage effect was enhanced by the behaviour of the Yugoslavs, who in a childlike way would often try to imitate our troops and their actions without really succeeding, but their whole behaviour gave our stay on Vis a feeling that the whole episode was just various acts of a comic opera, the dramatic story line of which might unfold upon us at any time with the impending German invasion.*

After this preliminary assessment of the town, I returned in hope that some breakfast might be coming. I found Frank and Dawson up and about and poking about the kitchen. Then LeBosquet appeared and started swearing because the District Acting Quarter Master General, Hamilton Hill, was asking all sorts of difficult questions. A very welcome breakfast eventually appeared, and so refreshed, we set off to find Heron.

Clearly I would be working closely with 151 Light Field Ambulance who were under him, so I was anxious to get to know him and his section as soon as possible. First we had to find him by asking his team, who were somewhat vague and noncommittal as to his whereabouts. Wanting to be loyal, they hesitated in sending a stranger to him so early in the morning. We did, however, eventually get out of them where he was to be found, and we arrived at his billet in time to see him sit down in front of a large cooked breakfast. He brightened at the sight of us, swallowed some tea, and offered to drive us around on a recce in his 15 cwt. truck.

Having located Heron, the next objective was to talk to the CO of the commandos, Lieutenant-Colonel Jack Churchill—"Mad Jack",' as he was affectionately called. He was no relation of Winston. He was a colourful character and unconventional in his military tactics. In dealing with the enemy, his tactics were subversion and surprise. He played the bagpipes and sometimes took them into battle to help rally the troops. In days gone by he had played them in an Italian nightclub. He also had a bow and arrow, with which he had considerable skill, having used it early in the war, In one particular episode he landed by canoe and stalked German sentries as targets.

After he had welcomed me, his advice was clear. When a medical hospital is set up, it is wise to make sure it is well away from the towns and both harbours. The best place would be somewhere high up on the mountain. Maintain a strict blackout, and don't plaster it with red crosses, which will be picked out for German favours in any bombing raid. This amply confirmed my earlier thoughts.

The next person to see was the District Acting Quarter Master General, who was a cheery soul called Major Hamilton Hill, known universally as Ham Hill. We found him in a small HQ in Komisa. He had the unenviable task of trying to satisfy the demands everyone made while somehow at the same time not treading on toes, particularly those of partisan feet. He was pleasant and helpful up to a point, but his "old boy" methods were not always particularly productive. He had virtually no staff, and as far as I could see, he had absolutely no hope of obtaining any personal help or even getting anything but the most meagre supplies coming through the Q department of Force 133. I discovered (but only by the hard way) that to achieve anything, one had to fight one's own corner and be endlessly persistent.

We asked him to recommend somewhere on the island where we could set up our unit. After some thought, he suggested two possible places to us. They would likely be already occupied by partisans, and we might have difficulty in getting possession. Anyway, off we went to inspect them.

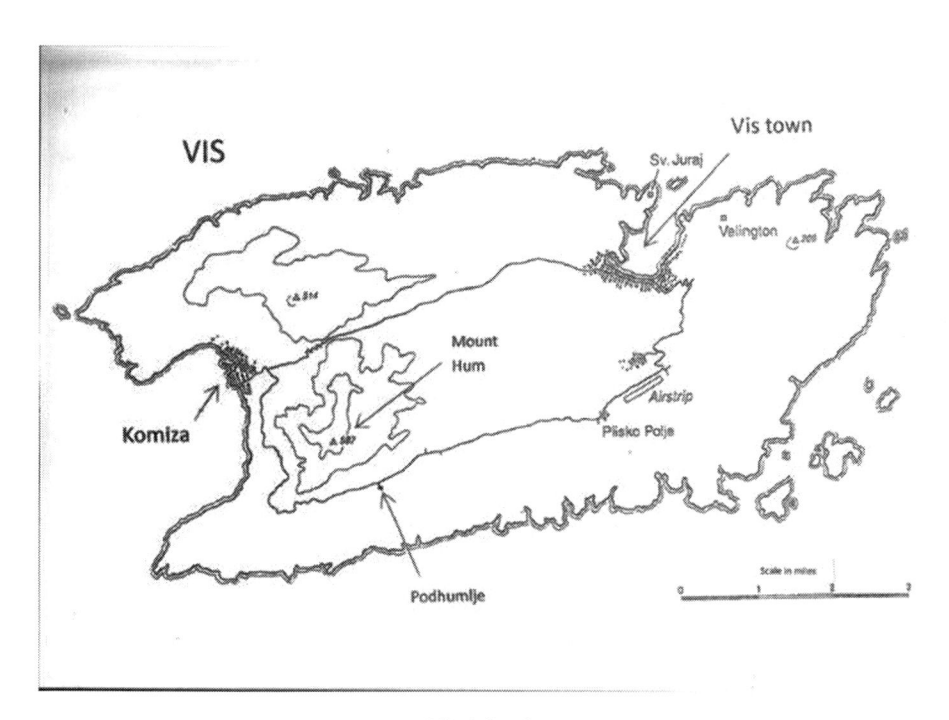

Vis island

Out of Komisa the road wound its way up, following where possible the contours of the mountain side. After about three miles and a good number of hairpin bends, it reached the plateau on the top. The ground there was pretty barren and rock-strewn, except for some small fertile and cultivated areas. Scrubby and stunted firs, bushes of rosemary, and rock roses abounded elsewhere.

The cup-shaped depression on the top was surrounded by minor peaks. All the soil from the hillside had lodged there, having been washed down from the mountain over time by rain. It formed a natural plane which had been cultivated as the island's main vineyard and was *thickly covered with vines. On the sides of the mountain that rose up over the harbour of Komisa were the more usual terraced small vineyards with their stone-built walls to retain soil from being lost down the steep slope. In between these little cultivated patches were heaps of stones placed so as to form a watershed. These were highly significant in some places, as they determined the local water supply. The water situation was later to give considerable anxiety, as the high plateau was the only rainwater catchment area. It was used as the bulk supply of water for the whole island.*

We found one of the houses recommended by Ham Hill that was potentially good but was, as he had suggested, already occupied by some partisans. It was situated on the higher part of the island amongst a tiny collection of houses called Podhumlje. So we returned with the intention of speaking to Ham Hill about taking possession. This seemed to me to be our best chance. A major drawback was the lack of electricity, so we would therefore need the promised generator, but we could initially work under daylight, though this would need to be supplemented with paraffin-vapour Tilley lamps.

Our quick initial assessment inspection was sufficient for us to decide it would need much work. The area on the ground floor could be used as a kitchen, dining, and sitting room. A narrow outside wooden staircase, wide enough to take stretchers, led up to the next floor, where there was a small landing with four rooms which seemed to be hardly more than about ten feet square each. The one on the northeast corner had been tiled and had a chimney where a stove had previously stood. This, we decided, would just make a very small operating room, while the room opposite on the northwest corner would make a sterilizing room. The other two rooms might at a pinch take three recovering casualty cases each, and above this floor in the attic there was room for possibly a dozen or more stretcher cases. This area would do for the more seriously wounded, while the lighter ones could go straight outside, where we might, given tents and stretchers, hopefully accommodate about fifty. Without any knowledge of what we might have to deal with, it was hard to make any plans at this stage beyond the barest outline.

The situation was clearly very far from ideal, and I could not picture coping with anything but lowest levels of received casualties. For instance, there was the question of the water supply. The only available water was from a water butt filled from a drainpipe from the roof. We would obviously need a regular water delivery and a holding tank. All this would have to be arranged. Then there was the delicate topic of a latrine, as the only one available was a small privy alongside the building. In the meantime we simply had to make the most of what we had.

To get what I wanted, I realised that I would really have to go for it. It was therefore with some trepidation that I went back to Ham Hill. One of the advantages about Podhumlje for us was that there were two other small houses nearby. If we were able to get at least one of them, this would make suitable accommodation for Heron and his ambulance crew. But of course at this stage this was a big if.

We found Ham Hill genuinely wanting to be accommodating, in that he realised the importance our mission, but in trying to find housing for other units there was a desperate shortage. There was, for instance, the signals section, which had nowhere. So the discussion was at times reduced to arguments and battles, but we eventually somehow obtained his agreement to the occupation by our unit of this house which proved to be, despite its small size, one of the best-built houses on the island.

Possession is, as they say, nine parts of the law. Therefore, acquisition from the partisans already installed there might be hard.

We learned it belonged to an unfortunate priest who, under partisan orders, had previously been summarily turned out. Whether this was done on account of his possible Nazi leanings or on account of a general dislike of the church by partisan radicals in the movement, I do not know.

We had to go through the partisan authorities to get their agreement to turning out the present occupants. There was the communist commissar, the commandant, Cerni, and the odbornin, who was the local administrator. So next we had to see Cerni as soon as possible. There would clearly be a language problem.

Yugoslavia was at the time a united complex of the various Balkan states. Serbo-Croat was the accepted language. Immediately I remembered that George Lloyd Roberts was working directly with Serbo-Croat-speaking helpers in the town. I must approach him. It was he whom I had been told to contact on arrival and with whom I would work as a functioning unit.

So with missionary zeal I went to find George in the town of Vis. The first thing was to get to the town of Vis, which was on the other side of the island.

CHAPTER 11

Although the two harbours on Vis were a mere three miles apart, the road had to climb tortuously up the mountain, with hairpin bends edged by a sheer drop. Then it went across the central plateau, before winding down to the town at the other end of the island. The distance travelled was at least double that of the crow's flight.

These two good harbours and this thickly planted vineyard supported a culture which had lived for centuries on fish and wine, and these continued to be the stable industries. We sampled both during our stay, and we found them to be excellent. The fish were mainly anchovy and sardines, both of which were exported in large barrels to the mainland. In addition, almost all other fish, especially shellfish, were available. The wine was a powerful heady white with a sweet almost cider-like flavour. The red was called "proscheck", some barrels of which were, I thought, a bit harsh, but with practise we came to thoroughly enjoy it. In addition there was "rakija", which was made from the distillation of wine with often poor quality grapes, crudely taken with stalk and pip after they came from the press. Rakija had a terrific kick, but it tended to be a major problem the next morning—to be taken, therefore, with extreme caution.

Here we were on this small island. We had invaded the lives of this quiet community. It is likely that the mode of living would have been little changed probably since the time of Christ. Goats and chickens were the usual diet, flavoured by herbs and cooked with olive oil and vegetables, all washed down with the good wine kept in goat-skin containers. Donkeys were the means of transport, and these docile little plodding chaps could still be seen all over the island. The women worked very hard, while the men tended to do little. They would sit around, often in groups, talking. Quite suddenly a force of about 12,000 partisans had arrived, along with a unit of commandos. The infrastructure of the whole island had been distorted.

The heavy influx would bring problems of drinking water supplies and, of course, also of drainage and sewage disposal. The system for sewage on the whole island was parlous to say the least. There were, as far as we could find, no lavatory arrangements except in a few of the houses. More typically there would be an outside hole in the ground that had been roofed in with a little hut to make a primitive privy. The less privileged locals for the most part used the fields or the vineyards. This habit of using open countryside without compunction worked for centuries for the original small island population. Thanks to the sun's rays and heat, the work of composting was effectively achieved. There was now, with the influx of partisans, a high risk of epidemic dysentery, not to mention typhoid or even cholera, which, in an epidemic, could potentially result in havoc. The provision of proper latrines required resources we simply did not have, nor were we likely to acquire them in the foreseeable future. Even an episode of food poisoning could potentially seriously affect the ability of the partisans and the commandos to provide a fighting force and defend the island in the case of an invasion.

George Lloyd-Roberts in 1947

Until I arrived, apart from a small clinic in Komisa, the only hospital facility was in the town of Vis at the north end of the island. I eventually found George busy at work in a temporary hospital, which was a converted schoolhouse on the harbour front of Vis town. With him were three RAMC orderlies, Zena, and a host of partisan helpers. When we arrived, we were at once warmly welcomed and received in what was called the sterilising room. It had, it is true, a sterilizer of a most ancient vintage in one corner, but apart from this, it appeared to be the surgical team's sitting room. There was a small table against the wall with five or six chairs. A kitchen stove, with its chimney leading out through a conveniently broken window pane, was burning merrily and not smoking as much as stoves like this do so often. On the table were a tea pot, cups, glasses, a flask of red wine, and a plate of gigorica. This latter was chicken's liver fried and chopped into small pieces and flavoured with local herbs. We were invited to help ourselves, and it was indeed a delicious snack. The place was a hive of activity. partisans were milling about in all directions, directed mostly by Zena.

Zena had sharp, aquiline features, with frizzy grey hair and nicotine-stained fingers. She was in her mid-forties. She was small in stature, but what she lacked in size and good looks she more than made up for in her effervescent personality. She was a dedicated partisan supporter, but by birth and belief she was an aristocrat and autocrat of the old order. She was the wife of the partisans' senior doctor on the island, Dr Milo Zon. Whereas he was quiet and unassuming, she was authoritative and had acquired a position as the matriarch for the administration of the island, and she was in contact with the higher orders of partisan command.

She ran her group of Yugoslavs with a kindly yet somewhat rasping tongue, somewhat like a corncrake, and comply they did. Lovro was also there, and under Zena's authority he would give us much help later.

Zena, in addition, organised the whole place and masterminded George's work. She spoke fairly fluent English and was an ideal go-between for the partisans and the medical service that George was providing. She immediately understood the problem I presented to her and agreed to go with us to speak to the commandant. She and George both said that Chicago Mary would be the person to approach about the houses, and she would also help try to get us some domestic and other manpower support. So we found Chicago Mary, and, along with Zena, we went off to see Cerni. We would also need to see the odbornin, but that would come later.

Cerni's quarters were higher on the mountain. A man in his early forties, he was slight, lean, dark, and dynamic. He had been a Chief Petty Officer in the Royal Yugoslav Navy before the war and spoke quite good English. After some discussion, he agreed to our using the houses at Podhumlje. This was a major victory, and so I decided on that basis to go further and try to get his agreement to the use of some other supplies which I learned had been sent over by the Allied HQ in Italy for partisan use. Up on the mountain we badly needed tents. In particular, if there was a serious raid, we would be extremely short of a place for the recovering wounded. I decided to try the softly, softly approach. Sadly, he was unimpressed. The answer was no. The tents were for his men, and that was that. However, we had got the main demand, and this was really all that mattered at this stage.

We realised that we needed to move quickly. To get possession of the houses in the little hamlet of Podhumlje was the first requirement—at least to get them quickly before anyone else laid a claim to them and moved faster than us. We needed the help of the odbornin, who would organise things at ground level. Chicago Mary came as our interpreter. She was invaluable, and she and Lovro together managed to get us to him.

We filled him with wine and insisted on his gang of workers clearing the place. The ground floor was taken up with wine casks, a wine press, goat skins, and equipment for feeding and harnessing mules and donkeys. Upstairs was not so easy. Five partisan girls doing night sentry duty slept there all day. With them was a very old woman *of eighty-six, wizened, toothless, bewildered, and speechless. Was it reasonable to wake them up and turn them all out just like that?*

I rather fled from this problem, thinking that if we moved in with all our stuff, they would get the hint, find somewhere else, and leave. We decided to go ahead and move in ourselves, so back we went down to the quay in Komisa to load up our gear into the trucks.

Alert to the threat of invasion as they were, the tension always rose to a climax each night towards dark, which was the time that an attack was most likely. The ragbag partisan army would move to their action stations as prescribed by their command. Those on lookout duty would wind their way up the road into the hills, singing as they went. During the day, tension was eased and action stations were abandoned. Rumours of the imminent invasion were often wild and frequent. This resulted in unease and nervousness on our part, which was quite scary. In point of fact, some scares were due to notoriously unreliable rumours which were hopelessly exaggerated.

That evening, our meagre little convoy started its perilous drive up the mountain side on this, our first day. The road, pitted and unmade, allowed only slow progress for our heavy truck, which would lurch precariously towards the precipitous edge on the frequent hairpin bends.

As we started up the hill, the sun was setting on the horizon. We passed bands of partisans armed to the teeth, solemnly winding their way on the road up the hill to their night action stations. They sang their national songs. The harmony of their voices was delightful and really quite moving. It gave an operatic atmosphere and lifted all our spirits. I felt that Italy and its ordered army life were part of a different world.

Somehow we safely completed the precarious journey without mishap and reached our new home. The last part of the journey was dark, and we had to comply with the blackout. Without lights we made our way up the rough track under the dim glow of the stars. Having got there intact and with so much at stake, we praised the considerable skill of the drivers.

Now installed in our new home, Podhumlje, that night we did no more than unload the essentials. We found the hurricane lamps and unpacked what we could of our gear and camp beds so that we could at least get a good night's sleep. Supper was bully beef and biscuits, cheese, and wine; we ate it standing in the future "sterilizing room". Late at night, mellowed by further draughts of wine, we unpacked our bedrolls and slept very soundly.

The next morning we woke up to find we somehow had acquired a goat. He refused to go away, and so we decided to adopt him. In fact it was more the other way round. Anyway he joined the team.

Then came a deputation from the signals section. They had heard of our acquisition of a useful house and thought that if there was some spare capacity, they could install themselves. The house was far away from the town where bombing would be targeted, and, more important, it was situated on high ground. Surely we did not need the whole house? The loft would be an ideal place for a transmitter. Important though the signals section was to the island, I thought we could ill afford to lose what precious little space I had for our own needs. The accommodation would be essential for the use of recovering cases and until then for the accommodation of our own staff. So after a slight altercation, we managed to turn them away and were then able to start to get our house in order. The signals section was run by Scottie, with whom over the next few weeks we would work closely. In typical fashion he held no

John Rickett

hard feelings, and I am happy to say they found another house nearby, so I felt justified in defending our territory.

Having established ourselves downstairs and having waited in vain for the sleeping partisan women to move, I returned two days later at lunch time to find Dawson had gone into the bedroom where the sleeping beauties were lying. He woke them all up and, using his most polite and best Serbo-Croat, asked them to leave. Then he solemnly stood over them while they dressed, and later he bundled them all out except the poor old eighty-six year old. She was just bewildered by the whole thing. In the end we decided to let her stay, and in fact she proved to be no problem. By that night we had acquired two young domestic girls, Anka and Felica, organised by Zena, who slept with the old lady upstairs, while we established ourselves in one of the other upstairs rooms. Anka and Felica were later going to prove absolutely invaluable when we got going as a surgical team.

The practicalities of how to make this small house into a functioning hospital were more than enough to focus the mind. Of the two-story building, which was of relatively modern construction, the downstairs was one large room with a stone floor and rough walls. It contained a wine press and seven barrels of wine. We, cleverly, had not insisted that the odbornin take these away. They were good-sized barrels, measuring at least five feet in diameter. We tapped them and found them all full, so at least one problem was solved—that being the restoration of morale after periods of stress! The shortage of water for washing and cleaning would need to be addressed. I had learned that water was available by delivery elsewhere on the island, albeit only in short supply. We would have to rely on a delivery truck. Of that more later.

Then followed some feverish activity to get our unit up and running. There was the portable operating table to set up, and then we had to find a place for the sterilizer to go, a place for the instruments such as they were, and, most important, we had to set up a light for the operating table. Without electricity all we had was a single kerosene Tilley lamp. This lamp was going to be vital to our work, and something had to be worked out to make it as effective as possible. Dawson immediately leaped into the breach. "Leave it to me," he insisted.

Any light in the operating theatre was also going to be a problem after dark, as there was a strict blackout in force. If abdominal operations were to be performed, the light direction has to be downward rather than sideways as is natural with the Tilley lamp. Having been used to a proper operating theatre light, I did wonder seriously how I could possibly cope and just how serious the wounded casualties would be. Dawson's ingenuity was going to prove absolutely invaluable. In addition, I was fortunate in having Frank as an anaesthetist. He had a practical and positive attitude to the various jobs in hand. The set-up was very far from ideal, but we simply had to do our best within our resources. After all, there was no one else, and all other facilities on the island were fully stretched and without any spare capacity.

Working without any senior officer in charge was most unlike anything I had previously experienced in the Army. In carrying out this work of sorting out the problems and working alongside other units, there could very well have been problems which would have made life very difficult. With Heron, however, we settled down to grasp the problems one by one, and despite one or two small teething troubles, we made a very happy partnership. We were able to work together most effectively—guided, I might add, by his basic and perpetual advice concerning the shortages of very basic equipment: "The trouble is that you f------ well worry too much!" This was very much a part of his basic philosophy, and in practice it was to stand us in good stead.

He had with him two ambulances supported by a three-tonner and a 15 cwt. Of personnel, he had twelve men. There were two ambulance drivers, a cook, a clerk, and a sergeant to oversee the smooth running of the unit. The unit lacked trained nursing abilities, and this we found was a serious omission. Then there was a RASC driver for the Heron's 15 cwt. and six orderlies who, thankfully, did have some practical ability, though this was not based on formal training.

With on-going commando raids on nearby islands, we should be in business right away. Clearly there was no time to lose. This was emphasized by a visit back to Komisa, during which we heard a report that the German invasion was indeed imminent. I have to confess it gave me a tight feeling in the chest to think how unprepared we were to deal with casualties in any number.

After talking with Heron, the serious need for tents dawned on me. How on earth could we accommodate the anticipated casualties? After a raid we would only be able to hold a very limited number before becoming completely choked. Jack Churchill, already had planned raids and these were in advanced stages. There was in addition a serious need to provide help for George's unit, as he was working full tilt on the partisans, who were coming to him all the time. He had no spare capacity.

I knew that the British Army had supplied a load of tents to Cerni and that these were not being used. This was ridiculous. So I determined to ask him again if we could have them. Having failed previously, on this occasion I should have to be clearer and more determined. When I saw him, I deliberately explained that we were setting up a unit to treat the British and the partisans alike. We were both of us fighting the same cause against the hated Germans. With the tents, I would be able to treat more wounded. Without them, the potential of our unit would be wasted. Cerni did not budge. His attitude remained unchanged. The tents were for his men and not for ours. So away we went, disconsolate and pensive as to how the recovering casualties could be accommodated.

It so happened that the next day the *Prodigal, which was an armed and disguised fishing trawler that had been converted and was used for carrying stores from Italy,* arrived on the island from base with stores. The boat always docked at night and in the blackout. It had become known that sometimes one could "acquire" items during the unloading. Heron and Dawson knew of this and stole down to the harbour to see if they could be lucky. Sure enough, they managed to get three crates of British Army boots which were intended for partisan use. This was a decidedly dangerous mission, as they had to evade the guards on the quay, and there was a risk of being shot for stealing or looting. The partisan boot shortage was clear. One often saw soldiers with makeshift shoes, the soles of which were repaired by stitching on rubber tyre patches.

Delighted with their success, they brought the crates back to Podhumlje. The following day I went back to Cerni. After talking further about the medical requirements, I ventured to ask how the partisans were off for boots. Cerni said that boots were one of their worst problems. This was now seriously affecting many otherwise capable fighting men. I then said, adopting as innocent a voice as I could, that I could let him have a crate of boots. Cerni lit up at this. I immediately added that we were still very short of tents. So a deal was struck. I got the tents, and he got his boots. Rather cunningly, I kept the other two crates with which to barter at a later date.

Before I arrived on Vis, the raids on the nearby islands were fairly small scale, and the injured casualties were being brought back to George for sorting out. He had arranged the transfer to a hospital in Italy of the worst cases which were able to travel, though the transfer was without any medical attendant and took over twenty-four hours. As time went by, the raids became more ambitious. The Germans were more prepared and defended the islands more effectively. As a consequence, the casualties increased both in number and in severity. This was just at the time that I arrived.

While Dawson and the others worked on setting up the makeshift operating theatre as best they could, I decided to visit the town of Vis and also see George once more. I went first to find Zena's husband, Dr Milo Zon. He worked at the small medical clinic in the town, where he was the island's chief medical officer. He organised the reception and care of the refugees who were being landed on the island in small open boats during the night from the mainland and neighbouring islands.

Often the arriving partisans were in a bad way. Some had been on the run, having escaped from the Germans after being tortured. Others had been wounded in skirmishes. There were very few medical units in partisan hands on the mainland, and getting a boat to Vis often took days of waiting. These unfortunate people were in a most miserable state. They arrived wearing totally inadequate clothing, having travelled often over long distances without proper food or shelter. Many of them were still clutching their guns, which they held with frantic possessiveness. The nights were very cold. Some were hypothermic, and many were seriously sick or wounded. The women, dirty, often looked about suspiciously, their peasant clothing in tatters. They were cachectic from infection, coupled by anaemia, half-starved and dehydrated from travelling for days with inadequate food and water. They were altogether a most pitiable sight. Some were so ill on arrival that only blood transfusions would save them from dangerously severe anaemia. Some died either before or soon after arrival. Dr Zon sorted them as best he could and sent to George those who needed surgical intervention or the fracture cases who needed some form of splinting.

For those requiring blood transfusion, George himself had a group of partisan volunteers who could be called upon. Blood was drawn off by an aged and toothless old man. After inserting a cannula into a vein, the old man would by suction draw off blood into washed-out wine bottles, which were then stored underground to keep them cool. George had then to check compatibility by cross matching prior to transfusion. He did wryly admit that if left too long underground, the blood tended to go, as he put it, "a bit off"! George sometimes needed blood urgently, and at these times he was helped by Johnnie who was group 0, the conveniently common blood group known as the "universal donor". In an emergency he was willing to supply a pint in exchange for a couple of bottles of wine.

I went to call on George, who appeared totally calm and completely unperturbed by the pandemonium with which he was surrounded. I would add that pandemonium is something I came to associate with the Yugoslav method of working. He broke off his work and offered us tea and wine when I arrived. He was extremely busy, and I therefore told him I would give him what help I could. I explained that my instructions in Italy had been that I was really to be concerned only with the British. However, I was most keen to provide help, and I suggested we first got our own house in order and then I would come down and give him a hand. At that time he was operating with the help of Suza. She was a good-looking girl who had once been a massage student and then a

John Rickett

radiographer. George was teaching her how to give anaesthetics. She was using intravenous Pentothal, supplemented with chloroform by an open-face mask. He was also training the totally uninitiated staff how to manage the sterile techniques of an operating room. Whilst doing so, he was operating all the while on desperately sick partisans. This arrangement was far different from what he had been taught in medical school, but when proper facilities were lacking, he had no choice. He was certainly making the most of what had been provided.

The result was impressive. He would work for about five hours and then take a break amidst the continuing chaos of the clearing up, stretchering, and cleaning. It was obvious to me that a great deal of good work was being done. His method was to start at about nine, when the first overnight arrivals had been sorted, and to continue working all day and, if needs be, into the night, until the last one had been settled in bed or prepared for evacuation.

The partisan helpers consisted of some large and strong men, who were excellent at the lifting, turning, and stretchering. They also helped in the theatre by holding and supporting limbs during the surgery. Their lack of experience in anticipating routines, coupled with the language difficulties, meant that their ability to help was limited. George clearly showed considerable patience, and without Zena's English, nothing much could have been achieved. Indeed, when she was not there the language barrier had to be overcome. He had found that raising his voice to emphasize and suggest priority and coupling this with gesticulations usually had the desired effect.

His operating room was a large room with windows on three sides. Again, as in the sitting room I had seen previously, there was one broken window. This was used as an exit for the chimney pipe of the iron stove, which was used as a sterilizer. The floor consisted of the *rough, well-worn and scrubbed boards of the old school room. The ceiling and walls had recently been lime washed. The rooms had been furnished partly from remnants of the small hospital that was originally on the island, and partly with kitchen chairs and tables. Knowing how scarce were all supplies of fuel, I enquired what he was using for the spirit lamps which provided his lighting. He told me he used rakija. Neither methylated spirits nor paraffin was available. He found this local distilled spirit of plum brandy burnt really well. Moreover, it was readily available and cheap.*

When I went in, there were two wounded men. One was lying on an operating table of primitive pattern, while the other lay groaning on what appeared to be an out-of-date gynaecological examination couch. Both had their hair clipped short on account of lice. The first, a man of about fifty with his short remaining hair bleached by age to iron grey, was emaciated and had that pinched look that is associated with the chronically infected wound.

When, with some difficulty, the dressings were cut from his leg, I was quite horrified. He had what must have been an exposed bone fracture of both of the lower bones of his leg. By its appearance the wound must have occurred many months ago. It had been untreated and the lower part of the leg was lying at a grotesque angle with the white ends of what was obviously dead bone sticking through a dirty sloughing wound with heaped up with chronically inflamed and indurated edges.

I would judge his haemoglobin to have been about 30%. His face had a hollowing appearance just in front of the ears that made all the bones of his face stand out as if under thin parchment.

George went up to him and very gently took the leg and tested it for union by putting light pressure on the fracture line. He found that in spite of the shocking position and the sepsis there was quite moderate union which had stabilized the fracture. He was obviously going to need corrective surgery, but this could only be carried out when the sepsis was clear. He turned to Zena and asked her to please arrange a back splint for support of the wound, a transfusion, and if there is a boat, to evacuate him that night. At least he would then be on the way towards proper definitive treatment. Zena signalled to Johnny and Lubo, who came in, to take the stretcher away and to leave him in a ward until he had his transfusion and was ready if a schooner was by chance leaving for Italy during the night.

Johnnie and Lubo both wore battle dress, with homemade caps of sorts on the sides of their heads, on the front of which was the red five-pointed star of Tito. They were strong but very good natured and kindly. In civilian life one might have dismissed them as layabout rough necks, but how wrong can one be, as here they were doing great work. These chaps, though they worked for the communist partisans, had no particular political leanings as long as they had food often and wine even more often, and a woman, if possible, even more often than that. The latter commodity was at the present time almost entirely denied to them, as there was a sort of amnesty between the sexes while the war was on. It had been made known by Partisan High Command that pregnancy was a hindrance to the cause until the war was over, the German occupation finished, and the communists firmly established. To encumber a woman with child was considered antisocial and therefore should be punished. In any case, all forms of contraception were quite unobtainable, so the truce was in force, and this was generally accepted and respected.

Most of the Yugoslav women, known as partisankas, were so tough that they were not easily distinguishable from men. Their hair was usually short, and the main noticeable sex difference was a rolling gait *and the enormous size of their buttocks, accentuated by the shorter battle dress blouse which they wore.*

The women were affected by their life in the hills, living amongst men and sharing with men the hardship, bad food, and all weathers. The result was that they were divided into groups. Those who liked the outdoor life and could hold their own in such tough surroundings soon began to exhibit characteristics new to them. They became markedly androgynous with coarse speech, greater breadth in the buttocks, and—interestingly from the medical aspect, as I only found later after having been consulted over some medical problem—as a result of stress and the poor conditions, their monthly periods became scanty or even absent. Their belts were often packed with grenades, and they usually carried a Sten gun, which might even be cocked and ready for action. They applied exactly the same carefree abandon as the men. They were certainly tough. They fought well and, when wounded, accepted their wounds with fortitude.

Then there were those who retained their femininity in a remarkable way. They could not stand the roughness of the life. They wilted very quickly and had to be weeded out. They were sent to do administrative work, nursing, Red Cross duties, or even simply carrying messages. After getting used to seeing just the tougher members of the female sex, I was so surprised to come across one day in the course of a morning's work, following a joke I made, a good attack of simple girlish hysterics in a young person with whom we were working. It was a spontaneous display of emotion, triggered purely by the tension in which we were all working and very much out of context in the normally fraught atmosphere. The episode gave us all a few moments of pleasure, and we all laughed together.

George's other case was a young man who looked fairly well, but he produced on demand a small wound in the thigh, through which, on close inspection, urine was seen to be trickling. This unhappy state of affairs had been going on, we found on questioning, for no less than thirteen months. For a month after he had been wounded, he had not been able to walk at all. From this account, I suspected he might have had a fracture of the pelvis with damage to the urinary tract, as can sometimes happen with these fractures. To escape from the Germans, who would certainly have killed him, he had hidden in the villages of the mainland, where there was no medical attention. In this particular case, giving no treatment at all could well have been better than inexperienced and ill-advised interference by catheterization to drain the bladder, which might have resulted in a permanent damage to the urinary mechanism. The injury would require full diagnostic facilities before a treatment plan could be carried out. To meddle around without knowing precisely where the problem lay would be likely to cause more harm than help.

When George had completed his work on the Yugoslavs, he turned to us, and we discussed together the practicalities of the reality of a German invasion. Vis harbour, where he was working, was the obvious landing place for a major assault. It would happen at night. George had developed a plan and invited us to inspect it.

Round the back of the building in which he worked there was a mule track. It ran straight up the hill. It was unused and overgrown, and the access to it was difficult. So his idea was to get hold of an old Austin ambulance. He had it lifted bodily round the corner of a narrow road so that it could be driven up the mule track. This was the old and original direct route between Komisa and Vis. It had not been used for years. Like all mule tracks, it involved a very steep climb, but it had the advantage that the German invading forces would not know of its existence.

He explained that when they landed, he would escape with his team, get in the ambulance, and retreat up the track out of the town. He would then be prepared to maintain his medical service on the other side of the island. He led us up the track, showing with some pride where he had turned it into a usable though rough road by manual labour. Going straight as a dye, this road might have been made by the Romans, as they had a settlement on the island all those years ago. Obviously there would be a few problems in the evacuation, but these could be addressed as and when the need arose.

We went up this road in the ambulance and had found a nice little sheltered valley. He stopped the ambulance and said this was where we were to get out and walk. He then produced a pair of Sten guns, with which we started to practice. We then held a target practice, in which the British took on the partisans in a contest, all of us finishing in a small hut where a crude wine was produced. We went back to his little unit in a pleasantly muzzy condition.

The threat of German invasion was at its height at this stage, and the tension persisted every evening as rumours of the attack continued to grow. The partisan news service was at best unreliable and tended to exaggerate the real situation beyond recognition. Action stations were maintained every night for all troops, and there was a continuous rattle all night long of small arms as the partisans loosed off at shadows or even the whisper of wind in trees.

Chapter 12

It was quite impossible to estimate the number of casualties we would have to treat after the raids. To add to the problem we had no details of the build-up of commandos and partisans arriving on Vis in the weeks ahead. Although our remit was to look after the commandos, I decided that on account of the help given to us by the partisans, it would be wrong to expect George to deal with them all. We would have to help him. The fact was that the partisan numbers had already greatly exceeded our own.

I thought further about the layout of the small house we had taken over. We felt it would be important to have a room alongside the operating theatre where we could rest and refresh ourselves between cases during what might be lengthy operating sessions. The weather in February was cold, but the room had a fireplace which we could use to keep warm, especially in the evenings. We pulled down a match boarding partition in the dark poky room upstairs to make a much better space. This then became a cheery room for the good open wood fire. We made use of the partitioning which we had taken down for shelving and for surfaces to be used in the operating theatre.

The following letter was written at this time. Whilst not wanting to worry Dorothy too much he needed to think about the worst case scenario.

CMF 8 Feb 1944

Future postal address given—Adv. HQ, Force 133

"Darling, A batch of letters written at Brookhill. How very sweet of you to go and see the old chap (*Jim's father*). I am sure he was delighted."

"I do wish I could adequately describe the scene here. An upstairs room in a house we had difficulty in requisitioning—I have taken it for my staff and myself! An enormous fire like we have at Jeremy's roars up the chimney, with a nice open fireplace, and sitting round a table lit by a vapour pressure lamp is a grand old girl who is our cook. She had become totally bewildered by the British Army invasion, but she has now preserved her isolated calm and goes on cooking under the most impossible circumstances. I started this letter days ago but have been so busy I could not finish it—busy with some work, but mostly trying to get my operating theatre in working order. Now if you don't receive letters from me for a month or more, you will know that it means I'm just busy and communication is very bad. I do assure you that at last I have the job I could have wished for myself."

"I loved your letters. Don't worry about the odd grey hair. I can't tell you the joy I will feel to be back with you again. Do you remember my once showing you a poem I saw somewhere?"

"Twixt you and me there's much emotion."

"That's the reason there's commotion."

"Take a lump of clay, wet it, pat it,
And make an image of me and an image of you."

"Then smash them, crash them, and add a little water."

"Break them and remake them into an image of you and an image of me."

"Then in my clay there's a little of you,

And in your clay there's a little of me,

And nothing shall us sever;

Living, we'll sleep in the same guise,

And dead we'll be buried together."

"Badly written all this, but a bad light and a continuous chatter of a foreign tongue with the two girls, our hard working housemaids, singing songs in a lovely harmony."

"At the moment Clynick and Dawson are teaching them English. Having taught them the English numbers, they insist that they should learn a) "Ten men went to mow, went to mow a meadow" and b) "Ten green bottles a hanging on the wall"—all as an exercise in their numerals. Hopeless laughter usually finishes the lesson. We are warm, well fed, well housed, good work and safe, and what more in this war could we ask?"

"I do hope you are well. I do love you so much and am so looking forward to our return, which, being an odd little unit as we are, might be earlier than being stuck in a general hospital."

My love,

James

The approach road to our unit was walled and would allow a three-tonner to get down with no more than two inches to spare on either side. This clearly would need widening to allow our transports and ambulances easy access. Fortunately, we managed to get a partisan labour force to do this for us.

Arrangements in the setting up were now coming on apace, and it was clear that without any beds we had to find an alternative for recovering casualties. The only possible answer was to use stretchers. These could be placed in tents on the ground or on trestles if we needed to keep a close eye on them. Stretchers had the advantage that they can be moved about easily. This would assist in both the triage and the postoperative care.

During a war, I fondly imagined, these should be readily available from base stores. So I talked to Heron. He had none available, and neither had the medical unit in Vis town. I calculated we would need about two hundred, and possibly even more if evacuation to Italy of the more severely wounded was going to be delayed. I therefore contacted the Bari HQ of Force 133 by telegraph to request the immediate and urgent need for two hundred stretchers. Straight back an answer came "Stretchers not—repeat not—available. To what use would they be put?" This sickened me much. Not only were they failing to provide our most basic needs, but what was even worse, they had no idea of why we should want them. There was even an implication of improper use!

We were on our own and very much felt that way. The Foreign Office, which was responsible for Force 133, had obviously neglected to provide the most necessary and basic resources for the very enterprise on which we were embarked. I realised that what I could not get from the partisans I would have to do without, and I would have to get on as best I could. Heron's remark about everything we lacked kept coming back to me repeatedly.

Fortunately, Chicago Mary was most helpful. It seemed she could, through the good offices of the odbornin, come up with almost anything. Tough, grey-haired, and middle-aged, she had spent sixteen years in Chicago. She spoke good English with a strong American accent. She

John Rickett

was a powerhouse in the communist organization. It was the great help I got from her through the partisans that had influenced me in deciding at the outset to make the medical unit available to both the British and partisan wounded alike.

Anka and Felica, our domestics, had come through her and also Marie, an old dear who became our cook. She, of course, needed a stove, and again Chicago Mary came up trumps and found us a wood burner. We put it downstairs and made a hole in the wall through which the flue went. To secure a good draught, we made a chimney out of biscuit tins.

She also got us the use of another local house, though taking possession was again difficult. Heron was able to use the ground floor as his base. Above this and leading from it by a rough wooden ladder was the second floor that was to become our home. There were three rooms, all very dark and divided by match boarding. This I removed, thereby making much more space and much more light. So now we had quite a good amount of timber from which we could make some primitive furniture for the hospital. We were even able to find skilled labour for different requirements, including a highly skilled carpenter who did excellent work with the spare wood.

George's hospitality was invariably open and welcoming. I found he was living and sleeping in Zena's house. This was one of the few comparatively large houses in Vis. It was in one of the best positions overlooking the harbour of the town of Vis. Outside was a terrace with a creeper to help provide some shade against the heat of midday sun, and there was a spectacular view over the harbour and out to the sea beyond. There was a real furnished room, with a table that would easily seat ten or twelve. He invited us to sit down to dinner, and we enjoyed an excellent meal cooked by a rather intense Bosnian lady who was called Cooky. She had Russian origins and spoke both Russian and Serbo-Croat. Like Zena, she was a character herself. She and Zena had plenty of arguments. They fought about the flowers that Cooky always placed on the table. Zena would come in and throw them away, saying that we are fighting a war and not having a carnival. They would be immediately replaced. If Zena attempted to go into the kitchen, she would be greeted by a scene and a flood of invective. Yet somehow they got on together. The atmosphere, however, was usually a little more relaxed on those occasions when Zena was not there, but then language difficulties reared their head, and to overcome these we had to communicate with gesturing and buffoonery rather like dumb crambo. In the end there was little she did not understand of us and us of her.

When we had been very busy, sometimes I would sometimes stay there for a night. I found that all the women slept communally together in one room on the ground floor, while George and his orderlies all had individual rooms to themselves. The food normally consisted of American rations, but with a few "little extras". Cooky was an expert at producing excellent food. One night after her four course dinner, we finished with a Bosnian cake which was so delicious it made one remember the days of peacetime. On Vis the living was rough and lacked creature comforts, but being able to sit down to eat and to be provided with such peacetime delicacies brought out sharply the contrasts in our lives. The partisans clearly had not altogether forgotten their cultural heritage, and it was good to enjoy it.

After one such a dinner a day or two later, someone was sent to find the one and only piano in Vis. Having located it, the evening finished round the piano with a good burst of song. After our very rough living *conditions, this was a wonderful way to relax from the tensions all around us.*

During these evenings after the work of the day was done, we would sit around, glass of wine in hand, and reflect. At such times I sometimes was prone to introduce controversial topics simply to stimulate open discussion and debate. These were usually topics that were uppermost in my own mind. The collaboration of the Allied forces with the communist Russians was one which invariably brought out strongly held views. Bearing in mind the communist ideals, there were profound ideological differences between us. At this time the Russians were in a different theatre of war, and we were sending large quantities of supplies to them. Hence our popularity with them was high. However, this popularity was very much supply dependent, rather than being based on any real friendship. It was therefore quite fragile. Russian policy changed markedly in 1944, when the Russians had advanced west from Leningrad and were appreciably closer. At that time our supplies were being reduced. Tito was then standing back and out of the limelight. Being a political opportunist, he was playing off one side against the other.

What was remarkable was that the partisan movement in general was a very mixed collection of different ethnic origins. There were Serbs, Bosnians, Croats, Slovenes, and others. They were, on this small island, working together under the inspiration of their leader, Tito. Their politics were diverse, some nationalists, some royalists, some communists, Roman Catholics and Muslims. Before the war started, they had been at each other's throats with intense internecine rivalry and jealousies. Here on the island and also on the mainland, they remained a united and cohesive force under the banner of an intense hatred of the Germans who had invaded their country.

Then there were times when close-to-home party politics would come up. Tongues were then loosened by the local wine. Often a good open talk would take place. Sadly, this was often impossible with George, who had such fixed and diehard right-wing views that he tended to get thoroughly steamed up. At times I confess I was a little embarrassed. I found later on talking with him that he thoroughly enjoyed the heated discussions, and in reality his views were a lot more moderate than he had made out at those times.

These evenings invariably ended happily with Cooky singing a series of sentimental Russian songs with her eyes fixed firmly on George. George's looks were a very good mix of the Messrs Redford and Donat, and before long it appeared to me that something was going on in the background, because Suza made a catty remark about Zena. Zena was no fool and realised that Suza might be getting involved in a relationship. This was a potential disaster which would work no favours for her. I later learned that local murmurings were even starting and that the commissar's ears had been pricked. Mysteriously, Susa was spirited away. Following this, there then developed a nice little storm, in which I believed that George was completely innocent. George was upset that his carefully trained anaesthetist was taken from him without so much as a by-your-leave. It would be back to square one. I dismissed it with laughter at the time, and I have no doubt it was taken all too seriously on the part of the partisans. The problem stemmed from the edict that Tito had issued. Love, pregnancy, and sexual relations were strictly forbidden. Any relationships other than the most platonic were slowing the cause. Therefore such practices were to stop forthwith, and offences were to be punished by death. George knew this was no idle threat, and it had him a little worried at the time, though I know that he would now pass it all off as a harmless joke.

During those first three days of our stay on the island, the team had worked like beavers in setting up our little unit. Dawson was the mainspring. He had found an old wood-burning stove, which he set up to heat a boiler for use as a sterilizer. Then he worked to solve the problem of the operating theatre light. This was no mean feat. He found some reflective mirrors and used hammered-out tins for additional reflection that he secured in a frame surrounding the light source to direct the light downwards, so that shadowing was eliminated just as a proper theatre light would do. Use was also made of the light from the window in a similar fashion. So we now had a light which might even allow us to work at night.

I was back in Podhumlje having just spent the day in Vis town with George, when a Messerschmitt flew over us, giving us a little peppering as it did so and forcing us to run for shelter. A short while later a dispatch rider arrived. He was quite shaken and covered in dust, having had to jump off his bike in a hurry to take cover. He said that Captain Morgan Giles had sent him up to us to tell me there had been an accident on one of the MTBs in Komisa harbour. A shell had hit the guard rail and had wounded three of his sailors. They had been taken to the little hospital in Komisa by the No. 2 Commando medical officer. He felt I should know about this but was unaware of the protocol for care now that we had set up at medical facility at Podhumlje. In the meantime he thought they had better go to the nearest place. Of course, there they would receive treatment from the Yugoslav doctor.

I immediately jumped on the pillion and went off to see what was going on. I met the commando MO, George McWilliams, who said that Dr Crylovic had been very good to us and whatever I did, I must not hurt his feelings. The casualties were now in the Komisa clinic and under his care. However, knowing Dr C.'s lack of experience with serious injury and the lack of an operating theatre in Komisa, I decided the care plan must take into consideration the best interests of the casualties rather than be based on Dr C.'s feelings. McWilliams was obviously anxious that I should not upset the good, friendly relationship he had established. At that point I also realised that if the casualties were serious and if we were to take them on, we would be under the close scrutiny of both the commandos and the Navy. If it went well we would remain in favour, but if we failed then in future we would have lost their confidence. It was make or break for us.

I went to the Komisa hospital. It was a building that would compare with one of our older hospital institutions. It was out of date but with several quite lofty rooms which served as wards. I found that two commandos had already undergone "surgery" on their wounds and that the other was waiting to be attended by the surgeon, Dr Crylovic. The "operating theatre" that I saw was simply his office, laboratory, and dispensary. It contained everything that he might want in any emergency, from agar plates for bacterial culture to cigarettes. It was lit by electricity in the form of one weak bulb on one of those adjustable flex cords.

Dr Crylovic had long grey hair and a pair of pince-nez glasses sitting askew on his nose. With cheerful enthusiasm, he tried to explain what he had done. The nearest approach to a common language was French, but his pidgin French was almost incomprehensible. It appeared that his previous surgical experience had been as an abortionist in Split. He was not trained, nor had he any experience in the treatment of war wounds as a surgeon, though we found later that what his medical knowledge lacked was amply made up for by skills on the piano keyboard.

John Rickett

I found that in one of the injured cases he had opened the wounds to explore them. This was, of course, in the principle of good surgery. However, in exploring the damage caused by a shell wound of the hand, he had divided the main sensory nerve. This was a serious mistake in that the hand would as a result be seriously weakened and would be numb and without any feeling. In another case, after the leg wound had been explored, it was stitched up and covered with plaster of Paris straight onto the skin. This again was mistaken, as the inevitable swelling, when encased in the rigid plaster, would compress the arterial circulation and might even result in gangrene. It offended against modern methods of how contaminated wounds and fractures should be managed.

The third case I found was a young fair-haired lad called Godby, whose wound had obviously penetrated the abdomen. Already there were signs of mischief in the form of increasing peritoneal tenderness—a sure sign of problems within. Using all my tact, I explained in the best French I could muster that, much as I would prefer to leave these patients in his capable hands, I must, under orders from my senior officers at headquarters, move them to our own unit on the hill.

We parted with expressions of everlasting esteem and goodwill, myself with the three lads in an ambulance. Having arrived at Podhumlje, I told Dawson to prepare the theatre for immediate operation on Godby, the lad from the MTB with the abdominal wound.

On the night of 27 February we christened the theatre with this case.

We fired up the Tilley lamp and got the mirrors positioned. Dawson got the instruments out, and Frank Clynick went ahead with the anaesthetic of ethyl chloride and ether. When he was asleep, with some trepidation I swabbed the abdomen with spirit and then put over the boiled surgical mackintosh drapes and made the incision. At that point the pent-up anxiety of doing our first case in our makeshift arrangement melted away. My surgical training and instinct took over. The routines took charge, with Dawson as my experienced assistant opposite me. It was the 95th General in Italy in a somewhat different context.

On opening the abdomen I immediately found free blood in the peritoneal cavity. In a sense this was a relief, as the decision to operate was clearly the correct one. The task now was first to locate the source of the bleeding and second to stop it. The source might be distant and inaccessible. Without a proper theatre light, it would be difficult to locate. That was worrying. With perfect timing, the Tilley, like a wheezy bronchitic, started to cough and splutter. But it kept going, and cautiously I sought for the source of the blood. He had a bruise on the rib cage on the left, and so the first place to look was the spleen. Indeed this proved to be the case, and much to my relief I found a tear on the anterior surface. This required removal of the spleen, so I reached down and delivered the spleen into the wound. I then carefully transfixed the pedicle and removed it. Release of the Spencer Wells clamp on the blood vessels was an anxious moment. Should the ligature slip at that moment, it would have been impossible to retrieve the large vascular pedicle without proper lighting, assistance, and the support of a major blood transfusion. I knew if this happened he would lose his life. Fortunately all was well: the ligature was secure, and I was able to close his abdomen.

I must confess to a considerable sense of relief that this case went well. It was our first and therefore very much a test of our set-up. We had established ourselves, but we needed to prove ourselves. We had to show that the commando casualties would be well looked after. From that point of view in particular, we had been, and would continue to be, under close scrutiny.

The other two men had contaminated wounds, and so I removed the stitches and plaster, cleansed the wounds, powdered well with sulphonamide as an antibiotic, and left them open to heal naturally. This way any continuing infection could drain. If needs be, the wound would be later treated by method known as "delayed primary suture". Repair of the damaged nerve could also be considered at a later date and possibly dealt with under better facilities.

We now came up against the nursing problem of how to look after Godby. Thus far all was well, but we needed to get through the next stage—the recovery. The bed was a stretcher, which for him we raised up on trestles. We had no pillows, and keeping him comfortable and free of bed sores was due to the hard work and enthusiasm of Heron's orderlies. With folded rugs we packed him up and made him comfortable. I am glad to say he went right ahead from the start, and before we left the island he was back on duty in his MTB.

Now that the operating theatre had been christened, we needed to sort out the remaining difficulties. For a couple of days after we had dealt with Godby, we were quiet. That proved a useful time to establish the team's routines so that we could embark on an operating list with a minimal turnaround time between cases. The instruments had to be washed and re-sterilized, and likewise the drapes which were used to surround the sterile area. We would also need help with lifting and carrying both to and from the theatre.

Then another marine commando called Harding was brought to us. He had been getting abdominal pains for several days, and after I had a look at him, I realised he had acute appendicitis. So we operated, and I found an acutely inflamed retrocaecal appendix with an abscess. It is not an easy operation to deliver the appendix when it is tucked away like that, but having done so, it gave me the confidence to know that I could handle abdominal wounds if needs be. Frank, at his end of the table, was also managing well and gaining confidence using just intravenous Pentothal on this occasion.

It was at this time that Col. Penman of the RAMC paid us a visit. From his base in Italy we were responsible to him, as he was in charge of Force 133 Medical Unit. He went round the island assessing not only our situation but that of the other medical facilities as well. There was from him a lot of chat, and then he left saying he would talk to the authorities. As he saw it, Force 133 would have to send over at least a full casualty clearing station to deal with the work that was anticipated from the raids the commandos were planning on the nearby islands. This was going to mean that a huge staff would come over to do what our little team of twelve men was doing.

I later heard the outcome of this visit. Force 133 authorities had apparently disclaimed responsibility for Vis! We heard that because we were a part of the SOE, a decision had been made to refer the whole thing to the War Office, whose responsibility we were in reality! This was serious for us on the island as, knowing army methods, it would surely mean a delay of at least three months. In the meantime supplies would continue to be very difficult. However, he did manage to get us a few things, including stretchers and blankets, and later even some Italian wooden beds and EPIP tents arrived. A pack of heavy sheepskin coats also came, and we managed to get one of these for our interpreter Lalla. It was still very cold at night, and though it was rather too big for her, she was delighted with it. Lalla had recently joined us. Speaking good English, she was extremely useful and helped George and me wherever she was needed.

After Penman left, Bryan Lees arrived. He was a 25-year-old ex-commando Medical Officer, who had been off sick with jaundice.

John Rickett

As we were still relatively quiet and he was not a surgical specialist, we had little for him to do, so I gave him the job of administrator and medical coordinator. I welcomed this, as it saved me a lot of bother and I could then concentrate on all the other jobs.

We were already getting ourselves known around the island, and soon our mess became something of a social centre. At no time were we in the least formal, and I was anxious that we should remain so. After all, we were still under the Foreign Office in Force 133, so we got the island to regard us as purely a medical and social unit. Therefore, in the relaxed atmosphere apparently so approved by the Foreign Office, without protocol brigadiers or corporals or anyone would sit down to relax, drink, and eat together. Bryan Lees knew the Brigadier well from Salerno days, so he was a sound connecting link. He had been provided with a jeep and with it a driver, who before the war had been a London drayman.

Things were now looking up, especially as Bryan, acting off his own bat, was available to round up stores and equipment. Probably the greatest need was electricity for a proper operating theatre light. There was a shortage of kerosene, and the Tilley vapour lamp with its reflective mirrors was very much makeshift. If the anticipated work turned up, we would need to work through the night hours. It was still early in the year and daylight was in short supply.

For another crate of boots we obtained the offer of an old single-cylinder Siemens generator from our old friend Cerni. This was our chance. It was clearly no good waiting for the generator that had been promised to us by base before we left Italy. An army generator might be more reliable whilst a partisan generator was clearly an unknown quantity, but this amounted very much to a bird in hand. We decided to take the risk, agreed to the deal, and got it delivered and set up. The next problem was to get it going. In this we were lucky to have Scottie of Signals, who found us a small contingent of helpers, including a skilled electrician from the newly arrived advance party of the RAF. They worked hard, and after several days we succeeded to get it chugging away turning out 220 volts. This was a start, but, alas, we still had no bulbs.

Just at this time we were joined by Dodd. He came up from the commando unit, and we never found out quite why he should have turned up. He was a private in rank, but as it turned out he was to become a highly effective member of our team, and he could well have been and certainly deserved a rank much higher. He was fair-haired and strong and took a keen interest in all around him, and in our own unit in particular. I think he was fascinated by our unusual set-up as he was a "fixer". That was precisely what we needed. He thought laterally and was plausible enough at times to get away with what many would have euphemistically described as "murder". He soon got his feet under our table, and because of his attitude and approach we were delighted to have him. He suggested that as nobody on the whole island had spare bulbs—neither British nor partisans—the supply boats might possibly help. "How so?" we asked. "They usually have powerful searchlights" was the reply.

But we had no cash. What did we have with which we could possibly barter? The answer was just wine and rakija. Then Dodd came up with the clever idea that they would probably like some fresh meat. We might be able to offload the goat, which recently had become a liability by wandering about the hospital and even into the operating theatre. The first problem was to catch the goat. After several unsuccessful attempts eventually they managed this, but only by summoning up their combined cunning to outwit the unfortunate animal. Then they set off,

Heron, Dawson, and Frank laden with wine and rakija, and Dodd with the goat slung around his neck. Having got down to the harbour, they found Le Bosquet and sat drinking with him until midnight when the boats came in.

Sure enough the Prodigal *duly arrived, and the team went aboard to negotiate. By a stroke of good luck Frank found an old St Andrews friend called Snaith on board. After chatting to Snaith he persuaded him to exchange some light bulbs for the wine, rakija, and yes, the goat. They could do with some fresh meat. This was a fair exchange, and all parties were happy. So away they came with a number of 110-volt light bulbs.*

The generator produced a 220-volt current, and so we had to wire up the bulbs with two together in series. In this way and without any sockets, by soldering the wires we got a very good operating lamp going. We could now, with blackout over the window, work at night, and we were no longer dependant on the Tilley.

No more than a few days later while we were enjoying a quiet drink in the now wired-up electrified mess, the Siemens roared up, and immediately all the lights went out. The throttle had broken and had fused all the lights. The question arose how to get more bulbs. We considered this carefully. Did we have any more goats? However, later on more bulbs were produced from somewhere, and we were then able to light our reception tent and even the tented wards.

With the help of fatigue parties from the commandos and Lovro, we pitched the EPIP tents which Penman had sent to us. We placed these end to end, making splendid wards, and with the field ambulance accommodation, we could now put up if needs be as many as two hundred patients here.

Poor old Lovro, the morose man whose wife remained on a German-occupied island, was under suspicion by the other partisans that he might be a spy for the Germans. I thought this was unlikely, but nonetheless he was treated to sidelong glances of suspicion by some partisans. We agreed to have him work with us. Even if he was working with the Germans, he posed no security risk whatsoever. Any information he provided to them about us would hardly be of strategic use to the enemy! I realised later that in fact he was quite an intelligent and well-educated man. In the end he acted as butler, houseboy, stoker, gardener, and odd job man. Later, after getting half a dozen cronies to do the work, he appointed himself as a general overseeing foreman.

A team from the field company of Royal Engineers turned up. They also did excellent work and over time became great friends with us. Using material we either found or otherwise appropriated, they made us a sink with hot and cold running water in both the theatre and in the sterilizing room. They also put up lights in all our rooms.

We now had a store—which was the old wine store—and this was reaching enormous proportions. Bryan had done a great job and saw to it that we would always had a reserve of three hundred pints of plasma and dressings in separate sections. All these necessary stocks were collected from the boats. These stores were officially Allied dispatches intended for the partisans. Knowing how unreliable our partisan friends were, we felt the handling of such important consignments was safer with us.

So some sort of order was appearing out of the chaos. During those early days, all of our time had been spent in poking round the island finding things we needed and contacting people who might be able to help. At this stage we now had a going concern for the care of the injured. In a small way the unit had been tested and had been found to work well, but the crunch surely lay ahead, as I was to find out. We had been very fortunate in getting the two girls Anka and Felica. Over the next weeks they were to prove absolutely invaluable. Anka, the elder, was seventeen; Felica, her cousin, was sixteen. These two acted as housemaid and parlour maid. They did all our laundry, waited at table, cleaned the house, mended the clothes and even acted as very useful assistants in the operating theatre. They scrubbed, they scoured, they cleaned all the bloodstained instruments and washed the operating theatre between cases. In truth they worked very hard from morning through till night. They were two very excellent girls. Shy at first, they soon adapted themselves to the peculiar English they were taught by Dawson and others. They spoke a little Italian, and this was useful, as Dawson was able to act as interpreter. Then there was Mare Repanic. Her face showed her sixty-five years, during which she had worked like all Balkan women do. They bear children, bring them up, and then cope with all the work of the house. These duties were forever worn as lines on her face. She acted as our cook and provided our meals. Her husband Miki had a donkey and spent his whole day cutting up pine and fir trees for fuel for the sterilizer and for the fire.

The mainstay of our team remained Dawson. So madly did he sometimes rush in to attack our problems, that we came to recognise these outbursts at the onset and make way whenever he started one of his surging revolutionary changes. When on one occasion he lost all our washed clothes, we shrugged and said "lost in the Dawson wheel", which, in its wild revolution, flings all useless (and also sometimes much useful) material aside. One's small but rather prized possessions were apt to be scattered to the winds as a result of these tornado-like sweeps. As an assistant during surgical operations he was excellent. The correct instrument came into the hand without our asking or even looking up. He was good at anticipating the next step, and his interest in the job in hand never flagged. He preserved the ideals of cleanliness and ritual to an extent that he would cheerfully wear himself out to make sure all was done in the strictest hospital manner. His conscience was keener than the best hospital theatre sister. He was impatient of obstruction and at times moody, but this was as nothing compared with all his excellent characteristics.

Frank Clynick was another mainstay. Frank was a man who seemed inwardly at peace with himself. He could forget everything while making some article of furniture or be so involved in his reading as to be two hours late for a meal. Time meant nothing to him. He was also imperturbable. If it came to a long night of carousing, particularly with the Air Force, he was tireless. He would stay up, and I could rely on him to see everyone off to bed. All in all, he was an excellent companion. I was so lucky to have him as my anaesthetist.

Bryan Lees was trained medically at Charing Cross Hospital. He had a young face, perched on which was a terrific moustache. In general he was rather self-opinionated. However he was extremely good at defending both our corner and his own even to the point of causing a fracas in doing so. Although always a bit unpredictable, he was, when needs be, really dynamic. He was a tremendous go-getter for awkward situations. Put him on a trail for something, and he would go for it. He was just the right type to look after our interests and, what is more, basically he was a thoroughly good soul. When he came to us, he had not been well, having only recently recovered from jaundice, so we had to make allowances for any stress-related lapses. In fact, he was never really fit during the whole time on the island. There were times when he quarrelled, and after a few drinks nasty moments threatened, but by keeping a tight rein, things never got seriously out of hand. As time went by, the pressure of work, combined with the threat of invasion and the way we were all pressed together in a small space, meant that nerves were bound to get a bit frayed.

Then there was Doc Heron. On account of his studious approach, we christened him the Prof. He was aged about thirty-two. He had been with his present unit since the outbreak of war. He had been overseas for at least three years. He was fair-haired, strongly built, and tough as a horse. He had been through the desert and was thoroughly browned off with the Army. He was, however, one of those incredible people who keep on a completely even keel and always remain cheerful. Despite spending virtually every night partying, he was always up for his work the next day. He could stand endless late nights and sing all the barrack-room songs, but unlike others he never once became incapable on account of having overdone it. During raids he would gather partisans around him and conduct their songs. His unit worked extremely well with him in charge. As head of the Light Ambulance, he led his team rather than commanded them. The leadership looked at times as if it might lead them astray, so wild was their path, but he never failed to have the work given pride of place and to have all the team on the job as soon as any emergency arose. He was a champion of the positive approach, and he would take everything with complete calm, as his trademark comment about worry indicated.

Chapter 13

The partisans themselves were an incredible mixture of the different Balkan states, brought together and united by a common hatred of the invading Nazi forces. Tito was their leader, and his charisma held them together as a cohesive force. Tito had strong sympathies with the communist ideals but did not accept the doctrine in its entirety. He had some royalist sympathies for the Yugoslav King Peter and stated there were to be free elections after the end of the war.

At the end of World War I, the Austro-Hungarian Empire was to reform as a Slav state. So under a Serbian king and parliament, a new country was formed called the Kingdom of Serbs, Croats, and Slovenes. The Serbs were the largest ethnic group. Over a period of time the Croats became nationalistic and wanted independence. This flared up in 1928, when Stephan Radic, the president of the Croatian Party, was assassinated by a member of the Serbian Radical party. Following this and in order to preserve order, the king decreed that a dictatorship should be set up. Thus was the Kingdom of Yugoslavia formed with the capital in Belgrade.

Subsequently, considerable resentment developed against the state among the different ethnic groups. The Serbs in particular dominated the army and police. Croatian extremist insurgents rose up and in 1934 assassinated the Serbian king while he was in France. Following this, the state recognised the need to bring Croats into the administration and formed an alliance with them, though this did not entirely satisfy the smaller ethnic groups, who formed together in an opposing alliance, uniting under the single banner of a loathing of Serbian dominance.

For many years the country had been in an economic crisis with mass unemployment. Peasants were attacking and plundering large estates, trying to acquire land on which to farm. It was in this context that the spread of the communist ideal took root. In 1920 the Communist Party of Yugoslavia was formed. It was immediately outlawed, but it continued to grow and flourish at a time when German economic and political influence in Yugoslavia was gradually increasing. When Hitler came to power in 1933, the Communist Party became very active against the fascism of Hitler. The king and state banned communism, imprisoning its members with long sentences.

At the outbreak of war in 1939 Yugoslavia remained neutral. She was asked to join the "Tripartite Pact" with Romania and Bulgaria and align with Hitler. This was agreed with signing of the pact in March 1941. There was an immediate antagonistic response from the Yugoslavian Communist Party, which hated fascism. There were mass demonstrations, and the government was toppled. A new government was set up which rejected the Tripartite Pact and incurred the wrath of Hitler, bringing the outbreak of war on 6 April 1941, on which date Hitler bombed the city of Belgrade. The army was in no position to fight, and the country was forced to capitulate to the German invading forces. The country was overrun in two weeks.

Yugoslavia had been overrun by the Hitler's Nazis in 1941. However, the main invading force had to leave soon after the surrender, as Hitler needed the army to attack the Soviet Union. It was agreed between Germany and Italy that Yugoslavia should be divided into two zones for maintaining occupation. Italy was to hold the coastal areas and Germany the inland area along the Hungarian border. The enemy occupation in Yugoslavia went as far as the main centres of communication and roads. Out in the country in the mountains and forests, resistance movements immediately arose. These were fired up by the reprisals and atrocities inflicted by the Nazis on the innocent Yugoslavs. Opportunistically, the Communist Party of Yugoslavia went on the offensive, taking advantage of German preoccupation elsewhere. With Tito as the commander in chief, all Yugoslav nationals were encouraged to join a guerrilla-type retaliation by forming clandestine groups throughout the country. There was a staggering recruitment to the partisans, as they became known, and by the end of 1942 their numbers had reached 150,000. They consisted of disinterested Croats, Serbians, and other groups, and they were united by a determination to be rid of the fascist German forces who had committed genocide on innocent people during the invasion. Initially those joining brought whatever they had for weapons—pitchforks, axes, and even sharpened sticks. Gradually they became an effective fighting force, and in places on the mainland they overran Italian forces and took over their uniforms and weaponry. In the success of their territorial gains, they obtained more recruits. The partisan uniform was very variable. They wore whatever they could get. The cap badge was a red five-cornered star. This was the most consistent part of their dress. Boots were always in short supply. They often had to make do with boots repaired with rubber from car tyres. Photos from the war often show soldiers in bare feet. They had little proper training, and many of the new recruits were young lads—sometimes as young as twelve.

Some Serbs joined the Chetnik movement, and Mihailovic became the leader. Initially he fought against the Germans. However, as the movement progressed the Chetniks began to cooperate with the Axis forces. There was also a group of Croatian extremists called the Ustase who favoured fascism, and they, too, joined forces with the Germans. They became known for their brutal atrocities against the partisan resistance fighters.

Initially the exiled Yugoslav King Peter and Churchill both supported Mihailovic, until, in 1943, he started to collaborate with the Axis forces. The Chetniks then became despised and hated intensely by the partisans. As a consequence, Allied support for them stopped, and help was provided to the partisans who, under Tito, had become a very effective fighting force and had recaptured large areas on the Yugoslav mainland. After Tito arrived on Vis in 1944, the island became the main partisan headquarters.

The account continues.

Both men and women joined the partisans. The women often made up ten to twenty per cent of the total. Not all the partisans were zealous communists, nor were they all politically aware. However, on Vis some were ardent communists. In number they amounted to about one in ten and were fanatic left-wingers who insisted on the proper procedures. "Smrt Facismo", *which means "Death to Fascism", was a proper greeting, to which the reply* "Slobodna Narodu", *meaning "Freedom to the People", was usual. Everyone was terrified of the communist commissars, who were authoritative and strong. Policy was controlled through them by "Uncle George" Tito, as he was known. They were ruthless and would not hesitate to kill anyone who was not toeing the party line.*

Sexual relations were strictly taboo, and if anyone was found guilty, the death penalty was carried out. This policy was rigidly enforced even on Vis. In practice, there were without doubt occasions when sexual relationships took place, but pregnancy was exceedingly uncommon, and contraceptives, until the British arrived, were unknown. Our own men had been warned and were well aware of the strict partisan rules. One sailor, having been discovered in a compromising position, narrowly escaped being shot. Two partisan girls on the island contracted gonorrhoea. They were found out and issued with an official warning. It was later discovered that they had passed the disease on to others. They were arrested and tried by a kangaroo court. Then they were summarily shot. When Heron heard this, he remarked dryly to me, "As a medical man, you might think that is rather radical treatment for the clap."

Working as a pharmacist in Vis town was a female commissar official called Jela, who ranked highly in partisan circles. She was a plump middle-aged woman with a strong chin and flaxen curly hair. She was the self-appointed guardian of morals on the island. She always carried a Beretta repeater rifle and a belt full of grenades. More outstanding than the weapons was her overdose of self-esteem. Her weakness was a neurotic love of the needle, and she would regularly call Zena at the hospital for injections for a variety of conditions. Rheumatism and neuritis required pain relief and a need for vitamins. It appeared she had no specific addiction other than a need for a needle and the attention to her personal health that it provided. She was universally disliked. On one occasion, so the story went, one of the island's other commissars, a highly efficient and well-liked man, "had kissed" a partisan girl. Jela got to hear of it and summoned him to her office. He was so frightened that the next day he committed suicide by shooting himself. When Cerni was told about this, he was absolutely furious. "That bloody Jela" was all he could say. Jela herself was apparently completely unmoved.

If Tito gave an order, it was rigidly and promptly obeyed, irrespective of every other consideration. We realised it was essential to go along with them and to cooperate with them in all ways, if only

John Rickett

for our own welfare. The partisan numbers were increasing all the time, and the island was becoming more and more of a partisan stronghold. Transports on the island were in short supply, so it was our policy always to stop and offer a lift to anyone we passed who was walking on the road. This was often appreciated and seen as a genuine act of trust and kindness, which we all thought did much to get the confidence of the partisans at that time. So different was our culture that many of them were deeply suspicious of the British. What were our real intentions, and could we genuinely be trusted? Much like the Germans, it was we who had invaded their homeland. Fortunately, my stock with Cerni and the partisans was high from the first and remained so. The small contingent of the Air Force was also on good terms. Sadly, several unfortunate little incidents with the commandos and the Navy showed that unpopularity lurked just below the surface. This gave some cause for anxiety, as we relied on the partisans for security and for information relating to raids the commandos were making on the nearby islands. The last thing we needed was antagonism.

The partisans were universally called "drugs" (pronounced "droogie"), which means "comrade". Women partisans, "partisankas", were addressed as "drugarica". I often had an interpreter with me when I had to say anything. At other times I found they responded to jocular bonhomie and teasing with slap-on-the-back type of humour.

During the evenings relations were improved when we joined in any drinking, the sessions of which might go on all night. During these sessions, we would often join in and end up singing their national patriotic songs with them. For their part, they would learn some English songs. We sometimes gave them "Green Grow the Rushes—O" and others.

Heron was an expert at this, and during one particularly unpleasant air raid in March, I found him with a circle of partisans, with arms around each other's necks, dancing, drinking, and singing. This approach went down very well. It seemed to show a defiance of the Luftwaffe and provided an opportunity to build up confidence in the common cause for which we were all working.

When we arrived, the partisans were an ill-assorted rabble wearing every sort of uniform, which had usually been taken from Germans or Italians from whom they had stolen or whom they had killed. However, later on, after being supplied with British battle dress and boots and having seen our troops drill, they started to become all very military-minded. They smartened up and drilled with vigour.

One of their weaknesses was their love of firearms, along with their unfortunate lack of training in the proper use of the weapons. The carelessness in handling them was phenomenal. Even when they had been wounded and admitted to our little hospital, they kept loaded Sten guns at their bedside. There was one instance when a Mills bomb dropped out of the pocket of a casualty on whom I was operating and rolled onto the floor. Fortunately, someone had the presence of mind to pick it up and get rid of it. After that experience, I insisted on detaching all grenades from their belts and turning out pockets before admission to our unit.

After watching commando training in hand-to-hand combat, the partisans were determined to have a go themselves. They wanted to pick up the tricks they had seen, but they had a more interesting idea, and that was to do the tricks without first disarming. A great trick was to steal up behind a fellow drug *and stick a revolver into his back. The* drug *so attacked, while at first appearing to submit, would then suddenly leap round and grasp the pistol, when a rough and tumble* would ensue. This became a great game, until in their enthusiasm they did it with cocked and loaded guns, with the result that two were shot through the kidneys from point-blank range.

Another source of danger was the landmines. It was the practice to send parties across to Hvar or Miljet to lie up and watch the Germans laying mines on the beaches. As soon as they returned to their garrison, the partisans dug up the mines and brought them back to Vis. Then, rather like squirrels and nuts, they would bury them and then immediately forget where they were, so the landmines were buried indiscriminately all over the island. Each section put them where its own ideas dictated with no reference to HQ, and no record was made. The result was a series of serious landmine accidents. One of our own British officers was killed, and other men lost feet or even legs.

When under treatment in hospital for wounds sustained, the sexes were not separated, and it was customary to examine even the more intimate parts of either sex in the presence of others, with no embarrassment or interest being shown. Despite this, there was an incident which made me not a little uncomfortable. One of the girls developed acute appendicitis. I said I would need to operate. When she appeared, I found she had been over-enthusiastically shaved—far more shaving than was needed for my purposes! I commented on this, and Dawson described a scene in the ward which he had witnessed. Lubo, the heavy black-moustached man who was our barber and stretcher bearer, was seen almost astride the patient in the open tented ward, puffing away at the pipe in his mouth, while using a cut-throat razor to shave this poor girl with excessive zeal and relishing every moment of it.

I found it hard to acclimatize to the type of warfare we were seeing. It was different from the fighting in North Africa and Italy. The tactics of guerrilla fighting were not based on the niceties of the Geneva Convention. Yet here we were in the midst of it. What attitude should be struck? One had to be mindful of the situation with which we had been presented. Yugoslavia had been overrun by the Germans because the country was not wealthy enough to sustain an army sufficiently well equipped to stand up to Germany. It was a poor country, but at the same time its population was intensely proud of their heritage and determined not to give up without resistance.

So the partisan movement arose, uniting the various ethnic groups. The Axis forces, realising what was going on, decided to suppress all resistance against them by force. So they adopted a brutal approach in the hope of scaring the local population into submission. This did not happen, and in fact the brutal tactics only helped to inflame and ignite the resistance movement. So the partisans responded with equal brutality against them. When husbands are shot in public in front of their wives, the feelings engendered and resentment which arises are strong. And they were passionately felt.

Lalla, our interpreter, who was working with me, showed me a picture of her husband. He was a small, rather fat, Jewish solicitor. He had been taken hostage on his way to work when the Germans occupied Sarajevo. He was taken to the market place, told to stand with his back against the church wall, and with many others, in front of her eyes, he was mown down with machine-gun fire. Lalla could never forget or forgive this, and she would spit in the face of every German prisoner who was brought to us.

It is difficult in comparatively civilized warfare to visualize to what straits and to what deeds of desperation this band of partisans had arrived. They had adopted guerrilla tactics. They started with nothing. To obtain just one rifle, a band of unarmed partisans had to mob a

German sentry and kill him with knives or bludgeon him to death. For their part, they neither gave nor expected mercy. The Hun, in an effort to quell the brutality, took to murdering hostages or torturing them to extract information. This lead to equally or even more brutal tactics on the part of the partisans, until it was open warfare of the most vicious type on both sides.

Our unit was now up and running. There were small routine jobs such as the incision of abscesses, dealing with cuts and minor wounds, removal of the appendix, and so forth. Jack Churchill's raids then came on the scene. In between times it was relatively quiet, but with increasing numbers of commandos on the island, the raids became more ambitious, often bringing in as much work as we could cope with.

During the last part of the hectic activity when we were dealing with the casualties of the partisan Miljet and Brac raids, a German prisoner was brought up to the hospital shot through the elbow. He was in such great pain that he pleaded strongly for his arm to be amputated. The ulnar nerve was intact, however, and it was clear that with conservative surgery his arm would be saved. The intelligence officer who came with him said that he had done a deal with him, in that he had provided some very useful information concerning the enemy positions and had bargained for him to be treated at the hospital and not handed over to the partisans, who would certainly kill him. At the time we were still dealing with the partisan casualties, and the team was also at the point of total exhaustion. There was a dilemma—what should we do with him?

Lalla said that she would have nothing whatever to do with him. In respect for her but in a quandary, I suggested George should take him on. Accordingly, he was transferred, and George sorted him out. He was able to preserve his arm and then took great care that he was not harmed by the partisans while he recovered.

Two days later he mysteriously disappeared during the night. No one had any idea of his whereabouts. At least if they had any information, their lips were sealed. So a search was made, but he was nowhere to be found. He could have been spirited away by the partisans and "eliminated", but no one would admit to having seen or heard him escape.

When George went back to work that day, he suddenly discovered in the middle of a surgical procedure that his best scissors were missing from the set of instruments laid out for him. This could not be explained. Again nobody knew anything about it. They had been in regular use all the time. George was furious. Surely they must be somewhere. Someone must have taken them. Someone must know something. Was it a conspiracy of sealed lips, he wondered? They could not have been lost. Was it something to do with the German prisoner? Scissors are one of the most important instruments for dissection work. They were irreplaceable, and he could ill afford to lose them. It remained a mystery.

So they scoured the camps, looking for the missing German, searching all the buildings nearby and questioning everybody, but no one had seen or heard anything. So the search went wider and was resumed the following day. He might have escaped and be lying up in the hills. He must be on the island somewhere. But where? After an extensive search, they eventually did find him. He was several miles from Vis town, hiding in the scrub on the mountain side overlooking the sea and clutching the missing scissors in his hand. He was in a poor way, having lost a lot of blood from a chest wound. He was hypothermic and had breathing difficulties. They got a stretcher to him and brought him back. He had a punctured lung. Using the scissors, he had attempted suicide by stabbing his chest where he thought his heart to be. He had damaged some lung tissue and had missed the heart. George put a chest drain in place, and over the next few days he made a remarkable recovery. The lung wound, which was superficial, healed.

There was then a further problem arose as to what to do with him. Neither the partisans nor the Allies had any accommodation for recovering prisoners. There was great pressure to provide beds for the sick and wounded, and now that he was better they had to move him on somewhere. The German prisoners taken by the partisans were invariably shot. To hand him over, therefore, to partisan care was almost certainly going to be a death sentence. In the end, Milo Zon, Zena's husband, agreed out of respect for the British medical team to take him for some convalescence to his ward. George agreed to see him every few days to check his progress. After a week without having seen him, George went to pay him a visit and found he was no longer there. He asked Milo where he was and found him evasive. "Very sad, very sad," he explained. "He had to have a further operation and died under the anaesthetic."

Imagine the weather now in February. It was cold with clear sunlit days and brilliant colours, the sea an ultramarine blue. In the distance mountain ranges stood out near the skyline. The nearest island was Hvar, then Korcula, and behind them the line of snow-capped Yugoslav mainland near Split in the distance. When the sun shone, one could immediately feel its Mediterranean warmth, but the north wind had a sharp edge to it which could cut like a knife. There were times when the Bora would descend on us. This wild wind was sudden and severe and might last for several days. From the north in winter and accompanied by rain or hail, it gave little comfort to those in tents on the hillside.

The approach to our grey stone house, lying a hundred yards south of the road, had now been widened for the ambulances and other *transports. In front we had two EPIP tents as a reception—neat and tidy thanks to Lovro—and alongside, two good wards made of six more EPIP tents.*

Our mess had a lovely old country-pub atmosphere with a roaring open log fire. It was so attractive that it became the port of call for all and sundry. Curiosity brought some of the visitors, while others came for all the wrong reasons—the hospitality. Whilst we were quiet, we welcomed all comers and enjoyed their company. It was a great place to relax in the cold winter evenings.

Chapter 14

Jack Churchill, was keen to carry out raids on the local islands, and in February he started a series of planned attacks. Some of these became known as the "ring-the-bell-and-shoot" raids. An account of the first of these was told to me by "Pissy" Parsons, a commando captain, who joined us one evening for a chat and a glass of wine. Pissy had heard from the partisans that the Germans on Hvar were putting on a cinema show one evening. This was going to be popular and would be well attended, so he went across by boat and landed. He stole up to the town and identified the German HQ, where he guessed the commandant would be. He then banged on the door, which was opened by the commandant himself. Pissy shot him in the stomach, pushed him aside, and went on into the building. It turned out he was alone in the building. He went through the papers he found and took away a load of files and intelligence material. When he got back to Vis, this was all examined and found to provide much insight into the Adriatic intentions of the German High Command. When news of this incident spread, guard patrols were increased.

On another occasion Lieutenant Barton of No. 2 Commando, again under cover of darkness, slipped across to Brac, where along with partisan guides he gathered intelligence about the whereabouts of the German forces on the island. Before leaving to come back, he decided on a plan try to spring a surprise on the commander, who had imposed some particularly severe conditions on the civilian population. He had developed a routine for the night hours, which were invariably spent in his billet in the town of Nerezisce. The question arose as to how Barton might get past the German guards, who patrolled regularly. He learned from the local partisans that although there was curfew between the hours of 6.00 p.m. and 6.00 a.m., some shepherds always drove their sheep past the German guards and on down into the town. So a plan was put forward. If he could possibly get past the guards, he might be able to get to the commander's billet. Obviously, he would need a Sten gun. This would be hard to conceal and would impose a risk to the whole idea. It was arranged that on the night in question a local partisan woman would carry the gun past the guards earlier in the evening by hiding it disassembled under a pile of wood on her mule. He then dressed as a shepherd and, along with a flock of sheep, walked past the guards into the town. He picked up the gun at the pre-arranged place and assembled it ready to use.

He had to wait until it was quite dark before locating and getting to the commander's billet. Leaving a partisan guard outside the house, he banged on the door. It was opened by a woman, who started to shriek and had to be quietened when it was explained what was up. A batman appeared downstairs, who said that the Commander was out, but if they did not harm him, he would take Barton to the house where he was dining. Thinking they had better check the story, Barton went upstairs and found in the bedroom an automatic pistol, a compass, and a pair of binoculars. He took these but hearing a noise next door, he went into the dining room which was in darkness save for a small candle burning on the table. It seemed the room was empty, but then something glinted in the corner, and he saw it was an iron cross on a man's tunic. He gave it a burst of fire. A figure rose up and then stumbled to the floor. They made a hasty getaway by jumping over a wall, with the German guards *after them in hot pursuit with barking dogs and under a hail of bullets. Official records later confirmed that it was indeed the commander who had been killed.*

These surprise attacks on the German positions in the island had the effect of making them very nervous. The impression the commandos sought to give was that the Vis force was much larger than it really was. On the down side, it meant that the German positions on the islands were all reviewed and where necessary strengthened. Future attacks on the islands would be much more difficult.

On 22 March, Jack Churchill carried out a full-scale commando raid on Hvar. In his planning, he used information previously gathered from an earlier raid. The idea was to steal across by night and take the garrison by surprise, making much noise with such a fierce and determined sudden approach that the German position on the island would think that the invading force was a large army.

Sadly the commando officer leading the sortie was killed early in the action. However, after some intense fighting the Germans were forced to surrender their defended position. The commandos then had to leave hurriedly, as reinforcements were approaching, and they were unable to pick up three men who had got separated. They had to be left behind. An arrangement was already in place, whereby there would be a rendezvous two days later when a boat would come across by night and pick them up. One of the men left behind had been wounded in the chest, and it was thought he would not survive. However, he managed to crawl three miles to the meeting place, eating his emergency rations and drinking melted snow. By then he was in a bad way. He was dehydrated and hypothermic. They took him to George's unit who despite the lack of equipment, did what he could. He was then transferred to Bari where, we learned later, he made a very good recovery. We dealt with six wounded commandos who returned from that raid.

All the time we were learning our problems. Fortunately we were helped by the commando units and were able to borrow two RAMC commandos from Col. Symmonds through the good offices of Capt. Crowther, who was Regimental Medical Officer. These boys were trained by Dawson as theatre orderlies and nurses, and though both were youngsters and without experience, they became very good.

Willett, Bryan Lees' batman and jeep driver, was given overall charge of the generator. This was as temperamental as a woman and so, inevitably, was christened Jenny. She gave endless trouble and like a woman would often pick the night hours to be unpredictable. She would be difficult in the middle of a night surgery list. We endlessly fought with her, but she eventually gave up the struggle against us and turned into a docile hard-working old lady, thanks to the RAF electricians and Corporal Sanderson of REME, attached to 255 Brigade, both of whom would come at any hour of the day or night. Both Sanderson and the RAF boys would come into the mess after a long session to enjoy a good square meal with a mug of wine comfortably in front of the fire.

Each morning we were visited by Messerschmitts. They would fly over, make a reconnaissance, fire at any target they could pick out, and then depart. We got used to them, learned their routine, and avoided them as best we could.

About this time there was an influx of Americans. They brought with them some heavy equipment, and this was put to use making the airstrip bigger by clearing more vines. Larger planes such as Lightnings and Liberators would then be able to land. After the work had been done, the airstrip became a hive of activity, with Spitfires using it all day to raid German provisioning transports on the mainland and then *return to refuel. The Liberators and Lightnings then used the strip to carry out bombing raids that targeted the industrial centres around Vienna. They passed over the island about 10 a.m. on the way out. They usually returned just about lunch time. Vis, in Allied hands, was the first opportunity they had to bale out into friendly territory. Any planes, therefore, which had been so badly damaged by enemy fire that they were unlikely to make the last ninety-mile stretch of water across the Adriatic, would take two runs over the island, baling out four men each time and leaving the plane to crash where it would. Sometimes this was in the sea, but on at least one occasion we watched a plane circle lower and lower until it crashed into the side of Mount Hum.*

Most usually the plane was destroyed by fire. On this occasion there was no fire, and the looters lost no time in getting what they could. Situated as we were up on the mountain, our men were first there and were delighted to get some heavy-gauge electric wire, switches from the gun turret, and some useful first-aid kits. The switches were then built in to make proper connections for the lighting circuits. We then had light in all the EPIP tents.

When parachutes or even planes came down in the seas around the islands, there would often be a race to make a rescue. Those planes that came down near the occupied islands were usually won by the German fast boats. They would take prisoners and search and question them in order to obtain intelligence. Those landing around Vis were attended by our own naval craft. Most often, however, there were no survivors from the planes themselves.

Zena found us a piano. It was the one around which we had gathered earlier after one of her dinners. It was in a house on the waterfront, which at the time was crammed with partisans, but they were not using it. A truck was organised, and it arrived up at Podhumlje amid cheers from the gathered assembly. Scottie of Signals came up to christen it.

Podhumlje Hospital

Podhumlje mess

John Rickett

The very next night the Luftwaffe paid us a visit. Immediately after the alert siren was sounded, the bombers came swooping over our hospital. Clearly, the net camouflaging had not disguised us. Incendiaries were dropped all around with an infernal noise. Heron thought the two girls could be panicking, so he dashed into their house, where he found them cowering and sobbing in a corner. He grabbed them and dragged them into the mess next door, along with Marie, the cook. He made them join the party. They each had a glass of wine, and with arms around necks, they sang and danced until the all clear went—though with the incredible noise they were now making, they had great difficulty hearing it.

Our mess quickly became the official club on the island. We had endless free wine and, latterly, the only piano on the island. A roaring log fire burned in the grate, and with Scotty being an indefatigable pianist, parties occurred nearly every night into the small hours.

The parties tended to get noisier, particularly at those times when the work was relatively quiet. After one unfortunate debauch, Bryan Lees' much beloved and carefully trimmed and twisted moustache was ruined with one sweep by somebody with a pair of scissors. Naturally, this brought a furious retaliation. Poor Bryan was determined to be revenged, so in future anyone who became incapable was liable to have parts of their hair cut. The result was that some people had a curious patchy appearance, with large areas of hair missing from their scalps and faces.

Considering my work the next morning and having surgery to do, I pitched a bivouac tent out on the hill and slept 150 yards away, where I could get away from the noise and settle down in some quiet. I could then get some useful work done the next day—not that I did not, on a good few occasions, stay and enjoy the entertainment.

With the news of the commando activity and the increasing importance of Vis in the partisan command, official visits were clearly expected. On one occasion a medical brigadier who was an orthopaedic specialist came over from Italy. He spent some time looking at the set up both at Podhumlje and in Vis town. He was entertained by George and Zena, and he much appreciated the informal atmosphere of the evenings when we gathered round the fire and the piano was the centre of attention up at Podhumlje. He freely admitted having enjoyed his time on the island and was indeed sorry to leave, but needs must, and reports had to be made. He got onto a boat for Italy just as a commando was brought in with a quite severe ankle injury. The question was whether there might be a fracture, and if there was, perhaps he would be best sorted out in Italy. I recalled how much the brigadier had enjoyed his stay and perhaps would like to enjoy another night with us, so I radioed out to the boat and requested an urgent orthopaedic consultation. Accordingly, a launch took him off and brought him up. The brigadier was able to give an expert opinion on the management of the injury. This benefited the patient and his more speedy return to duty, and the brigadier was able to spend another evening with us.

With the successes of the partisan raids on the islands, a supply of German prisoners was gradually building. They were a problem, as accommodation was limited on Vis and they had to be provided with food. In the early days, the partisans took them to the small offshore island of Bisevo, from which there was little chance of escape. Eventually a High Command decision was made to negotiate a prisoner exchange. This was to be arranged through intermediaries. Accordingly, on the appointed day under a white flag of truce, a partisan schooner took a group of captured prisoners to the previously arranged island rendezvous on Hvar. They were a mixed bunch. In addition to Germans, there were Austrians, Poles, even some Greeks and Chetniks. The Germans appeared at the rendezvous and went through the ranks of each in turn. They refused the Austrians and Polish prisoners and only took back the German officers. They then refused to release any of their own prisoners. Those they brought down to the rendezvous they took back, and we heard later that they simply hanged them all on Hvar. When Zena heard about this, she exploded into one of her now famous furies. Her greatest anger was focussed on the partisan decision to carry out this attempted swap, saying they should have known better than to cooperate in any way with the Germans.

On one occasion George was operating to remove a bullet from the leg of a German prisoner who was under an anaesthetic, given now by Zena who, like Suza, had no proper training. George knew of Zena's intense loathing of all Germans. After the operation was over, the prisoner remained deeply asleep, and the question arose as to whether Zena had deliberately given him an overdose. Zena strenuously denied this, but when the prisoner was still asleep later that evening, she herself was worried that perhaps inadvertently this had happened. George had by this time accepted that she had no evil intentions against the German and was able to reassure Zena that occasionally patients can react unfavourably to a combination of anaesthetic drugs, and especially of Pentothal and morphine when these are given simultaneously. Zena none the less remained worried.

In the event, it took him twenty hours to wake up. When he did come to his senses, he immediately, and in a very loud voice which echoed down the corridor, started to brag to another German prisoner about his exploits as a pilot. He shamelessly boasted of his achievements in the Luftwaffe. In December when the Germans planned to overrun and capture the town of Split, he remembered flying low over the town, *strafing and killing many partisans whom he enjoyed watching as they ran in all directions, terrified for their lives. Little did he know that Zena, approaching down the corridor, understood German enough to make out what he was saying. Naturally she was incensed. It was his brazen, loud-mouthed boasting that made it intolerable. This was a particular insult, as he had just received considerable care and attention from the very people whom earlier he had ruthlessly murdered. She reported the conversation to the partisan guards outside that a German Luftwaffe officer was in the hospital. They said they would need to question him, so George was then under pressure to allow them to move him out of the hospital. George refused, but in the end he had to relent and the prisoner was taken away. He never heard what happened to him. When he asked Zena if he had been shot, she said she did not know, adding dryly, "I hope they did."*

The now enlarged airstrip was used by planes for refuelling, for emergency repairs, and as a strategically important forward reconnaissance base. The enlargement had been done against the islanders' wishes, but assurances were given that after the war the area would be restored to the production of wine.

Liberators were landing regularly, and it was particularly useful for crippled planes returning, which would otherwise have had to ditch in the sea. On one occasion, a Lightning landed with engine trouble. The Lightning was a large twin-fuselage plane, and the airstrip was even now only just long enough for the landing. The pilot was a Chinese-American who was in quite an excited state, saying that he had special information about enemy positions that was urgently needed back at base. He demanded to know how long it would take for the engineers to work on the engine to get it airworthy again. The answer of four hours did not satisfy him, and he pressurized them to try to

John Rickett

get them to work more quickly. After two hours his impatience got the better of him, and he demanded to get airborne. It was pointed out this was extremely unwise, but he was adamant. He simply had to get back with this vital information. So they hurriedly cleared the runway, and off he went. The engines spluttered into life and seemed to be working well, so he decided to take the risk. He took off but had engine failure almost immediately, and the plane crashed back on the land amongst a group of partisans, killing fifteen men and catching fire as it did so. A big rescue took place, and he was dragged out alive but very severely burned. He was taken to us at Podhumlje. Evacuation, sadly, was out of the question, as he would not have survived the journey. So all I could do was to cleanse and dress the extensive burns, which I estimated as covering about ninety per cent of his surface area. I had to perform a tracheotomy, as the swelling in his throat region was making it difficult for him to breathe. Afterwards it was felt the best measure was to encase him in a plaster to help prevent the inevitable infection of the raw burnt areas and to keep him comfortable with morphine. He was fed by a tube which led into his stomach. In this way we kept him as comfortable as possible, but despite these measures, he died a few days later. His was a very lonely death so encased and lacking the care and attention a Burns Unit would have provided, though the end result, I have little doubt, would have been no different.

Gerke was an early beneficiary of the airstrip. He ran out of fuel and had to crash land his Spitfire on the small strip. He was a lean and dark Australian pilot, and in a short space of time he found his way via Scottie to the Podhumlje mess, where he and Heron found they had a lot in common. He was all for a night of drinking and had some good stories to tell. He fitted in well. He made the most of it and after several days, when questions were being asked about his whereabouts and progress, he thought he had better return to Italy. Several days after he left us, there was news of another Spitfire emergency—again a fuel shortage. Gerke had re-emerged, and this time he had brought his toothbrush and pyjamas. Unfortunately, the plane's undercarriage had buckled when he landed, and so this had to be repaired, further delaying his return.

During these quiet times, the late nights were fairly regular and fully enjoyed by Gerke, who was patiently waiting for the engineers to do the necessary work. After one such evening, the next day Heron came up and asked me if I would take a look at Gerke. He said he had a pretty bad hangover. They didn't usually last this long which was into the afternoon. I saw him and straight away I said we must get a theatre ready. He had an appendix. So we took him down, and sure enough, I found and removed a gangrenous appendix in the nick of time before it burst. After that he recovered from his "hangover" pretty quickly and went back to Italy. Within three weeks, he was back flying Spitfire sorties, returning from which he would come over Vis and send via Scottie rude joking messages to one and all.

The Prodigal's *crew would occasionally come up to see us. Occasionally they brought mail and this was always welcome. On one occasion Dorothy wrote that she hoped I was having a wonderful time on the isle of Lissa (she used the Italian name for Vis). I think she thought an Adriatic island after all couldn't be too bad. How she had guessed where I was is hard to know, as all mail going back home was very strictly censored. We never put anything that the censor would blank out with his pen, as this defeated the whole purpose of writing. On this occasion I also learned that my family had moved back to Sussex from Scotland, as the fear of heavy bombing along the South Coast had* ended. This was excellent news. Hitler had more than enough to keep his army occupied in Europe.

Along with the letters they brought with them the goat which we had given them in exchange for light bulbs. Somehow he had avoided the cooking pot and was now called Herbert. He appeared very happy to be back with us, though this was not exactly what we had in mind. However, we were persuaded to take him, as they pleaded that Herbert had never taken very well to life on board and was now a pet, and nobody was prepared to kill him despite the fact that he would have made quite a nice dinner for one and all. So back home he came, and very soon he got up to all his old bad habits.

There was news of trouble down at the port, where a couple of sailors had been fraternizing with two partisan girls. Morgan Giles had been told, and he was under pressure to have the culprits dealt with in a manner appropriate to the partisan system. The sailors had been sent back to Italy ostensibly to be "shot". Dodd became rather quiet after he heard this, and later it transpired that a partisan girl he had been seeing was pregnant. White as a sheet, he confessed this to me. His regrets about what he had done were of course totally inadequate and irrelevant. We simply had to deal with the situation. I immediately thought of George. After all, he dealt with the partisans. I discussed this with him, and of course he pointed out that the problem had been caused by Dodd, who as a commando was my responsibility. I pointed out that it wasn't Dodd who was pregnant. Well it so happened that the girl developed "sudden and rather acute" abdominal pain. She saw George, and he immediately diagnosed appendicitis. He decided he should operate at once. I saw George after the operation and asked him how it had gone. He said just fine. He found and removed the appendix, which had looked a bit pink and was "slightly inflamed". He *checked down in the pelvis in case there was any incidental problem, and in doing so, he confessed "I just gave the uterus a little friendly squeeze."*

Midwifery facilities were more or less non-existent on the island. Maternity cases were shipped to Italy. However, I remember a sad case of a lady in a small cottage on the hillside. She was in a bad way, lying in the dark with the shutters closed against the cold and too ill to be moved. She gave birth to a baby, but soon after she died from what must have been, judging from her poor condition and terrible cough, tuberculosis. The refugees from the islands were often infected or were carriers of the infection. The baby was taken into care in Vis, and a few days later one of the refugee women going through the hospital was told of it. She had just lost her own baby when her village had been burned, and she immediately took this little scrap into her arms as an emotional substitute for her own. She went on her way and was evacuated to Italy by boat, taking the baby and almost believing it to be her own. I never heard anything more, but I had the rather disturbing thought that the baby would likely have caught TB from her mother, and having it could well have endangered both lives—that of the baby but also that of the new mother.

I was asked to see Melitsa. It had taken eighteen months for her to get to Vis. She had a compound fracture of her leg, which had healed in a bad position with the leg at an angle and bone showing through the wound. There was osteo-myelitis with chronic infection, and maggots were crawling about in the open wound.

The story was that as a partisan fighter she had laid explosives to blow up a section of the Zagreb-Split railway. The fuse was faulty, and the explosion had gone off before she could get clear. She had crawled away and was picked up by comrades who carried her on one of their *blanket stretchers into hiding. No medical attention was possible, and the group that had saved her had to keep moving to avoid the attentions of the Germans. In the end, they could not take her with them, and she had to stay hiding in the cottage for several weeks. When she was only partly recovered, she decided her best chance was to go on the move, using crutches as best she could. As a consequence, she spent the next months scavenging for food and shelter in the woods amongst people who gave her shelter but begged her to move on for fear of the Germans and the reprisals they would seek if she was discovered with them. So disorientated had she been that she could remember little of the detail of those months on the run.*

So now she was with us. Gaunt and emaciated with the cachexia of chronic infection, she presented a pitiable picture. Our immediate problem was to see to surgical means for draining infection from the wound and to build her up as best we could. This would obviously take time, and when she was fitter, she could then undergo the necessary corrective orthopaedic measures to give her a useful leg again. Pleased as she was to be under medical care, her main concern was a worry about her menstrual cycle. This had dried up. "Would it come back?" she insisted in continually asking me. She did not really believe the reassurances I gave to her. She appeared more worried about this than whether she would have a useful leg on which to walk.

CHAPTER 15

Brigadier Tom Churchill arrived on Vis on 1 March two weeks after his No. 2 Commando force. His remit was to support his colourful brother Jack, whose raids were now well known at the commando base in Italy. He was to take over as overall commanding officer. At the time No.2 Commando arrived all the available billets had been taken and a decision was made to put them on the high ground outside Vis town where they bivouacked in tents. Here they should be able to keep an eye on the small offshore island of Ravnik, which was a potential landing spot for a German invasion. Tom himself and his staff moved into Borovic, occupying a couple of houses fairly near Jim Rickett on the lower slopes of Mount Hum. Immediate plans were made for a raid on Solta island. This was coded Operation Detained. This had to be a more substantial raid than those planned earlier, as the enemy was more prepared. There would be a combined commando and American force, supported by the Navy to make the landing. Finally, the Air Force would come over with bombers and fighters to help finish the task.

The geography of the island was such that it was relatively easy for German installations to defend from a position on high ground, which was surrounded by rocky terrain. Equally, it was going to be difficult to get heavy artillery from the landing place over the ground in order to support the combat of the final assault. First, a preliminary reconnoitre was made, in which two commando officers, Jenkins and Macminamin, along with two men, accompanied the partisans who had been working on the island. They observed the defended positions and timed the night patrols during the hours to be used for the raid. Having got the information they needed, they went to return to Vis, but they were taken by the partisans along a new track which the partisans assured them would be clear and safe. They met a troop of Germans who saw them and opened fire. The commandos split up. Macminamin escaped and made it to the pick-up point, but, sadly, Jenkins was shot and captured as he tried to scale a seven-foot wall.

Macminamin then returned to the island a few days later in a further reconnaissance to determine whether the German positions had altered as a result of the disturbance. It appeared they had not, so they decided to go ahead. They would go under cover of darkness. During the night, they planned to move as silently as possible into positions surrounding the village of Grohote, where the Germans were installed. At dawn the RAF would come over and bomb the German position. The crossing went ahead, and the positions were taken up by dawn, though the difficulties of getting the men and equipment through the difficult terrain was such that by the time they were installed, the Germans had realised an attack was taking place and were starting to open fire. They knew that their positions would be exposed in daylight and were relying on the Air Force bombers to arrive at the time agreed, which was one hour after dawn. Jack Churchill had his loud hailer with him, and a man who could speak German. At the break of dawn, using the loud hailer, he shouted to the German garrison, "You are entirely surrounded by British and American troops. In one hour squadrons of bombers are coming and will blow up and destroy your installation. Come out now with hands above your heads, and you will be taken prisoner unharmed." After this some Germans came out carrying a white flag. Cox went forward to receive it and was immediately machine-gunned by the Germans, receiving severe abdominal wounds. This provoked a fierce counter attack. Later, as arranged, the bombers came over. The Germans still held out, and the attack had to be finished with a fixed bayonet charge by the Allied forces on a house-to-house basis, before the Germans surrendered finally. There was loss of life on both sides, and a number of German prisoners were taken. The evacuation from Solta after the raid had been planned in advance. The garrison on Vis was too small to sustain the depletion involved in the event of long-term occupation of the island. A fast launch was to take the wounded back to Vis, but they had to wait until dusk to avoid a German air attack.

The account continues.

By the time poor Cox got to the small hospital at Podumlje, he was in a bad way, profoundly toxic and collapsed, some thirty-six hours having elapsed since his injury. I asked him to open his tunic and found a penetrating abdominal wound with seven feet of small intestine lying inside his vest. I had to resect about five feet of ileum[22] and carried out repair of other areas of damage. Following this, I replaced the bowel, repaired his abdominal wall, and got him off the operating table. Sadly, but much as I had anticipated, he died four days later of the overwhelming infection which was already established. We took about twenty hours continuous operating to complete the work on this lot of casualties.

---

22 The operation register starkly reads "19th March—Cox MG (machine gun) wound perforating abdomen. Excision of 5 ft. of ileum." Exteriorizing the small intestine outside the abdomen by the gunshot wound in fact probably delayed the onset of peritonitis, which otherwise would have killed him before he got to the hospital.

DATE	NO	NAME	RANK + UNIT	DIAGNOSIS		OPERATION	ANAESTHETIC
1.	27.2.44	P/MX 99459 MTB 651	GOOBY LMM	Prejudic?	Abdomenal wound.	Lacerativ spleen. Wormin peritoneal cavity. Splenectomy	E.C. + E Pent.
2.	28.2.44	D/JX 217625 MTB 651	ROSS AB.	T+T SR (L)	Arm. Ulnarpalsy.	Toilet SVG	Pent.
3.	16.2.44	MTB 651	SLACK. J.	T+T UR (R)	Thigh	Toilet SVG.	Pent.
4.	29.2.44	43 CM Commando	HARDING	Acute Aft me ach? Aseilory Abs.		Grid-acuta inflama Retroseccid bu ciu	Pent 12.
5.	2.3.44		DEANE				Pent.
6.	11.3.44		SAYER	Multiple Acc	Nim wds.	Toilet Deb + SVG.	Pent.
7.	13.3.44		HIGGINS	A.A. shell wd	Fractus r L Hand.	Toilet Deb. SVG.	Pent.
8.	18.3.44		WILSON	Acc Nim wd		Toilet Deb. SVG POP R Right to toes.	Pent.
9.	19.3.44		PEMBERY	Bomb wds	(L) Hand.	Toilet + SVG.	Pent.
10.	19.3.44		NICK	Natur wds	(L) Knee.	Toilet + SVG.	Pent.
11.	19.3.44		AMYGDALITIS	Dohn or			Pent
12.	19.3.44		COX	MG wd rt buttock	abdomen	Excision of silicon	Pent.
13.	19.3.44		POFFIE	Panetratig wd	(L) Knee	Excision + P&P.	Pent.
14.	20.3.44		BOKERS	JSW (L) calf		Deb. SVG.	Pent.
15.	20.3.44		RITCHIE	GSW (L) Thigh		Deb + SVG.	Pent.
16.	20.3.44		EAGLESON	GSW Bck Thigh		Deb + SVG.	Pent.
17.	20.3.44		SHINKS	GSW R Thigh		Deb + SVG.	Pent.
18.	20.3.44		SAWYER	GSW Ant Leg		Deb + SVG.	Pent.

Operations register

Stretchers Not Available

Working through the night with great care to avoid showing any light over the blackout was our first test of a dose of really heavy work. All went well, but we were to learn our weak spots. One of these was quickly identified as we operated that night. There were still enemy planes overhead, prowling after boats returning from the raid. We had to douse the flames of the sterilizer whenever we heard an enemy plane overhead. This made for some delays in between cases, but Dawson did a fantastic job, making clean and sterilized instruments and mackintosh drapes available for each case.

The following morning, I went out in daylight to find another problem. With no mortuary those who had been killed and brought back were brought up and left literally on our doorstep. This untenable situation needed sorting out.

I now came to realise after this how the whole of the medical arrangements of the island depended on us. More stretcher bearers were also needed urgently on the occasions when we were very busy after a raid. They would help to ensure a faster turnover between cases. After requests were made, we were able to get partisans to be ready and standing by for these duties. We got over the language problems by using gesticulations. Somewhat surprisingly, this seemed to work fairly well.

About this time, a touching incident was described to me by Zena. She saw in the sky an Allied Liberator on fire and about to crash into the sea. A solitary parachutist baled out from it. He landed on the high ground nearby, and after disentangling from his parachute, he stood up, but it was clear that he was hurt. She said he appeared to be just a young lad who was apparently the pilot of the doomed plane, but as he hobbled along, making his way towards a woman walking up the road, he called out, "Mother, mother". When he got to her, they embraced, with her crying, "My son, my son". Zena was on the scene, and realizing he needed help, she got him into a truck, though he was extremely reluctant to leave the embrace of his mother. He was brought in to see me to deal with his damaged leg. Having taken a look, I realised that without an X-ray we were very much in the dark. A fracture was likely. I explained this to Zena. He would need to go to Italy unless, of course, she could find me one. I simply put this in as an afterthought. Zena thought about this, and realizing the British supplies had all but dried up, she said, "I will get you one!"

Zena had heard that requests had been made on the Yugoslav mainland for her services. She realised that if she ever went, she would need some knowledge of proper warfare. So she determined whilst in the relative safety of the island to get some experience of weaponry by using the expertise of the British Army. She approached the commandos to let her have some grenades. She practised with these away on the hill, throwing them at imaginary German targets. After one such practise, she returned to harangue the commando officer who had supplied her.

"What sort of joke is this?" she asked.

"Why? What is wrong?" asked the officer.

"The grenades are empty!"

The officer, taken aback, thought for a few moments and then asked, "How did you find that out?"

Zena replied with withering scorn, "You stupid man, I need to know how my grenades work, so I took one to pieces."

Soon after we had sorted out the wounded from the Solta raid, the Germans, in retaliation, decided on a heavy night bombing raid on Vis. They went mainly for the towns, first to Vis on the northeast where George and his team worked, then on to Komisa. With the initial raid *they severely damaged the bakery, a sardine cannery, and a score of partisan billets.*

The military command had issued instructions that in the event of a raid, shelter should be taken under the stairs, which was considered the safest place in the house. So George went to shelter under the stairs, where a hysterical Cooky was already crouching. He thought he had better look for Zena and found she had ignored the recommendations and was asleep upstairs. He had the greatest difficulty in getting Zena to join them, despite the bombs landing so close that the house was shaken with each blast. Only when he threatened to literally drag her down did she agree. She then appeared in a nightgown. This was completely against the regulations—staff were under instructions, in readiness for an evacuation, to have at all times at night clothing ready and packed. Then one bomb landed on the quay outside their house, shaking the house badly and sending Cooky into a further attack of hysterics. This irritated Zena, who said, "Cooky, you are stupid. Is it better to die of a terrible illness or by a bomb?"

Cooky came back, "That's just like you! We must even quarrel when we are about to die! You even take my flowers off the table. You have no heart. I will not work with you any more!"

Eventually the bombing stopped, and immediately there was a knock at the door. A partisan had come to say there was work to do. The hospital had been hit, so there were clearly considerable problems. Fortunately, George was able to make a start, mainly by assessing the casualties, some of which were severe. There were traumatic amputations, crush injuries, chest injuries, shrapnel wounds, and more.

An old expatriate American called Joe was badly hurt with a severely crushed chest when the hospital was hit. Joe had left a comfortable life in America before the war started, where he been a meat packer and a salesman, amongst several other jobs. Instead he had opted for the somewhat Spartan life on this island. Speaking good Serbo-Croat, he had helped George as an interpreter from time to time. When asked why he had left America, he replied, "It's okay for the dough, but it ain't no place to die." Dalmatia was where he had always said he wanted his life to end, and that night he was granted his wish.

Having shaken the town of Vis, the Luftwaffe went on to Komisa, where they concentrated their effort on the harbour area. The defending Bofors guns were woefully ineffectual in the defence of the town. Prof Heron had been enjoying a drink in the town, and he reported quite unshaken and in the best of spirits, "We only had half a dozen casualties."

Admiral Sir Walter Cowan had come over to the island with Tom Churchill. He was in his element during the raid. He persisted in marching up and down the Komisa quay in the midst of the blitz, castigating first our own artillery for poor aiming and then the Luftwaffe, sarcastically, for the same reason. Some partisans were lying down on the ground while the blasts were going all around them. Sir Walter shouted, "What on earth are you doing down there? Did you drop a coin?" Finally one bomb landed in the water just by him, and after the spray had cleared, he said witheringly, "If all the buggers can do is wet you . . ."

The story went that in Tobruk he had tried to hold up a German tank with his revolver, emptying it out at it as it approached and finally throwing the gun at it. He was taken prisoner after this but was later released in an exchange deal.

The commandos had welcomed Sir Walter almost like a mascot. His energy was incredible and his spirit indomitable. Despite being retired for many years, he had made the habit of becoming attached to fighting units in different theatres of war. He now had joined the commandos. He was seen regularly wearing their green beret, riding up the hill past the Podhumlje hospital on a donkey or taking a constitutional walk up to the mountain. He regularly went on the commando raids and even on gunboat trips. On one occasion, I saw him outside our unit and invited him into the hospital. However, he refused, saying that he did not want to cause any bother.

Tom Churchill told me the story of a group of a hundred or so German prisoners, who had been captured in the Solta raid. During the bombing, they became hysterical with fear. They rushed out into the street, flattening themselves on the ground. So an order was given for them to be marched out of the town up onto the plateau in case there was a further bombing assault. A cottage had been evacuated to take them. As the men were dispersed into the accommodation, their leader thanked the officer who took them, choosing his words carefully. "I want to express my thanks to our captors for this humane act by moving us out of the town and saving us from the Luftwaffe. We consider this has been a most chivalrous act, and we thank our captors accordingly!"

George continued to operate on the wounded in Vis for forty-eight hours without stopping. The brief breaks taken for tea and a snack were all he made time for. I came down from Podhumlje when I had finished my work up there. I had some interesting and difficult cases, including a ruptured spleen and a wound necessitating a nephrostomy tube, which had to be inserted into the kidney for drainage of urine. Eventually, an exhausted George was led away to take a rest and have a break.

Zena was also simply exhausted and just wanted to sleep. Little did she know at that very time that the partisan authorities had been considering her services and had felt they were now needed on the mainland in Bosnia, where Major Rogers, who previously had been working in Vis, was now running a medical unit with the partisans. He had demanded that Zena was to give his anaesthetics, as she had done so previously at the time he was working there.

She was told a schooner was waiting for her that very night. Ever faithful to the cause, she got up, dressed, and prepared to go, remonstrating as she did so with Dr Zon, her husband, who was to stay behind on the island as one of the few much-needed medical officers. It was he who persuaded her of the necessity to obey the partisan High Command. There was a brief emotional farewell, during which she said her heart would very much remain on Vis.

So she was gone, leaving George wondering how on earth he was to cope without her energy, ability, diplomacy, and language skills. And I was also left with doubts as to how we would, without her, get the partisan cooperation we had previously enjoyed. As she left, she said to me that she had not forgotten her promise about the X-ray machine. She would do what she could.

The severity of the last raid, especially with the damage to the hospital, brought home to George the need to move away from the town, which would obviously become a target yet again. I found him accommodation up on the mountain in two nearby houses, which were to become another treatment centre. As they would be dealing mainly with the partisans, this became known as the "Juggery". They were able designate a new "sterilizing room" like the one they had in Vis town in which to relax between cases. As we were to find later, this was highly fortuitous.

Within a few days of Zena's departure, we heard that an X-ray machine was to be delivered. Sure enough, it was landed from a schooner and was brought up to Podhumlje. It arrived in pieces—all gleaming and obviously new. Zena—what a girl! How on earth did she do this?

Later in the day, Milo Zon came up to find out if the parcels had all arrived and to see how we were managing to put it all together.

He told us the story of the capture of the X-ray. Before Zena had left, she had scoured the island for anyone who knew of the existence of an X-ray machine anywhere on the mainland. After she had gone, Milo and a group of partisans had kept the enquiries going. Eventually it was reported to them that there was a medical clinic in Split where a new X-ray had only just been delivered. So a plan was hatched. They contacted a mainland-based partisan group. They would provide a truck. On the day of the plan, a section of armed partisans stole over by night to the mainland in a schooner. Split was a large and important port and was heavily protected by German guards, so they had to be very careful. With local knowledge, they were able to get this boat to a small landing place some distance down the coast from the town. When it was light the next day and wearing ragged clothing which concealed their guns, they were picked up by an arranged truck and driven to the clinic. Once inside, they held up the staff at gun point. Sympathetic to the partisan cause though many of them may have been, they would have been terrified of the reprisals that would be taken by the Germans later. However, they were given no alternative. The new X-ray was dismantled and parcelled up into relatively small packages, covered in the same brown paper in which the machine had been originally supplied. The partisans then walked out of the building to the waiting lorry, loaded up the parcels, and were driven to the boat on the coast. They would again need the cover of darkness to escape. Waiting for this was an uneasy time, in case word had got to the Germans of what had happened.

Of course, the next problem was putting the machine together and getting it to work. There would likely be voltage problems, but this

John Rickett

seemed to be the least of our difficulties. After all, we had a team of people whose inexperience of X-ray machines was more than made up for by their enthusiasm. In fact, putting it together went well. Rather like a large jigsaw, the various bits fitted together presumably where they were meant to go. At least that is what we hoped! So it all came right, and there we had standing before us a brand new machine. The voltage needs were stated on the machine, and though they were considerable, the lads sorted it out for us. The high voltage wiring, together with switches, came from the recently crashed Liberator gun turret.

Then the moment came when we had to switch it on for the first time. Everyone stood well back waiting for the blinding flash. No flash, just a gentle purring noise of the machine warming up. Who's first? But, hang on for a moment, what about the dose of X-ray needed? We had no instruction book to guide us. We would have to do it by trial and error. So someone had to volunteer, and I could see the assembled group all looking at me. No point in beating about the bush—just do it, they said. I remember thinking I had been lucky enough to have already had three children and had no plans to have any more, so let's quietly forget about the effects it might have on my testicles! I stripped off and stood with my chest firmly against the plate. Again no blinding flashes—just a stunned silence from the onlookers and then the obvious facetious remarks, which, of course, I ignored. The initial screening had gone well. The dose of X-ray was adjusted through the experience we gained with the early cases. So now we were in business. This would make a great deal of difference to our work, in spotting fractures particularly, but also in looking for embedded fragments of metal from shrapnel and mortar wounds.

Later that very same day, I was treated to a very different but again unique experience. We were quiet, and I was taking a nap in one of the messing tents. I awoke feeling some warm liquid on my chest. Opening my eyes, I realised that Herbert the goat was urinating on me! That did it. Enough was enough. He had to go, and I called Dawson who, when he saw what had happened, most tactfully stifled his desire to fall about laughing. He caught Herbert and took him off. To celebrate the arrival of the X-ray, we ate him for dinner that night and enjoyed the varied moments of the day over a glass or two of wine.

Within quite a short time the X-ray was proving to be a great help. However, its use was restricted because it could only be used for screening. This meant that relatively large doses of radiation were required, and this would be a risk factor not only for the casualties but also, of course, for the staff of the unit. So we needed X-ray film, cassettes, developer, fixer, and, of course, proper dishes for developing the film. Only then would we be able to take X-ray films so that the potential of the new machine would be fully realised. During his recent visit to Italy, Brian Lees had been unable to obtain any X-ray equipment, so we would have to think again.

A stroke of luck occurred soon after when a commando sergeant was having lunch with us. He pricked up his ears when he heard us discussing our X-ray difficulties. He said, "I can get you all these things without any problem, as I have a brother who works in the base medical stores in Italy. The only difficulty is that to get to speak to him, I will need a leave pass."

Straight way I went up to Borovic, where Colonel Tom Churchill was in conference with a group of commando officers and partisans. I got in to see him and said, "Ask no questions, but I would be very grateful for four days leave for Sergeant Purcell to go to Italy on a special medical mission." Tom Churchill smiled faintly, agreed, and immediately issued a leave pass.

The plans for further raids were going ahead, and this meant that we could within days be inundated with work. X-ray film would make all the difference to the management of the wounds, so we got Purcell down to Komisa with the pass and managed to get him aboard an LCI which was just about to leave.

Sure enough, within a few days he was back with a large packet which they got up to Podhumlje. We now had film, developer, and cassettes. The next problem was to get trays to take the developer and fixer for the film. We also had to find a dark room. In the end we made wooden dishes out of the room partitioning we had taken down. These trays leaked rather badly, resulting in much wastage of the precious chemicals.

A few days later, a new padre came up to join us. We welcomed him, as he seemed a good chap who would fit in well with our curious ménage. I thought to myself that although Italian HQ could not provide us with physical help, at least we had spiritual support, and this must be better than nothing. The padre said he needed to be close to the action to be able to provide support for the injured men, so he pitched his tent right outside the operating theatre. After a little while, we found this was rather too close for comfort, but we could not think of a tactful way of getting him to move. His presence seemed to be hinting to those we treated that last rites were needed for everyone on whom we had operated. He was, however, a good member of the mess, and he put up with quite a lot of teasing, which took many forms.

In trying to get him to move, first they told him that pitched where it was, his tent would need to be taken down each day for camouflage purposes in case of bombing raids. However, he had a batman to help, so with this he readily complied. Then the ribbing took the form of teasing about the celibacy of his profession. Rather twisting the knife in the wound, I said to him one day that with the tent so close to the operating theatre day and night, there was a slight risk of radiation from our use of the X-ray machine. I said that he, as a priest, need not worry, as sterility would not be a concern. The very next day, he had taken his tent off the theatre site and to a place well away on the mountain side. When I next saw him, he confided in me, "Oh, I did it for my batman, of course. He is a family man." Needless to say, the mess guys were merciless.

One of our most pleasant guests was Squadron Leader Britton, who was a dentist. He walked in for breakfast one morning, having arrived during the night. "Hello chaps, I'm Britton." We acknowledged this with a blank stare. He seated himself down and proceeded to eat two eggs, a bowl of porridge, and a good deal of bread and marmalade. Apparently, on hearing on the grapevine that Vis was a "good spot", he had told the dental authorities that he ought to go over to review the dental situation. This indeed was necessary, but as there were no facilities at all, he was unable to do any work, so he settled with us. Both he and his sergeant helped us in the theatre; they played usefully with the X-ray machine and filled in the rest of the time with little practical jokes. He lived with us for a month. At the end of this time, I wrote out a glowing account of his activities, with which he reluctantly returned to Italy. We missed him a great deal after

John Rickett

he had gone, as the mess was usually in fits of laughter over what he was up to.

As the weeks went by, gradually signs of spring appeared. The bitterly cold nights were fewer, and the sun's rays became hotter. The mountain side started to show spring flowers, gentians, and then rock rose in particular, but everywhere there were signs of the fresh green of new spring growth on the mountain. It's a sight that lifts the spirit as did the thought that as time had gone by, so the immediate threat of German invasion had been reduced rather than increased. This did not mean that we could relax. The visitations of the Messerschmitts in the morning were a timely reminder, and so we maintained a state of alert. It would have been very mistaken not to do so, as to be taken by surprise would be a disaster. We ourselves, in dealing with the commando raids, had found this out. The commandos were making plans all the time.

The Navy for its part, having previously been involved a great deal with escort and protective work, had recently become effective in carrying out surprise attacks on German sea traffic. This was now hampering the German mainland supply lines. Their technique was based on piracy. Morgan Giles, senior naval officer of the Coastal Forces Unit, entered into the spirit of it in a way that I am certain would have impressed Billy Budd.

Lieutenant-Commander Tom Fuller over time became the chief exponent. During the first week of April, he captured eight German ships and sunk three more. On the first of these attacks, a motor torpedo boat accompanied by a fast gunboat waited under cover of an island. When the approaching convoy appeared, the gunboat charged out and down the line of the convoy, spraying *the ships with fire. Fuller then raced out, picked a target, and rammed into it to come alongside. Yelling and shouting, his party leaped on board with Sten guns. They overwhelmed the dazed crew and took the vessel in tow back to Vis. The very next night, they attacked two more schooners, using the same tactics, and brought them back. After that, the German air force got to hear and came looking for them with Messerschmitts, but they managed to get back safely and hid up under camouflage in Komisa harbour during the day. Other men followed Fuller's success, but Fuller proudly held the speed record of twelve minutes to board a vessel, subdue the crew, and take it in tow.*

For their part, the partisans tried similar tactics. They did not have the fast gunboats and had to use caiques—and these were much closer to the Billy Budd model. What they lacked from a technology point of view they made up for with enthusiasm and dash. And they had some successes. There were, however, a few problems when both parties were out at the same time. There was an agreed system for identification that was designed to avoid the otherwise inevitable clashes. This was to be a rapid flashing of lights in a certain sequence. The problem was that when the partisan boat was challenged, the lantern that should have been immediately available for the response was not always to hand. It first had to be found. It might well be down below deck or even in the hold. The result was that on occasions the delay was taken to be a failed response, and, consequently, shots were fired, thinking that this was a German gunboat disguised as a partisan caique. These incidents did nothing to help the rather precarious relations between the two forces on the island. Even a later apology did not always calm the situation.

John Rickett

With the experience gained, Fuller on one occasion went for the Libecchio, a 400-ton schooner, no less than fifty-two miles away. She was overcome and brought back to Vis. The risks increased considerably with ships further away. On one occasion, a MTB was damaged badly by an enemy aircraft attack while returning. Five men were seriously hurt. They were brought up to me at Podhumlje. Two men had such severe damage to limbs that it was impossible to save them, and I had go ahead with an immediate amputation. Another man had a nasty gunshot wound involving both of his hands. He lost several fingers. The worst case was Lieutenant-Commander Smyth. He was lucky to be alive, having been wounded in the chest and abdomen. I had to do a combined thoraco-abdominal approach to sort him out. This in itself was most risky surgery, and it was clear that he certainly would need expert aftercare during the recovery period. Without it, the risk of chest and other complications would be considerable. We had inadequate and totally untrained staff to handle the recovery of such casualties. Our best hope was to try to get him to Italy. A boat transfer was out of the question. There were no facilities for such a case during the long sea passage. There was no accommodation at all for the sick or wounded, nor could we spare any medical person to accompany him.

After a few days in the tent recovering, he looked tired and unwell, and the flies were on him. In fact, they were everywhere in the heat of the sun. I realised that unless I did something we would lose him.

Just at this time, the first of the American Dakotas landed on the enlarged airstrip. Scottie, as was his wont, invited the crew for a drink. They had to go on straight back to Italy, but Scottie asked if they had any spare room on board. "Why, yes," came the reply, "we could take four or five." So an ambulance was arranged, and they took away five of our worst cases in the plane. This included Smyth.

The Dakota crew were so impressed with the nature of their mercy mission that within a few days they returned with an American nurse and offered to take another five cases, and we were indeed pleased to supply them. This seemed too good to be true, but the American authorities then clamped down on these trips, saying that the British should be responsible for their own casualty transfers.

Sometime later, I had an opportunity to visit Smyth in hospital in Bari. He was making a slow recovery, having had a pelvic abscess and other complications, but recover he certainly would. I was most relieved to see him in good spirits and to know he was going to be all right. I kept thinking to myself with frustration and anger that despite the advent of penicillin, we had until recently been denied supplies on Vis. It was available in Italy, where it was revolutionizing the aftercare of dirty mortar wounds. For us on the island, where wounds would arrive several days after the injury, we needed it just as much, but it had not been available. We had to make do with sulphonamides. They were not as effective and had drawbacks relating to side effects when used by tablet and for long-term control of infection.

Did the authorities know what we were doing on the island? After the famous "stretchers not available" message, one did wonder. At times we had been visited by emissaries from Italy. One never knew exactly the scope of their visit, nor what was their remit, and I was given no opportunity to comment on any report submitted. Occasionally things did happen. Penman's visit had produced a few things, but not what we really needed, which was an X-ray machine and a generator. One question that worried me was whether the authorities were relying on us using the partisans to get us what we wanted and needed. At the outset, we had been given a portable operating table, but they must have known that we had no proper operating theatre lights and if we were able to carry on without such luxuries then we should not need other things normally supplied to active surgical units. There had been no supply of proper equipment for normal hospital use and the situation for anaesthesia was pitiable. We were expected to deal with severely wounded commandos and naval men with the most inadequate resources.

Bryan Lees had been very effective in getting us some supplies it is true. Transfer of the severely wounded was an obvious serious deficiency. Now that the airstrip was enlarged so that Dakotas were able to land there was every reason to provide proper evacuation facilities. All the time the island was becoming more important in the battle for the Adriatic with forces building up all the time. Over five thousand Partisans were now here with the two Commando units and the active Naval force.

The War Office had sent out a young man who turned up in a smart service suit complete with his Sam Browne. He had blond hair in tight, rather effeminate, curls. He certainly looked incongruous in the context of the island. He had one of those swagger sticks with which from time to time he would whack against his leg. He showed us some amiable but rather tired interest, staying for a few days. On one occasion he went to the recently enlarged, communal latrine at Podhumlje and a Partisan *girl came in while he was there and sat down next to him. He was somewhat nonplussed by this experience and later, when an opportunity arose to have a quiet word with me, he asked in a dazed way if this was literally the sum total of our facilities for this particular activity. He imagined there must surely be a privileged facility for officers somewhere. I wondered if his report back to the War Office addressed the real issues or was relevant in any way at all.*

Another chap came over to inspect us, but he was a partying man and spent the whole time either enjoying the social scene, or recovering from it. After he went back to Italy it was reported to me that he had no recollection whatsoever of his visit to Vis! No wonder we failed to get the attention of the authorities!

During the month of April we were kept busy mainly with partisan casualties from raids and from accidents on the island. On April 21 and 22, I had to deal with severe accidental wounds caused by grenades exploding. Four children were badly hurt. Two had perforating abdominal wounds, and one of them had a damaged liver with embedded shrapnel.

The partisan wounds were mainly gunshot wounds and lacerations with metallic foreign bodies to remove, but one never knew what was coming next. I thought it would be most helpful to get some warning in advance of what might be on its way up the winding road from the harbour. We could then do some planning to get accommodation ready and the decks all cleared to receive them. So I had a word with Scottie to see if something could be set up.

Chapter 16

A decision was taken by Partisan High Command to make use of the strategic position of Vis, to strengthen the garrison, cooperate more with the Allies, and carry out raids on the neighbouring islands. Colonel Zujovic was sent to organise and lead them. He was a personal friend of Tito, and he had been a most active and vigorous leader and a prime mover in the Serbian uprising in 1941. He came from a well-known Belgrade family and was over six feet tall, had a swarthy complexion, and was charismatic and impressive. On arrival, he contacted Brigadier Tom Churchill, who agreed to cooperate with him in an immediate attack on the islands of first Miljet and then Korcula.

The Navy also agreed to help with the raid. There was much pressure from Colonel Zujovic to get the raid going within a few days. For our side, Tom Churchill was forced to comment that he did not feel the reconnaissance information was complete. However, stalling for time was not welcomed by the partisan colonel. At that time, the weather was so bad with very high winds that landing troops in a small rock-strewn bay was going to be hazardous and difficult. A postponement was inevitable, and this allowed slightly more time for the Allied forces to provide the best combined operational support.

Though it was still considered premature by the Allies, the attack went ahead on 22 May. Some 3,000 partisans and 500 commandos took part. After some fairly bitter fighting, during which casualties were sustained on both sides the island was captured save for a single mountain top position which had been heavily defended with barbed wire and land mines. There had been no plan by the Allied forces to occupy Miljet so they decided to withdraw to the small island of Lagosta before going on the next day to land on Korcula. The fighting there was again fierce, and during the subsequent three days they overcame the German positions and captured it. There were again casualties. The partisans showed themselves in this attack to be extremely brave and effective. They fought with tremendous enthusiasm, but not always with the best strategy. Nor was their equipment ideal. In particular, they relied heavily on Allied signals support. The returning troops brought with them a considerable amount of German booty, including guns, howitzers, German military lorries, and motor cars. Their triumphant return to Vis brought rejoicing and did a great deal to lift the morale of all on the island.

The account continues.

In support of the partisan raid, a commando doctor, Captain Fletcher, was sent to set up a Regimental First Aid Post on Korcula. Fletcher was in the Australian RAMC. He was RMO of 43 Commando. Fletcher was well known on Vis and, in particular, at the now regular gatherings at Podhumlje for his social skills, which included the ability to tell a good story and to drink fairly heavily. His CO was Simmons, who was a friend of my GP partner at home, Toby Mc Dowell. Fletcher quarrelled endlessly with him, and he would come to see us simply to get away from his unit. He knew he could always get a good square meal, and wine was there for him to help himself. The trouble was that he had an unpleasant habit of demonstrating the points he wanted to make with his Colt 45, which we all knew must be loaded. The only doubt was whether it was cocked. It was always best to give him quite a wide berth at such times. He usually tended to start drinking in the morning. By the evening he would be well away.

In fact, everyone was very happy to learn he had been delegated to this duty on Korcula with the partisans. It would at least make the mess a safer place for a few days.

After landing on Korcula with his equipment, he was not able to keep up with the partisans because of the very rough terrain and the fact that he had not been given enough support help with his equipment. However, he eventually found a suitable house for the first-aid post, and like so many similar, it contained some barrels of wine. He thought it was a good place to install himself. The fighting got close. Still no first-aid work had appeared. Then a group of partisans came in to reload magazines and confer to make a plan. They took no notice of Fletcher, and after a while they left. Fletcher then closed and bolted the door so that he would not be disturbed and could enjoy more of the refreshment provided. A little later, some German soldiers came up. They tried the door, and, finding it bolted, they hammered on it, demanding it to be opened. Fletcher ignored them, but in the end they practically broke the door down, so he was forced to open it. Once inside, they discovered Fletcher was British and immediately surrendered to him and begged him to take them prisoner. By this time Fletcher was, thanks to the wine, somewhat incoherent.

"Why me?" demanded Fletcher.

"We do not want to surrender to the partisans. They will kill us," came the reply.

"Push off," growled Fletcher, and he went back to his barrel.

We were warned that the casualties would be heavy, and so we had early nights in preparation. On the night the raiding troops left, we had been to see them off, while they loaded up into LCIs in the port. They were in high spirits and singing. It was quite an inspiring and emotional sight, women as well as men, armed to the teeth and setting off with little regard for the outcome.

The storm broke with the expected flood of casualties the following afternoon. Navy House were to phone immediately they had any news of the timing of the evacuation. We were to receive information about how many casualties to expect. The report came from the RAF observer who was flying with the attacking party who radioed to Scotty to tell us to prepare for thirty or forty. This proved to be a serious underestimate. A batch of eighty very serious cases—what we call priority I and II—arrived in this initial phase. The stretcher cases came first, some of whom had plasma transfusion drips already running in an attempt to correct the blood loss. We started operating at half past eight in the evening and kept going till five in the morning, by which time we had cleared the worst. At the end of this session, we found that Morgan Giles had sent up a bottle of naval rum for us to enjoy and in order to restore morale. So I supplied a stiff tot for all the boys and sent them off to bed. Shortly after, a message came that he was bringing up another one hundred and fifty wounded. So at eight thirty, after three and a half hours sleep, we started getting ready for the next batch.

Transporting the large number of wounded men on the narrow rough track and up the winding roads from Komisa to us was difficult. Our most severe cases, having been operated upon, were taken by transport to Vis, where arrangements were now in place to take them by boat to Italy. This arrangement created a one-way traffic system on the island and ensured that the lorries winding up the narrow road from Komisa should not have to meet and pass the lorries going down with the cases we had treated.

We operated from ten until one thirty in the afternoon, and then from three until eight. We stopped for a good supper, and I made all the boys rest for two hours on their beds. We started again at 10.00 p.m. and carried on until 3.00 a.m. Then to bed and rest, but up again at seven, when we started again and operated all that day and most of the night.

This spell lasted for three days and nights, working about fifteen hours at a stretch with three or four hours sleep. I found I could get the most out of the lads was by stopping every four or five hours for a good square meal.

Many of the partisan soldiers were brought into the operating theatre still clutching their weapons, and these were mainly Sten guns. They were usually very reluctant to part with them, as they had been acquired during the course of the battle, usually wrested from the enemy. To avoid an unpleasant struggle to disarm them, we usually adopted a policy of checking that the gun was unloaded and tucking it under the covers to transfer with them when the surgery was over. It was on this occasion that the hand grenade I mentioned before dropped onto the floor during surgery.

In the middle of this session and while I was still operating, the theatre lights flared brightly and then started to die. The generator throttle cable must have gone again. We only had three spare light bulbs remaining, and these would have to be soldered to replace those which might have burnt out. Frank kept the wounded man nicely asleep while we investigated. We had organised that Dodd was always sitting under the stairs holding the throttle cable whilst we were operating. This normally seemed to work all right. Something must have happened. A quick check on Dodd revealed him fast asleep. Anka and Felica had taken pity on him, crouched under the stairs beside the generator. They had supplied him with refreshment consisting of wine.

In the middle of this frenetic activity, Lt. Col. Orchard, the hygiene RAMC expert from Bari, arrived to spy out the land as No. 2 District was apparently already feeling rather hot under the collar about the curious set-up that seemed to exist here on Vis. A sudden wild idea struck me that he might he be the one person with influence enough to able to get us some penicillin. Officially, we were still under the Foreign Office, and at some point we would be passed over to the War Office, who would have to pick up the loose ends and sort them out. Intensely practical, he buckled to, coming straight into the theatre and taking off his coat. He immediately began shaving limbs and holding on to wounded arms or legs, while we excised wounds, cleaned, debrided, and removed all foreign material and plastered. After the last session started, we decided to put the generator throttle duty rota onto a half-hour change over. We could not risk losing the lights a second time.

We got so tired that at times we rested on the floor between cases while Dawson was re-sterilizing the instruments. And eventually I became so tired that I could not think enough to diagnose the cases, so then we simply had to stop.

During this whole time we never, thanks to Dawson's energy and foresight, ran out of sterile towels, jaconet gauze, and dressings. Anka and Felica scrubbed the theatre out at the end of each session. It was wonderful the way those two young girls kept going.

In eighty hours we sorted, dealt with, dressed, and evacuated three hundred and fifty casualties, all heavy ones, since the minor puncture and simple flesh wounds were sent straight back to their units to await

John Rickett

their turn for first-aid attention. We did forty-seven major surgical operations. We retained about fifty serious cases unfit to travel. I cannot speak too highly of the work of the team. The entire RAMC personnel of the island came over to us to help, and each did their bit, and all the while our dear old Marie kept us all going with hot meals.

This extremely heavy burst of work was obviously more than the two of us, George and I, either could or should be doing. Might the authorities at last come to our aid? Our activities must be reported back in Italy. Surely they must know the figures for the wounded.

During April and May, we were just about coping with the often large volume of casualties. At quiet times our heads were well above water, but after a raid we would be completely inundated with work. Then the unit was stretched to the absolute limit. However, I have to say that despite the pressure, our little unit worked incredibly harmoniously. We were there to do a job, and that was what we did. All the team pulled their weight unstintingly. We operated on commandos and partisans alike. The transfer of casualties by stretcher was done by Johnnie and Lubo, the anaesthetics were given by Frank, and the instruments were all cleaned and then boiled to sterilize them. This latter task and all the theatre arrangements were done by the heroic Dawson. Anka and Felica worked tirelessly to clean up the theatre after the dirty cases, and then they helped look after them in the recovery period. We had become a viable established team.

The original garrison of several hundred commandos and partisans was now in May swollen to as many as 5,000 commandos and double that number of partisans. It was no longer simply an outpost, but an important part—one might say the key part—of the Allied strategy for the Adriatic. Vis had become a fortress. The commandos has formed into specialist sections, including a regiment of field artillery, two anti-aircraft regiments, and field support in the form of engineers, a bomb disposal squad, and a beach group. Naturally enough, as a result of the sheer numbers on the island, there were more ordinary medical emergencies. The day-to-day operating lists would often include hernias, opening abscesses and dealing with emergencies like acute appendicitis. All the time, stores and equipment—even penicillin—were arriving from Italy, and this gave some hope for the future.

A newspaper was now published, and this appropriately was called the Vis-à-Vis. There was some evening entertainment for the troops, and our official name had now become Number One Forward Base! We were on the map!

May Day came. This was a special day in the partisan calendar. It called for a communist-style celebration. There was much to raise the spirits, as the partisan successes under Commander Zuljevic had been considerable. As a main feature they decided to stage the public hanging of a German prisoner. So a prisoner was accordingly singled out and kept aside.

The night before, there was some preparatory celebrating which got a little out of hand, and a group of partisans set out to find the unfortunate prisoner. During further drinking, the party became rather boisterous, and the German was kicked to death. There was a bit of a row about it in partisan circles, and this had a slight dampening effect on the planned hanging ceremony the next day.

A further incident occurred the same night. A severely wounded partisan was recovering in hospital. He had been wounded and had a very severe facial wound, with the loss of an eye and a very badly damaged jaw. In order to feed him, a gastrostomy tube had been inserted through the abdominal wall into the stomach. Despite his serious wounds, he was making good progress. On an impulse he took a fancy to a passing nurse. He leaped out of bed, pinned the unfortunate nurse to the ground, and assaulted her. He then immediately dropped dead. Cynics were later heard to remark that at least he would not have to face the terrible Jela!

With the very large numbers now on the island, the problems of water shortage had become acute. A team of our engineers came over from Italy to carry out a survey looking for possible sites for underground supplies and to make an exploratory bore hole. There was a site near the harbour of Vis town which might be hopeful. They bored down and found water, but it was decidedly brackish. Up until now, water from Italy was being brought over every two days in a converted LCI. They had it pumped into the new well, and this produced an acceptable blend which was just about good enough for drinking. It was then piped all over the island, but of course water still remained very strictly rationed.

During this time George Lloyd Roberts began to look very poorly and tired. He developed a nasty cough and was running a temperature during the evenings. In fact, these could well be the typical symptoms of early tuberculosis. We decided to send him back to Italy for a thorough medical check-up, including, of course, a proper chest X-ray in case he had picked up something from one of the refugees he had been treating.

While George was away getting his chest sorted out, I had to run both our hospital units at the same time. In quiet times this was feasible, but when a rush started I found it was quite hopeless. A team of surgeons was really needed to give full and adequate treatment to casualties arriving at the rate they did.

Despite the pressure we were under, frequent signals were continually coming for us to send Prof Heron and his ambulance team back to Italy. Brigadier (Tom) Churchill, however, was worried about the medical situation—in particular the care of his commandos was his concern—and fully backed us up. He said Heron could not possibly leave unless he and his team were replaced by an adequately trained and fully equipped theatre staff and the necessary supporting ambulance personnel to go with it.

It was in late May that No. 2 Field Hospital finally arrived. The LCI which brought them over contained over 200 hospital beds, much equipment, tents, and all they were going to need. It took them all next day and every available island transport to get everything up onto the plateau. Along with them were one hundred personnel, including six officers, NCOs, and a quartermaster to sort things out in the proper army fashion.

Clearly things were going to change at this point, and change they did. I met the CO, whose name was Charlton. He was a nice enough guy. He seemed easy-going, though somewhat war-weary. From his attitude I thought he might possibly be content to allow our own unit to continue without too much interference from his own machine. We might then work harmoniously alongside one another. This would be, I thought, good under normal circumstances, but in the event of a raid, some planning in advance would be essential. I talked to the new staff and found that in themselves they were individually pleasant to talk to but seemed not to have had the experience needed to deal with a heavy work load. They had spent the last two years just doing garrison duty at Setif in North Africa and later at Messina. I came to realise that they were quite out of touch with front-line casualties. What was worse, they appeared smug and unwilling to discuss plans in the anticipation of a heavy raid.

They had no idea about the triage that would be needed as casualties came streaming in. I tried to talk to them, but my remarks fell on deaf ears, and I could see my advice was not welcome. Rather than allow a row to develop, I decided to let them go their own way. The best way of keeping the peace was to be independent. They would go their way, we would go ours. They would therefore take over the original operating room, and we would move in with George in what had now become known as the Juggery.

The new team had brought all their army forms and comfortable base habits. The quartermaster wanted to list everything to make it official. Immediately, he made himself unpopular by trying to appropriate our equipment, much of which had been provided by and was for partisan use. He even wanted to take over our X-ray machine. He wanted to list all the gauze and dressings and make Dawson sign for them if he needed any! Naturally enough, Dawson became speechless. He had "acquired" these dressings himself from American supply ships. After several altercations, Dawson approached me, explained that he could not work with the new field hospital, and resigned. He said he would join the commandos. This was indeed a sad blow, particularly after all he had done for us. But we had work to do, and personality clashes can be a serious impediment and must at all costs be avoided. In the end, I felt he would be happier anyway with a change and the new challenge that working with the commandos would provide.

We invited the new field unit team to use our mess. They were, however, unhappy with the informality, which they regarded as against army discipline. They wanted to turn it into an exclusive *officers' mess. Other ranks would not be welcome. This was not acceptable to us, as we had always welcomed all comers without regard to rank or status.*

When all was said and done, it had become clear that our curious ménage would not answer in the atmosphere of the "proper" unit. We would have to make a formal break. I felt it was best if in future we just dealt with the partisans. I pointed out that of course I would help at any time should there be a spillover from the field hospital during busy spells.

We decided, in particular, that the piano in the mess was not the property of the quartermaster sergeant and would not anyway be required by them, and so it was shifted by some willing partisans up to its new abode in the Juggery. At that stage fate stepped in. The surgeon of No. 2 Field Hospital went down with a gastric haemorrhage. He had to be transferred to Italy for hospital treatment. As a result of this, I found myself officially "posted" by Charlton to No. 2 Field Hospital, where I remained effectively in sole charge of the surgical services. I confess I was disappointed, as I then realised I would not then be working amongst our old team with whom we all got on so well. Charlton, however, was very understanding and said I need not sleep or live in their mess, so I stayed on to enjoy life in the Juggery. I would be working with George who was now returned from Italy and in much better health.

Spells of hectic activity continued. These were very unpredictable. We would be relatively quiet with just routine work, hernia repair, appendicitis, incision of abscesses, reduction, and plaster of fractures. Then after a raid or even an accident on the island, we would be rushed off our feet. At that point we had to say goodbye to Prof Heron. This was indeed sad. Together we had set up the unique and highly effective team. Previously there had been nothing. We had got together a fully functioning medical unit, based on the close cooperation with his field ambulance unit. Could or would this be repeated now he had gone and the long-awaited field hospital were here? I had the greatest of doubts. On thinking about it I found his obvious reply ringing in my ear.

During this period, we had examples of how partisan casualties should not be treated. The Yugoslav doctors who had gone to Lagosta to deal with the battle casualties had treated the contaminated wounds in a field tent hospital, and having done so, they stitched them up and immediately bandaged and encased them in a plaster cast without any padding. Inevitably there was swelling in the wound, and this resulted in pressure on the circulation to the limb, which eventually resulted in some cases in gangrene. The result was a number of cases in which amputation was required as a life-saving measure.

The typical example was a man who was brought up to us sitting, moaning making wild sweeping gestures to have his leg cut off. On exploring the wound by opening it all up I found he was only too accurate in his diagnosis. I found the surgeon who had treated him initially had ligated the popliteal artery. This artery is the main artery of blood supply to the lower leg. He had then stitched up the large wound and had then put on a skin-tight plaster without any padding to allow the natural swelling of the leg to take place. Sadly, amputation was then the only possible treatment.

After the postponement of Operation Freischutz, a further German plan was devised. Hitler's intelligence had suggested that the partisans were a highly unstable political force and were only held together by Tito's charisma and leadership. If he could be removed, they would be like headless chickens and would be destroyed by their own ethnic in-fighting.

They had located Tito. He was hiding on the mainland in a cave near Drvar, which the partisans had taken and established as a small HQ. Parts of Yugoslavia were under partisan control, but each undercover unit had to be under constant alert. The threat of a German raid might occur with little warning, so they had to be ready to move at short notice. The partisans knew that the Germans were closing in on Tito. So a message was sent to Colonel Zukovic in Vis to create a diversion.

At this time in late May, the details of the Brac raid were already under way, though they had not been finalized. This major distraction was required and should therefore take place without delay. Brac was thought to be the best choice, as it was close to Vis and would be an ideal base from which to make a landing on the mainland at Split. Making plans at short notice inevitably results in problems. The island was strongly held, and it was never going to be easy. The German positions had been recently reinforced with artillery and were on well-prepared high ground, surrounding which was rock strewn maquis. The surrounding cover had been cleared and laid with mines and wires. Numerically, the invading force was much larger than the small defending force, but any attack on the German positions was going to be fraught with problems, and the casualties would be high.

It was, in fact, the largest attack undertaken from Vis. The partisans and commandos would work together, making altogether a force of nearly 6,000 troops who would be, in the absence of Tom who had been called to England for consultations, under the command of his brother, Jack Churchill.

The plan was to land by night and use the darkness to get into positions undetected before daylight. This was clearly going to be difficult because of the heavy artillery, which had to be carried over the very rough ground.

No. 43 (RM) Commando and the Highland Light Infantry, together with considerable artillery support, embarked on Royal Navy vessels. George went with them, along with Lalla, Lubo, Visco, Johnny, and all his band of partisans to set up a forward unit on the island to deal with immediate casualties with first-aid measures and to provide plaster splints for wounds prior to evacuation. There was also a partisan surgeon delegated to the raid, who would work independently. The more severely wounded were to be returned to Vis to be treated by Jim Rickett and the newly formed field hospital.

There was to be a three-pronged flanking assault on the German strongholds. As the raid progressed, heavy casualties were sustained, but after some bitter fighting, the Highland Light Infantry took one of the positions. Against the German defences, the artillery could not manoeuvre over the impossibly rocky ground. It remained ineffectual.

Then there was a change of plan by the partisans. The reason for this was not clear, though their commanding officer was adamant. Jack Churchill was faced with an awkward decision. Should he withdraw or carry on without them? Playing on his bagpipes, he called for an advance. He reported later, "The partisans buggered off to God knows where . . . I never saw them again." The Spitfire air support then came over, but some of the strafing, unfortunately, was at our own troops. Jack then decided to pull back and call for reinforcements from Vis. These arrived on the third day, when Lt. Col. Manners came over with troops of 40 Commando. Colonel Jack then led a further commando force into attack, again playing his bagpipes. The last anyone saw of him was by the light of a shell explosion. He was seen attending to two wounded officers. Unfortunately, both he and another officer were then captured.

The unfortunate last minute change of plan made by the partisan commander meant the commandos were not supported in making the final strike at one of the main strongholds. There had been great problems coordinating the different attacking units because of the poor wireless reception in the hills and valleys. This, coupled with a serious depletion of many commando officers, meant a withdrawal was inevitable. The German garrison, however, had been hard hit, and they were unable to attack during the withdrawal. As a consequence, the passage by sea back to Vis was unimpeded.

The account is resumed.

George had set up his field unit in a small stone building. As the wounded started to stream in, he realised the work was going to be extremely heavy, so he thought it was essential to warn me that I would be overwhelmed and that evacuation of the severely wounded by air to Italy was going to be needed. This should be organised right away. He telegraphed a message to the SMO (Senior Medical Officer) on Vis. "Expect heavy casualties. Suggest air evacuation the only hope." Unfortunately, this message was taken, misread, and mistakenly directed to the SNO (Senior Naval Officer) on Vis, Captain Morgan Giles. He made nothing of the message, and it was redirected on to Admiral Morgan, his senior in Taranto. Obviously, there the source was questioned, and no sense was made of the content. In any event, no action was taken. As a result, there was no air evacuation, and the hospital on Vis came to be inundated. George worked hard on Brac, using the daylight to work outside the house in which he had installed himself. His anaesthetist was an artillery doctor who had been lent to him for the occasion. By night he had to work inside and use what meagre light there was available. While dealing with an abdominal wound, he fell through some rotten floor boards and landed in the foundation of the building up to his waist in dust and filth. He had to scramble out and carry on as best he could, cursing and musing to himself on the problems of front line surgery.

After two days of continuous work, a Yugoslav doctor called Beliakov came up to him and boasted that he had performed thirty-eight amputations. This sickened George. Knowing what he did of Yugoslav surgery, it meant that most of these unfortunate partisans would have lost limbs not only unnecessarily but also by an unfortunate and out-of-date method of amputation. This was the so called "guillotine" method. This had the merit of being quick and simple, but without covering the stump with skin flaps, re-amputation would inevitably be needed later and at a higher level. The technique went out of date years ago because of improvements in aseptic technique and on account of the problems it caused when attempting to fit an artificial limb.

The casualties from the fighting were very heavy, and the medical team of No. 2 Field Hospital back on Vis were shaken to the core. I found they could not even do the essential triage of sorting and deciding which of the casualties were the most urgent and then making arrangements and dealing with them first. They were junior medical men who were completely bewildered by the vastness of the task, and they would walk about amongst the wounded men in a state of dazed confusion, not knowing where to start. They were without training even in the basics of resuscitation—putting up drips, looking to airway problems, and assessing blood loss. This was obviously a serious problem, and the result was that, as their commanding officer, I had to take over. At the same time, I found I had to get Simpson, the resuscitation officer, organised and also arrange all the necessary evacuations and transfers. In essence, everything was simply up to me.

One outstanding case comes to mind. It was a commando soldier who had been shot in the groin. On examining him, I found he also had a through and through wound of the scrotum. Despite the journey over from Brac, which had taken over twenty-four hours, much of which was on a stretcher and over the rough mountain terrain, he was in other respects fairly well and had not lost much blood. I got him onto the operating table, and as I was exploring the wound under anaesthesia, a huge spurt of blood shot into the air. I found that the femoral artery was completely divided and jutting into the wound. Having been severed by the original bullet, it had gone into spasm, and this had stopped the bleeding. This was just as well; otherwise he would not have been with us. By disturbing the wound, the clot which had formed in the artery came out, and thanks to a quick arterial clamp, I was able to control the haemorrhage and keep the situation in hand. The wound was contaminated, so I had to ligate the artery. Saving the leg was going to be touch and go, and I decided to make pressure-relieving incisions in the leg to reduce tension in the muscle compartments. This would encourage the remaining circulation while the leg was healing.

I worked for three days and nights until I could no longer think straight in order to make a diagnosis. Despite having about ten times our usual staff, the work was poorly organised. Standing out in my memory of this time is a typical incident illustrating the poor training of the team which had arrived on the island. I had to watch an orderly flatly refuse to undress a badly wounded female partisan. In the end I had to give him a direct order. Then with averted head and eyes he proceeded to expose her wounded chest and abdomen. I was then able to assess the urgency for operation and labelled her appropriately.

Without the old team, we did not do as well as previously, and with both old Prof Heron and Bryan Lees away, I realised we were facing a gaping hole in the team. However, we finally got through and finished, and when that happened, the whole attitude of the field unit altered from that time. It was no good telling them, "I wish you had listened to me." Their respect and friendliness increased beyond all recognition. Needless to say, I was grateful for that.

Several bold attempts were made to recapture Jack Churchill. These were made more difficult on account of the German reinforcements which had been sent over to Brac. In retaliation, they took reprisals against those who had cooperated with the partisans. A house that had been used as a dressing station for the wounded was torched with the couple inside.

A plan was devised, and three troops of commandos landed to establish contact with the civilians on the island. The prisoners, they learnt, had been taken to Supetar, which was the harbour on the northern side. It was likely that they would be transferred to Split by boat for questioning. Morgan Giles sent three MTBs through the mine-infested channel between Brac and Solta and into the harbour at Supetar. The plan was to lie there and challenge any boat leaving the harbour and force them, using a German speaker with a loud hailer, to release any prisoners. In the event, it was a clear starlit night, and the moon was full. Fuller led the mission, and the MTBs made the passage successfully and stopped at the harbour mouth without a shot having been fired. They waited there all night, and then one hour before dawn they went right into the harbour in order to take a closer look. There were no boats obviously preparing to leave for the mainland. At that point gunfire opened up and, as it was getting light, they decided to make their getaway.

Sometimes prisoners were involved in working gangs in the fields, so a party of Allied scouts were landed and took up positions around Supetar. At an agreed time, a flight of Spitfires flew over, causing the locals to scatter in panic. They hoped to expose working gangs who might then escape and hide up. They would later be picked up by the scouts.

In a further plan, the planes were to target and bomb the largest of the seafront buildings in the hope that prisoners might escape. As it happened, no prisoners appeared, and at that point the plan to rescue Jack Churchill had to be abandoned.

The Brac raid had meant that at least that some German forces were drawn off the hunt for Tito. There had been no Allied plan to occupy the island after the raid, and the withdrawal was always part of the original intention. A large German force massed at Split in fear of an Allied invasion of the mainland. What was surprising was the failure of the German forces to use their significant E boat force at Split to harry the retreating Allies while they returned to Vis.

It was as they sailed back to Vis after the Brac raid that the news came through on 4 June 1944 that the Allied forces, advancing from Anzio, were now entering Rome. In a further two days came the news of the landings on the Normandy beaches on D-Day.

Despite the distractions of the Brac raid, the German plan to close in on Tito was coming off. One day the partisans noted a

John Rickett

reconnaissance plane flying low over the HQ on the mainland taking photographs. This was obviously significant, and they realised the attack must be expected at any time. In fact, as anticipated, it came a few days later.

A glider containing parachutists came over the cave. The glider crashed in the forest, killing the pilot, but the parachutists landed successfully. Well-armed, they immediately moved to gain positions overlooking the mouth of the cave. It appeared to them that Tito was cornered. In fact, the prearranged escape plan was then put into action. He got away by climbing up a rope through a narrow cleft in the rock and away into the forest. The Germans had followed up the air attack with forces surrounding the whole area, but Tito managed to evade them and escaped to the hills, where he laid up in hiding.

The Germans, having failed to capture Tito, then took reprisals against the local people. There were extensive massacres of men, women, and children whom they accused of collaboration with the partisans.

Tito spent some time on the run. He hid during the day and moved by night. There were several close encounters with German soldiers. The food ran low. Allied air drops were used to support the local partisans, and these were useful. Eventually Tito came to realise that he could no longer command the partisan force without a proper base, and the mainland of Yugoslavia had become untenable. He needed to get to Italy at least temporarily. This message was signalled to the Allies, and an immediate night air evacuation was organised, using a small airstrip that was still in partisan hands. This was going to be a hazardous mission. It was late May, and on the night in question it was raining. There was low cloud, and visibility was extremely poor. Could the plane possibly land? A gap in the cloud suddenly appeared, and the Dakota flew in. It was in fact piloted by a Russian crew under a lend-lease arrangement. Tito, his dog and the immediate staff got aboard and flew to Bari.

The failure to take Tito was a bitter blow for Hitler. The Adriatic offensive was now not looking good. For his part, Tito had to decide his next move. The mainland of Yugoslavia was out of the question, and Vis was the obvious answer. He was always partial to caves, which were inconspicuous from the air and relatively safe from bombing. They had already served him well. There was a cave on Mount Hum.

Tito arrived on Vis on 9 June aboard *HMS Blackmore*. He set up his HQ in the cave on Mount Hum. Initially Tito's presence on the island was kept a close secret. The cave on Mount Hum was heavily guarded, but after two weeks he broke his cover and appeared to the troops. He then gave lunches and made lavish speeches of praise for the bravery, gallantry, and comradeship of all. It was clear in late June 1944 that Hitler was on the run and that the Allied forces would win. At this point in the war it was only a matter of time.

The account continues .

A few mornings after we had dealt with the all the Brac casualties, an American Major in command of a troop of rangers came to us with the story that one of his men, having been drinking a lot of rakija the night before, was found dead in his bunk. I remembered the large insurance compensation, which I understood amounted to the equivalent of over £2,000, that an American soldier's widow received if the death was "in line of duty".

A request was made that I carry out a post mortem and report my findings. However, without having any instruments for this particular purpose, I was not relishing the idea, and in the end I persuaded the young major to send the body to Italy to an American field hospital for examination by one of their own pathologists. Accordingly, it was decided he should be put on a schooner. Unfortunately, the weather took a turn for the worse, and the schooner did not sail but lay in the harbour weather bound. The following evening our old friends in the Prodigal *came in. The corpse, much to their indignation, was under orders transferred to them. The Navy has a very strong superstition about carrying corpses, and a very subdued, morose crew set off with their unwelcome passenger to Italy, where on arrival in harbour, they unfortunately dropped him into the sea while getting him ashore. They then had a lot of difficulty rescuing him from the water, though they eventually succeeded.*

The body was now several days old without refrigeration in the height of the Mediterranean summer. The unfortunate American pathologist would have to draw conclusions and write a report. I shudder to think what the report might have said.

News came through that a hospital ship was at this moment heading for the island. This was too good to believe, but none too soon. At last there would be some relief. We would be able to transfer some of the most severely wounded to recover in a proper hospital with adequate nursing and food, away from the intense heat of summer and the flies which were now everywhere. Proper medical care would be available for them. Of the casualties lying about everywhere, we could carry out some sorting so that those who needed it most could be transferred to Italy. Soon after we got this news, a message was received that there had been a terrible accident on an MTB. Some men had been washing down the walls of the MTB with petrol to be ready for action that night. In the heat of the sun they had stripped down to their shorts in order to keep cool. Someone then started up the generator on the boat, and a small bar fire, which had been left switched on from the night before, started glowing. Immediately the place became an inferno in an explosion of petrol. The three men were all very badly burned and had to be dragged out. They were burned from head to feet, save for the area protected by their shorts.

They were brought to me, and since I was on my own, I could only deal with them one at a time. The first, though this was the worst, took six hours to get sorted. I was then told the hospital ship was now moored up actually in harbour. This was, I thought, in the nick of time. There were still the other two severe burns to be treated. All three would need immediate transfer to a proper burns unit in Italy. The sooner this happened, the better. The facilities on the island were hopelessly inadequate. We certainly could not cope with the nursing and management of such severe cases. I contacted the MO in charge and negotiated with him to take them. However, it turned out that this wonderful hospital ship was no more than a Yugoslav schooner with one medical man on board. What was even worse, the medic in charge, Mc Williams, was not surgically trained and had absolutely no instruments to do even minor surgery. I realised, in spite of this, they would be more comfortable on board than under canvas on the island, and they would at least be transferred straight away to a proper unit in Italy. He would get them transferred as quickly as possible. In the meantime, the immediate treatment was to urgently set up an intravenous infusion to replace the tissue fluids lost through the burnt tissue. McWilliams asked if he could borrow some instruments from me so that he could put up this drip into the saphenous vein, which was the only available site. This put me in a

John Rickett

dilemma. I could ill afford to let him have any instruments, as I had none to spare and was using them all the time. However, in gratitude for McWilliams taking the casualties, I loaned the necessary instruments so that at least the desperately needed fluids could be started. I asked him to be sure to return them to me before leaving the island. He agreed to do this, but later I found that the schooner departed, taking my precious tools of trade. When I realised this, I dropped everything and asked Morgan Giles to send a fast motor boat to catch up with the schooner to collect them. This he did, but sadly I learned later that despite getting them to the unit in Italy, they lived no more than a few days.

Work in the field hospital continued in repeated spasms of hectic activity, and it was during another such spasm late in June that I pricked my finger whilst operating on an abdominal wound. It started to swell and become red and painful. I lay in my bivouac tent and thought, "Jim lad, you cannot operate with that infected finger. You had best get it sorted out." This might anyway be the best time to wind up.

Already rumours had come of more commando units having landed, which made it evident that Vis as the small community it had been a couple of months ago was long since gone. The whole atmosphere was undergoing an inevitable change to accommodate what was a large commando and partisan army. The close knit community of the happy island as we had known earlier it was over.

I wrapped up my finger, put on a sling, and saw Charlton. He signalled for another surgeon to come and take over from me. Jimmy Waterston then arrived in the Prodigal two days later so I hopped onto an Anson plane and flew back to Foggia.

It seemed quite strange to be in Italy after living in our very small community. On landing, I got a lift from the airport in a post jeep, which took me into Foggia town, where I found the officers' club. By that time I was hungry and pretty desperate for a meal, as I had been travelling for some time. They would serve nothing—not even a cup of tea or a drink or anything. The regulations stated it was "after two", and they were closed. In thinking about all we had gone through in the last few weeks, this upset me, so I hotfooted round to the Major's office, where I expressed my displeasure. Thankfully, a meal was then served! Later I found an ambulance and managed to get a lift all the way to Trani, where I stopped and located and stayed with my old friend Fen. At that stage I am pleased to say my finger was just starting to improve.

I received a terrific welcome and arrived just in time for a surgical division party with Jimmy Brown and all the ladies stationed at Barletta officers' club.

The next day I took myself off to Bari and called at No. 2 District. There I found an absolute turmoil. Brigadier Cameron had at last woken up to the Vis problem. I stayed three days to be thoroughly debriefed and spent my time with him trying to describe the set-up on the island. One afternoon during the debriefing, I was left temporarily alone in the office and took the opportunity of running through the files. A recent high-powered communication about Vis and the Yugoslav problem had appeared from the War Office. It was impressive. At last in their eyes we existed and were in the overall framework. However, I knew it was effectively a little too late. I learnt that quite a lot of wounded men were even being flown straight out from the Yugoslavia mainland in DC3 American planes.

John Rickett

On Sunday the ADMS, Col. Hunt, and I took a car to the BRCS officers' convalescent wing, where Brigadier Cameron was trying to get a few days rest after dislocating his shoulder. He agreed Hunt should return to Vis with me. We then left by car, dined at the Imperiali in Bari, and then kept going north till we got to Barletta, where I knew the old *Prodigal* would be. Sure enough, she was there, but she was not sailing for two days. By this time it was 10.30 p.m. Helpful as always, they phoned Manfredonia for us and told me that two LCIs were due to leave for Vis at 8.30 the next morning. To leave by day rather than make a night crossing was good news, as it meant the risk of a German air attack was now officially considered most unlikely.

So on we went again, boarding the LCI at 3.30 a.m. We turned in to the aft saloon which was designated as "troop space" to get a little sleep for the remainder of the night.

With all the rush and the roughness of our quarters on board, I think Col. Hunt was quite horrified as, in his position as a senior officer, he was more used to the calm atmosphere of HQ, which included the attentions of his batman. His spirits, however, improved gradually as we sailed in glorious Adriatic weather, and I felt almost like approaching home as Vis grew bigger from a dot on the horizon to take its old familiar shape.

After we arrived at the island, I took Hunt around. He was intrigued with the whole atmosphere and was amazed at the amount of work that had been put through the makeshift Juggery hospital in the days before the field hospital had arrived. He could see the continuing need to support the partisan army and became seriously perturbed that George might be called back to Italy suddenly and have to leave the island without a replacement surgeon. The reason *for this was that George had become somewhat frustrated, easily irritated and very allergic to the vagaries and interference of the seniors and also of the partisan commissars. When any requests made were turned down, bickering would start, and more so latterly, he tended to lose his temper. I saw that it was high time for the sake of peace, quiet, and good relations generally that George had a change. Back in Bari later, I searched out Penman, his immediate superior, and talked it over with him. He agreed to his leaving Vis.*

Although I had asked for and been given leave, I volunteered to stay on in the island in case George was sent on an immediate posting. There would then have been nobody to do his work. How they might expect any movement on our part either to or from Vis to be sudden I can't think. Out here we were sufficiently out of touch for personnel movements to take at least a week to filter through the system.

I told Hunt that I too would like a change. With the arrival of the field hospital and the accompanying staff, my own position was no longer needed. Finally, my own posting to 45 came through. George and I would leave together.

The farewell party for the two of us was a memorable one! The Jugs gave a sit-down supper for about fifty people. There were the brigade HQ men, the beach group, Colonel Meynell, Brigadier Tom Churchill, partisans, RAF fitters, and others—in fact, all our friends of whatever rank. We got under way at 7.00 p.m. in our EPIP tent with gin, whisky, and anchovies on toast. Dinner followed at nine and lasted until midnight. Then the more serious drinking, singing, and dancing started. It broke up at 6.00 a.m., when we were all ready for bed. It was a wonderful send off. There were speeches and dances, with the most senior officers staying on till long after midnight. Not

John Rickett

content with this, the party started again the next day, so when we finally went on board the Prodigal, *we'd had about enough of parties to last for many days to come!*

On Vis we had two jeeps between us. One belonged to 43 Marine Commando and had a driver called Strudwick; the other one had been brought over from Italy, having been made from cannibalized and broken-up old vehicles. We loaded the cannibal with our luggage. She was hoisted aboard Prodigal, *transported over, and lifted off again at Barletta. So George and I were able to drive in state to Bari, with the back of this very disreputable jeep loaded high with all our goods.*

It was a painful leaving; Lalla was tearful, poor Dr Zon made the most extravagant speech in his faltering English, and Johnny, Lubo, and Visko were quietly drunk. Strudwick was also somewhat under the weather. There was only Frank hovering around to see that all was well. I was indeed sorry to say au revoir *to him, as he had been just a fantastic and unswerving support all along.*

Jim Rickett left Venice in August 1945 to come home on a month's leave. He arrived before VJ Day. Now that the war was over, he appealed to the War Office to be demobilized on the grounds that his GP practice was being run by doctors past the usual retirement age and he was needed more in Havant than in Italy. Dorothy and the children went to see the film of *National Velvet*, and on returning home, they learnt that he had been released.

On return from Italy he was found to have contracted TB, having caught it in 1944. He was treated with streptomycin, had to undergo some surgery, recovered from TB, and went back into general practice in Havant and Emsworth. He died in 1968.

Appendix A: Special Operations Executive (SOE)

The Special Operations Executive was formed in 1940 from three separate organisations to assist local resistance groups and to promote sabotage and subversion throughout occupied Europe—in Winston Churchill's memorable phrase, "to set Europe ablaze". The chief executive of SOE was responsible to Hugh Dalton at the Ministry of Economic Warfare. It was divided into three organisational branches reflecting its origins: SO1 (propaganda), SO2 (active operations, subdivided geographically), and SO3 (planning). Its broad remit often led to confusion and interdepartmental disputes with the War Office, the Foreign Office, and MI6 regarding its responsibilities and priorities.

In 1941, following a dispute between the Ministry of Information and the Foreign Office, the bulk of SO1 was transferred to the newly created Political Warfare Executive under Foreign Office control, whereupon it was amalgamated with the Ministry of Information's Foreign Publicity Department and the BBC European Section. Thereafter the remainder of SOE continued as a planning and operational entity until it was disbanded in 1946. When the Ministry of Economic Warfare was wound up in May 1945, responsibility for SOE was transferred to the Economic Warfare Department of the Foreign Office.

Unfortunately, the vast majority of SOE operational files have not survived. Many were destroyed in a fire at SOE's headquarters shortly after 1945, and some files, particularly personnel files relating to administrative staff seconded from the armed services, were destroyed at the end of the war. As there was no central registry and no indication of the file series, it is difficult to estimate overall file losses, though these have been estimated as being as high as eighty per cent. However, surviving SOE records can be found in the department code HS.

Appendix B: First Aid Nursing Yeomanry (FANY)

The movement was not recognised until 1907, when warfare methods had changed. The role of the movement remained unclear until 1914 when six FANYs went to Calais with just £12, found the place littered with untended wounded, set up a hospital in a local convent, and treated over 4,000 wounded over the next two years. In other theatres of war, they ran soup kitchens, drove field ambulances, carried spare clothing up to front-line soldiers, and came to do espionage work. During the First World War, they won seventeen military medals including one *Legion d'Honneur*.

When the SOE was formed in 1940, FANYs were recruited to pack supplies and explosives and then to become agents in order to do intelligence and carry out subversive operations behind enemy lines is Europe. Some women were trained secret agents and posed as typists and clerks, orderlies, and drivers and in consequence were captured and at times tortured and killed.

Copy/jrk.

SUBJECT:- Appreciations - Major J.R. RICKETT RAMC.

H.Q. 2 District, C.M.F.
Tel No: 13611
9588
10 Aug 44.

O.C.,
45 General Hospital.

Will you please inform Major J.R. RICKETT RAMC that I have received a communication from the Senior Naval Officer, VIS, forwarded by Rear-Admiral C.E. MORGAN, TARANTO, in great appreciation of the surgical work performed by Major RICKETT on the Island of VIS.

The following is an extract :-

"Not only did officer and ratings receive some extremely skilled attention from Major Rickett personally, including major surgical operations, but the reputation which he and his unit quickly and deservedly established for themselves was a major factor in maintaining the morale of the crews of the small craft engaged on offensive patrols, who knew that if wounded they would receive prompt and excellent medical attention."

It is with great pleasure that I associate myself with this appreciation of Major Rickett's work.

Will you please convey to him that I consider his work and devotion to duty on the Island of VIS has upheld the finest traditions of the Corps and also convey my personal thanks to him.

(Sgd) W. CAMERON.
Brigadier,
D.D.M.S.

WF.

Certified true copy.

14th August, 1944.

Major,
Registrar,
45 (UK) General Hospital.

Appreciation

Appendix C: Letter from Brigadier Tom Churchill, 6 June 1946

My dear Rickett,

It was a real pleasure to hear from you, but I am exceedingly sorry to learn that you have got this pulmonary tuberculosis: what vile luck and what a rotten return for all you did for us in Vis. I shall never forget the splendid spirit that you engendered in our slender medical team and the sterling service you provided. I enclose the certificate, which I hope will ensure your adequate consideration by the Ministry of Pensions for there can be no doubt in my mind that this spot on the lung was caused by your work in appalling conditions in close contact with the Jugs.

Funnily enough, I have an old Vis inhabitant on my staff now—one Captain Finnigan who was in Tommy Thomas' Light AA Bty and we often gossip about those days.

I was so very glad to hear only about 3 weeks ago that you had in the end been given the MBE that we put you in for—one was never better earned.

Jack came out of the bag alive and kicking and none the worse for his experiences in concentration camps and solitary confinement following escape attempts. He did finally get away and walked into the advancing Americans in the Brenner Pass.

I am in Austria at present and having a wonderful time skiing and shooting stag. It is the best of all the occupied zones. My wife and two children have recently joined me, which is fine for us all.

I will certainly look you up when next I come home, though my present object in life is to avoid returning to England at any cost, as it seems that conditions are as bad now, or worse than they ever were in the war.

Could you, in your spare time, write out for me some time the words of that song you and the other MO's used to sing. It ends "and ever more shall be so" and includes such phrases as "the lilywhite boys", "the knockers at the door", etc. It always intrigued me!

Yours ever,

Tom Churchill

Appendix D: The Night of the Portsmouth Fire Blitz in January 1941

To add to the scene that night, the following was written by an eye witness at the time. The first-hand account provides the atmosphere of what it is like to be in a bombing raid. This was written for the BBC's *The People's War*. It tells of a teenage boy, who had literally to run for his life on a cold January night in 1941. The account has been paraphrased.

John Rickett

ON BEING BOMBED OUT
10TH JANUARY 1941

BY PETER ADDIS

On being bombed out one had a certain status. The Government had no time to deal with you and that was accepted. Relatives and friends gathered round, providing lots of sympathy, food, shelter, clothes, and even furniture. One could never talk about it. That was just not done. It was very bad form, and any mention of the subject brought glazed eyes and a frantic effort to change the subject. One could talk about the rationing, and other things—people would tell with bated breath where they got a piece of extra cheese off the ration, but the bombs, no.

In the summer of 1940 I was sixteen and in the School Certificate class. Hopes of success were slim as I was too excited about the war. At school we all cheered when the Air Raid Siren went, as it meant we could play around in a very interesting shelter and skip the remains of the lesson. I remember our teacher said that one day we might stop praying for air raids. How right he was!

We lived in Portsmouth, and for the past 6 months we had been frequently attacked by the German Luftwaffe, first by day but as winter drew on by night as well. My parents tried to evacuate me but I was just old enough to resist. So I lived in a thrilling world, of interrupted lessons, and sleeping in a cellar at night with a picnic of sandwiches and a flask of tea or cocoa. We did this on a regular basis to save getting disturbed at night as the air raid warnings were so frequent. My parents kept a Newsagents shop and I had to rise early for the paper round. I did this using my bike.

One quiet night I sneaked out to see my pal Jack and we drank a bottle of port between us. I had a job to walk back to the shelter and my poor Mother had to hide me from our neighbours under the blankets because I kept talking.

Reading the history of the 2nd World War one would assume that this period must have been a very anxious time. Disaster was close to us and around us all the time. That very precarious period might have been a bit depressing. On the contrary it was one of the most wonderful periods I have ever known. The atmosphere was euphoric. The Germans were regarded as comic figures goosestepping around wearing coal scuttle helmets shouting *achtung*. The fact that they had conquered most of Europe in a few months was ignored. The word Blitz was adopted into the English language as it had a nice descriptive sound. The retreat from Dunkirk we regarded as a victory.

There was a rumour that British bombs captured by the Germans in the retreat from the continent were being dropped on Portsmouth. A friend of my parents lost his house and thinking of this rumour said "well at least they are very good bombs!"

Then came the time when silly boys stopped praying for air raids. It was a January night 1941 (10th Jan). The bombing started at dusk and the first bombs put out all the lights. Continuous incendiary bombs set whole streets alight. Then H.E (high explosive) bombs and land mines were dropped on the fires. I was not thrilled anymore, I was scared. As we sat in the cellar we could hear the whistle of bombs and the crump of the explosions and feel the vibration of the earth. One particular sequence, I remember when the whistles got louder and the tremors got more violent first on one side then across to the other side of us as the line of bombs straddled our house.

At about 10 p.m. it went strangely quiet. There was no all-clear siren, as all the power was cut. Someone asked my parents if they should go upstairs to check that the building was still OK. The cellar was under a big department store and they went up to the first floor they found the building was on fire, so we all had to get out and go to the shelter

Outside we were greeted with an awesome sight. Kings Road, which was one of the town's main shopping centres was burning all down one side, and to get to the shelter we had to run a gauntlet on the opposite pavement slippery with broken glass, threatened by high blazing buildings. As I started, a soldier, taking out a cigarette, said to me "got a light mate?" Then as I ran a whole side of a building collapsed into the road, I will never know how near it was. I saw a lady lying on the pavement, a couple of wardens were looking at her. One said "She's dead." At that moment she sat up and started screaming.

Later we went back again in a lull to check the house. Our home just off the main street. The place was still standing but had been very badly blasted. The shop was a wreck, all the goods strewn on the floor mixed up with the glass from the windows. The whole scene was lit up by the flames of the shop burning fiercely opposite. The Bush Hotel on the corner was ablaze, but the Landlady had gone back in and was clutching the cash register and would not leave. My mother went into the burning building and persuaded her to leave, much to the relief of an anxious warden. Meanwhile I had gone into our shop to retrieve the money from our own till. As I had my hand in the till a special policeman appeared and for a moment I thought he might think I was looting. But the poor man seemed dazed and asked me if I had seen his wife. I had no idea who he was. Then my friend's brother Bill popped in, looked at the remains of my Dad's lending library and said "can I borrow a book Pete?"

If things should ever get hot Mum and Dad made me promise to meet them in an air raid shelter on Southsea Common. This shelter had always figured in the family plan because it was about half way to Old Portsmouth where some very old and dear friends lived and it had been arranged that if things got really bad we would all meet there.

So I went round to my friend Jack. His house was intact, and having a basement they always stayed at home. I was there for about half an hour, when without warning the bombers came back. I expect the family tried to persuade me to shelter with them there but I was obstinate and remembered what my parents had said. I borrowed Jack's bike and set off for the Common.

I could not go direct as the fires had closed the road, so I went a different way. After all it was my local area. I had not gone far however, before the incredible noise made me dump the bike and rush into a nearby street surface shelter. This sort is a bit vulnerable, but you have the comforting thought that you may go quickly and not be buried alive under tons of masonry. The shelter was packed and I could only stand in the doorway. Everybody was very quiet at first, then suddenly a woman had hysterics and made an awful row. I don't know why, I just could not stand it and had to go outside again and rode off on my bike. No one tried to stop this stupid boy. Everyone had their own problems. I rode a circuitous route avoiding the streets on fire. After all I was a newspaper boy

John Rickett

and knew all the dodges. I can only remember riding as fast as I could avoiding broken glass and debris and aware of the great noise. I don't think I saw anyone the whole journey which was a long way with the detours I had to take. When I arrived and I found my parents in the shelter.

Now I have been a parent myself I realise what a relief it must have been for them to see me. It's only just occurred to me, now.

Our friends were there were there, "Uncle" Jim, "Auntie" Vera and their daughters Betty and Valerie. The Common, ringed with fire, was an incredible scene of destruction. Even the roller coaster on the side of the blazing pier was on fire. Peering out from the shelter door was my Uncle Jim, who was a great musician. He had played the piano years before for the silent films said to me as I came in "All very dramatic but one misses the incidental music."

Daylight came and the raid finished. We arranged with our friends to go back to their place in Old Portsmouth if our house was not usable. Then we went home. It was gone. All that was left was a small square of rubble. I could not believe that small space had been my home for nearly all my life. It must have been flattened by the blast of an H.E.in the 2nd raid. I could hardly believe the house I had lived in nearly all my life could only leave a tiny square of rubble. It was a bitter blow to my parents. Not only was it their home but also their shop and their means of livelihood. I remember it was at this time that my mother started to tell me to take the bike back. She opened her mouth to speak when someone threw out a smouldering eiderdown from a window and the hot feathers went into her mouth. I rushed to help her as she spluttered and pulled out the feathers, then she turned to me and started laughing. She always had a great sense of humour.

We set off towards old Portsmouth to Jim and Vera's house. We got about half-way when we met them. Their house had gone as well. We walked out of town, carrying a small bag that Mother always took down the shelter with her. It held all the important family documents. I have it still.

We travelled up to Maidenhead to relatives, getting lifts and local buses. No official help was ever found. I think our arrival was a complete surprise, phones and communication were not great in those days[23].

We were given a great welcome. We were given everything we needed, but it was all from the family. We eventually got a clothing grant from the government but that was all. The next night we went over to Marlow and met more family, all evacuated from London, they took us to the local pub, where there was an impromptu dance. It was a tribute to the general spirit of that time that my mum and dad were dancing less than 48 hours after losing everything. My Dad, always good for a quote, said "I'm dancing with tears in my eyes", which was the title of a popular dance song at that time.

My Dad had had a rough time with war, back in 1916 he had been very badly wounded in the Battle of the Somme and then this loss in the 2nd war. However he recovered well, getting a new job and eventually buying a house in Marlow without any help from anyone.

---

23 So severe was this raid that in the interest of local morale there was reluctance to broadcast the true severity of the destruction that night.

About the Author

John Rickett FRCS
Son of Jim Rickett.

He was born in 1935. Education was at Repton School and then at Jesus College, Cambridge University. He represented the university in cross-country running before going on to Guy's Hospital, London where he qualified medically in 1959. He obtained the specialist surgical degrees of FRCS (London) in 1965 and MS (Cambridge) in 1973.

He worked as a consultant general surgeon at Torbay Hospital in Devon, retiring in 1996. Previous publications have been professional medical articles which were published while he was working.

He now works as a volunteer for the charity Royal National Institute for the Deaf (Action on Hearing Loss) and runs an active (non-commercial) internet website reporting on listening devices for those with hearing loss. Other interests include walking on the moor, butterflies, other wildlife and sailing.

ABOUT THE BOOK

Jim Rickett was a family doctor in 1940. He was called up in 1943 and was working in Italy in early 1944 when he received an urgent posting to join the commandos. They were working with the SOE (Special Operations Executive) on the Adriatic island of Vis. His job was to set up a hospital to deal with the wounded who would be brought back from raids on the nearby islands under enemy occupation. He had to get out there immediately and was told the supplies to the island from Italy would be very difficult. There were no evacuation facilities. A German attack was imminent. The island was to be held at all costs.

At the outset he had nothing. He had to set up a makeshift hospital from scratch. Initially he had to operate with a kerosene lamp for light. Later they managed to get wiring from a crashed Liberator plane and set up electricity using an old diesel generator. They bartered and stole to get the unit operational. A hospital clinic on the German occupied mainland was raided to acquire an X-ray machine.

When a heavy influx of casualties was expected from a commando raid, Jim Rickett wired to Italy for two hundred stretchers. The unhelpful reply came back "Stretchers not—repeat not—available. To what use would they be put?" Despite the setback, they managed to get a hospital facility running and operational by working continuously for days on end. The small unit became highly effective, provided some light-hearted moments, and became the social centre of the island.

What was family doctoring like prior to the NHS? Told as a first-hand account Jim Rickett's diary builds a cameo picture of the community under the stress of the 1940/41 blitz. His GP practice was near Portsmouth which was heavily bombed. He was a surgeon (with no formal surgical training) and carried out much routine surgery in the

John Rickett

local hospital. Much of it is now unthinkable. A caesarean operation had to be done on the dining-room table. The story tells vividly of the severe bombing at the time of the "Fire Blitz" on Portsmouth in January and in April 1941. This was one of the most severe raids of the blitz.

Lightning Source UK Ltd.
Milton Keynes UK
UKOW03f0657210414

230286UK00001B/30/P